My DAD, ORAL ROBERTS

Roberta Roberts Potts

ENDORSEMENTS

Here is the life of a great Christian and a great Oklahoman, told by his daughter with love and admiration.

-**Tom A. Coburn,** M.D., U.S. Senator

Few know a father as well as his daughter does. Roberta Roberts grew up in the home of one of the most intriguing, famous and complicated men of the last century. To the rest of the world he was an evangelist, a visionary, a gifted healer and the founder of a major university. To Roberta he was Dad. This is an intimate memoir of a remarkable man, a fascinating family and an unforgettable era in American religious history.

– **Mark Rutland,** Ph.D. President, Oral Roberts University

As a child, I remember having to sit in the balcony of the movie theatre, because the seats on the main floor were reserved for my white friends. But Oral Roberts, a maverick in his generation, fought such segregation in his healing crusades and later, refused to allow it at Oral Roberts University. The famous Oklahoman was not only ahead of his time in that regard, but was one of the first who understood that Jesus sees all of us in the same way. Not only did he preach it, he practiced it. Oral Roberts understood that God looks through our skin color, He looks through our faults and even our strengths — straight through to our hearts. Reading *My Dad, Oral Roberts* gives me a new hope that people can begin to see each other as God sees us.

–**J.C. Watts Jr**., Former Oklahoma Congressman

Oral Roberts' children have received spiritual DNA from their parents which is an inheritance from God. Children who have obtained Godly knowledge have been empowered beyond the normal with a message that can provide one with supernatural wisdom and insight for living today. Roberta has a rich reservoir of heavenly insight that few children will ever understand. Her amazing story is a powerful demonstration of how the message of healing and hope is not for "God's favorites" alone but for everyone of God's children.

Here is something extra.

Rev. Oral Roberts and my father, Rev. Gordon Lindsay, were men who received similar callings and supernatural giftings. Both ministers received calls to spread the message of redemption and that healing is for the body of Christ today. Both the Roberts and Lindsay families have been friends for more than 60 years.

–Dr. Dennis Lindsay, President/CEO Christ for the Nations

Roberta Roberts Potts has captured the essence of her father's life like nobody else. She knew and loved the real Oral Roberts and gives us a wonderful window into his heart and soul. Don't miss her incredible insights into the life and family of her beloved father.

– **Ed Hindson**, Ph.D., Th.D., D.Min. Distinguished Professor, assistant to the Chancellor at Liberty University, President of World Prophetic Ministry and speaker on "The King is Coming" telecast.

First printing: October 2011

ICON Publishing Group
Customer Service: +1 877 887 0222
P.O. Box 2180
Noble, OK 73068

ISBN: 978-1-933267-21-0

Cover and Interior by Brent Spurlock, Green Forest, AR

Printed in the United States of America

www.icontitles.com
www.iconpublishinggroup.com
www.mydadoralroberts.com

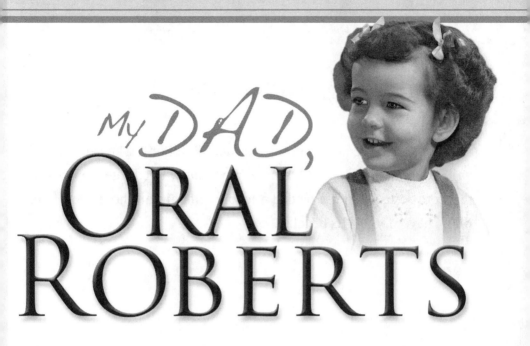

My *DAD,* ORAL ROBERTS

Roberta Roberts Potts

ICON
PUBLISHING GROUP

DEDICATION

This book is dedicated to my husband, Ron Potts, who said I could write it in the first place. And more importantly, I dedicate the book to my Lord Jesus, who befriended a lonely little girl all those years ago. May I never forget His benefits.

TABLE OF CONTENTS

Return to thine own house, and shew how great things
God hath done unto thee. And he went his way, and pub-
lished throughout the whole city how great things Jesus
had done unto him.

–Luke 8:39 (KJV)

"HE KEEPS ME SINGING"
Introduction

Have you ever dreamed of spending your birthday in the hospital with an elderly man? Well, that certainly was not anything I had ever envisioned. It was on a late Saturday evening, December 12, 2009, when my husband and I were driving home from dinner with friends that I realized I had missed a call on my cell phone. I was told in that telephone call that my dad, Oral Roberts, had taken a serious fall and was by that time prostrate on a hospital bed, having been given large doses of morphine in order to quell the terrible pain due to several fractures throughout his body.

As my husband and I live in Oklahoma and Dad had steadfastly insisted upon living in California (well, just because Southern California has better weather!), I was unable to arrive by his bedside until late the following morning.

My brother, Richard, and I were joined by our nieces, Brenda and Marcia, along with two of Dad's caregivers. It did not take long to determine that Dad's situation was most likely irreversible from a physical standpoint. As it was, I felt blessed to still have my father who was already 91 years old. And, while Dad's eyes would shine to a degree when I spoke to him of Heaven, I cannot honestly say that he was truly coherent during the first hours after our arrival.

The following day I awoke rather depressed, remembering that it was my birthday and I was, I must admit, feeling slightly sorry for myself—for obvious reasons. As soon as I dragged myself out of bed, I immediately called Sunny, one of Dad's faithful caregivers who had stayed through the night by his hospital bed. Dad had always had difficulty tolerating pain medications and this time was unfortunately no different. I could hear him yelling in the background—of course in terrible pain. I immediately burst into tears.

That day at the hospital was very much like the first until the late afternoon. Richard and I had just finished lunch at a nearby cafe when Sunny called. She advised that Dad was asking for us. I thought, "Oh no—now what?" When we exited the elevator on Dad's floor, I noticed a strange noise.

The closer we came to Dad's room, the noise became increasingly louder.

When we opened the door of his hospital room, we were flabbergasted. The strange noise was emanating from my father. He was singing! And I do not mean he was humming with a weak voice. No, he was singing—and he was singing with a very loud voice. It was an astounding noise. He was singing the old songs I had learned throughout his ministry, such songs as: "When He Reached Down His Hand for Me," "God is a Good God," "The Healing Waters," "Something Good is Going to Happen to You," "Expect a Miracle" and others.

What was even more amazing was that he was remembering all the words—exactly. He remembered all three verses of "When He Reached Down His Hand for Me." Richard and I were the only ones in the room who knew the songs, so we attempted to sing along. I found myself getting mixed up on some of the verses at which time Dad corrected me—more than once. Well, I cannot say that surprised me all that much, as he had corrected me on many such things all my life!

Then Dad would stop singing and yell at the top of his voice: "I'm going home!" "I'm going home!" "I'm going home!" During a lull in the singing, a nurse would enter to ask: "Mr. Roberts, what's your pain level?" He responded quickly: "I don't have any pain." What's more, it seemed to shock him that anyone would even ask the question!

This continued for about forty-five minutes. Here was a 91 year-old-man who was clearly dying—singing before the Lord with all his might, as David had done all those centuries ago. But remember, David had not been given mega-doses of morphine! And yet, for those few minutes, for that short, 45-minute window of time, Dad was as coherent as I had ever seen anyone. Then, almost like a veil, that small, last window closed and suddenly, Dad's body returned to its basically comatose, terminal state just as it had been for the past few days. And while his death certificate does not record Dad's passing until late the following morning, I believe that at the close of that time period of absolute bliss and joy, Oral Roberts went home, just as he told us he would. Oh, what a wonderful birthday it was for me. I look back on that day as perhaps one of the greatest of my life.

I remembered Dad having said to me on many occasions over my lifetime that he wanted to die while preaching. There was a time about one year earlier when Dad proposed to come to Tulsa from California in order to speak at a homecoming banquet at Oral Roberts University. Several thousand alumni were to be present and Dad knew they would be so pleased and thrilled if he could indeed make the trip despite his advanced age. My brother, Richard, strongly opposed that visit—out of concern that Dad would die as a result of such grueling travel. When Dad asked my opinion, I remembered that old desire of his and said something like, "Well, what do you hear the Lord saying to you?" He said: "I feel He wants me to come." My response was: "Then what do you have to lose?" Well, he came—and what a great time it was. Clearly, the Lord was not quite finished with him yet.

Over the months since Dad's passing, I have mulled over and over in my mind the meaning of the things I have just been relating to you. Upon reflection, I have come to believe that my father was reliving his entire ministry during that forty-five minute window. He was remembering the great things God had done for him, through those songs. I realized that it is those songs that tell the story. Thus, the origin of this book—a song for what I see as every chapter of Oral Roberts' life.

If you are an Oral Roberts critic, I pray you will perhaps see him in a different light as a result of this book. Folks either seemed to love him or hate him and never the twain shall meet. If you are an Oral Roberts friend or partner, I pray this book will help you to better understand what drove Dad, and more importantly, I pray that you will understand his heart. All who are brave enough to finish this book will see that while Dad's critics have demonized him and some of his adherents have deified him, both were wrong.

I welcome your comments about this book, whether they are positive or negative. And finally, let the reader be aware that I do not have access to my father's ministry materials. My little dream, therefore, is that this book will inspire Dad's friends to supply me with their own pictures or materials which belong to them—perhaps to be included in a reprinting of this book at a later date.

Roberta Potts
August 24, 2010
Tulsa, Oklahoma

God be merciful to me a sinner.

–Luke 18:13 (KJV)

"WHEN HE REACHED DOWN HIS HAND FOR ME"
Chapter 1

Dad's story begins just before January 24, 1918, with his mother and a stormy night. Claudius Priscilla Roberts seems like a pretentious name for a Cherokee Indian woman who was not even close to reaching five feet above the ground. And yet, it was "Sister Claude" as she was called, pregnant with her fifth child, who became my grandmother. Sister Claude was apparently the one who was notified in Pontotoc County, Oklahoma when someone was sick. Dad's family lived near Ada, Oklahoma, which is in the central, southern part of the state. They lived in the country and were gratingly poor.

On this particular evening, Sister Claude was visited by a little neighbor boy whose brother was dying with pneumonia. The brother was not expected to live through the night. Being far along in her pregnancy, it could not have been easy for Sister Claude to venture into the night, however she went. On foot, and having cut through one of the farms that dotted the landscape, she had to pull her short little—dare I say fat?—body through the rungs of a fence. While she was making the slow tortuous walk, she prayed. She told the Lord that if He would heal that little boy when she prayed, and if God would give her a blue-eyed, black-haired little boy of her own, she would give that baby to God and that she would name him "Oral."

Now as I understand it, most Cherokee children have brown eyes, not blue ones. So what my grandmother was requesting from God on that stormy evening would have to have been quite a miracle. The little boy was in fact healed, and Granville Oral Roberts was born soon after. Sister Claude's little boy had piercing blue eyes and she and her husband, Ellis Melvin Roberts, dedicated him to the Lord, as promised. Reading through the lines of Dad's descriptions, I have a feeling that in his mother's estimation, Oral was much more than just what one might describe as special.

I do not know why "Granville" became my Dad's first name because from the very beginning, he was called nothing but "Oral," his *middle* name. There was a problem however. His name was "Oral," a word which typically dealt with things which are spoken or also, things having to do with the mouth, and yet he stuttered and stammered terribly. He often could not speak more than one or two intelligible words at a time. And sometimes, particularly when he was nervous, he could not speak at all. How ironic. Perhaps that is why his fellow students at school laughed at him during his first day to attend school. When asked, he could not even say his own name. The teacher laughed as well. Apparently there was more than one occasion when Sister Claude was obliged to appear in her son's schoolyard, shame the other children, and take her embarrassed little boy home!

The reproach of others was not limited to outsiders. It also included his own uncle, his father's brother, Uncle Willis. In Dad's presence, Uncle Willis announced to the family: "Why that little Obadee will never amount to a hill of beans!" Perhaps if *his* childhood nickname had been something as draconian as "Obadee," he might have struggled as well! (Do you detect a rather defensive attitude coming from this author?)

But apart from his speech problems and even the disdain of his own family members, I think the hardship that weighed most heavily upon my father during his childhood was the deep poverty in which he found himself. And, to be honest, that deep sense of frustration due to the terrible economic straits was intermingled with what he saw as the bondage he felt in the churches he was required to attend.

While Dad loved his father, Rev. Roberts was apparently not all that interested in being the economic provider his family might have expected. My dad's stories about his father were not generally positive, at least in my recollection. I remember him talking about his dad sitting around until the kitchen shelves were bare. Then Sister Claude would "ream him out" and tell him to go preach somewhere. Dad's father would go preach (one wonders where) then return a few days later with a box of groceries. And that is apparently how they survived over the years of the Great Depression. In the meantime, the Roberts family was very involved in the church and unfortunately, I do not remember happy stories of Dad's attending church during his childhood.

God was—at least in Oral's mind—someone who either was not for real or who simply did not care about him. After all, to the mind of a sensitive boy, a thinker from his earliest years to his last days, living in a family who were as "poor as church mice" must have been almost soul-destroying. A preacher could go to the pulpit and preach about his people getting to go to Heaven when they died, but if they had to live… wondering where their next meal was coming from, you can understand why Dad and so many others felt that talk of a place called Heaven meant no more than the proverbial "pie in the sky!" Dad had needs *then* that going to Heaven when he died could not solve!

Is it surprising then that although his family made several attempts to draw Dad into their love for Jesus, my dad wanted no part of it? For most of his early years, my father rejected the claims of Christ on his life, seeing God as an ogre "up there somewhere" who was just waiting to swoop down and knock him off his feet if he made the slightest mistake. Perhaps the church never actually portrayed God in that manner, however, that is apparently what Dad and oh-so-many others perceived. And most would agree that our perception becomes our reality.

One bright spot in Dad's life, however, was his grandfather, Pleasant Roberts. Pleasant had been a judge in territorial Oklahoma. This was long before the days when lawyers were required to pass a bar examination, at least in Oklahoma. In those times, an aspiring attorney "read the law." While I am unsure of the exact process, I know that Pleasant had gone through whatever hoops were in existence at that time and become a judge. Later when the requirements changed, he was no longer qualified to practice law.

While perhaps it was his grandfather who inspired Dad's desire to later become a lawyer and governor of Oklahoma, I believe the greatest inspiration Dad received from "Pleas" as he was called, was his storytelling. Apparently, Pleas would sit on the steps of the courthouse in Tahlequah (the capital of the Cherokee Nation) and captivate his audiences by telling stories. Dad always said his own gift of storytelling was greatly eclipsed by the ability of his grandfather.

Raised to New Life

When Dad began high school, he quickly realized that he had at least a modicum of athletic ability, particularly in basketball. He made the team and was so excited about it that when he was only fifteen years old, he packed up everything he owned (apparently it wasn't much) and left home with his coach, having no intention to return within ten lifetimes.

It was while my father was playing in a basketball tournament at the age of 17 that he collapsed on the gym floor, after having made a long drive to the basket of his opponent. His coach and some of his teammates carried my dad to the back seat of a car and took him home.

I doubt that it ever occurred to my father that Sister Claude had been praying for him ever since her little boy left home. She had pleaded with the Lord to bring Oral home at any cost, and...He had done so. The doctor pronounced a diagnosis of tuberculosis, a death sentence in the year of 1935. This was of course long before the discovery of many of the prescription drug regimens available in our day. The dread disease was formerly referred to as "Consumption," for it unquestionably consumed a person's very life. As Dad was not the first one in his family to be struck with that deadly illness, it appeared that the family would simply settle down and wait for Oral to die.

They did have the pastor come to pray for the recalcitrant young man. The problem was, however, that those prayers went something like this: "Oh God, give Oral the strength to bear this terrible disease. Let him meet you before he dies so he'll go to Heaven, and not to hell." You can imagine the response of a red-blooded American boy. He was only 17 years old! He wanted to live, not learn patience while he was in the throes of death! How terribly uninspiring those prayers must have seemed to a boy panting merely to breathe!

Dad was bedridden, spitting up blood so often that his room had to be re-wallpapered at least once during his confinement. During that time Dad could not take a deep breath, but only short, small breaths. While his father may not have had the faith that God would heal Oral, Ellis was in fact very concerned that Dad could die and end up in hell. He made a vow to pray on his knees beside Dad's bed until Dad got saved.

By the word "saved," I mean that my grandfather wanted Dad to accept Jesus as the Lord of his life. Ellis wanted Dad to believe Jesus was the Savior of the world and was therefore the only One who had the power to take Dad to Heaven when he died, and therefore keep him out of hell.

My grandfather steadfastly kept his vow. One evening Dad was watching his father pray for him, angry at God for the terrible fate which had befallen

him, when he saw something he had never seen before. Ellis' facial characteristics faded into the background and Dad saw Jesus—in his father's face. I don't know what Jesus looked like, but what my father saw signaled a gigantic change in his life. Dad did in fact get "saved." He did accept Jesus as his own, personal Savior. God was no longer someone his parents loved and worshipped, but someone *He* now recognized—with everything he had in him.

Of course as good as that must have felt, Oral Roberts was still dying with tuberculosis. However, a few nights later, Dad's sister, Jewel, showed up in his room. She said only seven words: "Oral, God is going to heal you." Dad's reply was not particularly enthusiastic, but merely "Is he, Jewel?" Very soon after that bold pronouncement, Dad's brother

Elmer borrowed a car, came to Dad's bedroom, and with few words, unceremoniously wrapped Dad in a blanket, picked him up, put him in the backseat of the car and drove him to a nearby town where Rev. George Moncey was scheduled to pray for the sick.

On the way to that fateful meeting, Dad, while in the back of the car, heard the voice of God actually speaking to him. The voice told him that God was going to heal him that very evening. God told him then and there that He would be sending that young man to pray for the lost and suffering all over the world and to touch his generation for God's Kingdom. God also told him that one day, Dad was to build God a university. How strange that must have sounded that evening. I might have believed I had just eaten some bad pizza, but not my father. While he did not know how or when, he did believe God's voice—every word of it.

When the time came during the course of the evangelistic service for people to be prayed for, Elmer somehow got Dad to the front of the tent. He was so weak by this time that he was unable to do much to propel himself. I think it might have been the words the evangelist used which ignited a fire in Dad that night. Instead of praying as every preacher Dad had ever heard before—asking God to give Dad patience to endure the suffering, this preacher prayed an entirely different prayer. It went like this: "Thou fowl, tormenting disease of tuberculosis, come out of this boy, in the name of Jesus of Nazareth!" Apparently this man spoke with an authority that my father had never heard.

As soon as the man prayed, my father was instantly healed. What a sight it must have been. How I wish I could have been there to observe for myself the spectacle of what God did for Oral Roberts that night. Instantly, Dad was able to take a full breath, from the very bottom of his lungs. How amazing that must have felt after all the months of shallow breathing. And such breathing did not cause a coughing fit, nor did Dad spit up blood. He was completely whole, inside and out. God had done the work and done it completely, just as He had said.

To simply say that everything changed for Dad at that point would be a gigantic understatement. While it took several months for his strength to return from having had such a debilitating malady, it was not long before Dad was on the platform himself, telling others about God's delivering power. He told people of what had happened to him. He now saw God in a totally different light, not as someone who wanted to knock him down, but as someone who wanted to help him and to help others. And when he told his story, Dad often sang a song called: "When He Reached Down His Hand for Me."

> Once my Soul Was Astray from the Heavenly way.
> I was wretched and vile as could be.
> But my Saviour in love gave me peace from above.
> When He reached down His hand for me.
> When He reached down His hand for me.
> When He reached way down for me.
> I was lost and undone, without God or His son,
> When He reached down His hand for Me.

The Anointing

The truth is that Dad had a rather gravelly, vibrato-filled voice. In some ways I suppose it is a wonder that anyone would have listened, and to all three verses, no less. And yet, Dad's rendering of what he often referred to as "his" song was so heartfelt and so very real to him, that people were deeply affected when they heard it. Dad's lack of choral grace notwithstanding, his rendition of the song became a favorite for his audiences.

Now if you have any desire to understand my father, you must have some understanding of the phenomenon known as being "anointed of God." I would define God's anointing in this manner: It is when God decides to temporarily use an individual for His own purposes, assuming the person is willing and has the faith to believe God will do that. For a tiny moment in time, when that person preaches or sings or perhaps prays for the sick, it is as if Jesus were preaching, and as if Jesus were singing or praying for the sick. Now don't get weird on me. I'm not talking about anything magical or psychedelic, but I do believe that from time to time, God exhibits His own presence in people, in order to help others. And during that tiny moment, it is as if Jesus is walking again on the earth, reaching out to help people and to meet their needs.

When a person is anointed of God, it is as if they are acting outside of themselves. It is as if the Lord takes over temporarily and gives them good things to say or showers them with talents they do not ordinarily possess. But don't get too excited. The "anointing" of which I speak is temporary. It does not change that person on the inside. In my experience, it is very short-lived and after it is gone, that person is his old self again, sometimes full of attitudes unworthy of God's Kingdom, not necessarily loving his brother as he should, for example. In short, he or she is a normal human being again—just as before.

But for that one brief, shining moment, it is absolutely mind-boggling when God chooses to use a person for His glory. Again, it is not intended for the glory of the person, but for the glory of God and to help people. While I personally witnessed the "normal" man who was my father, I also witnessed on many, many occasions an anointing upon him as I have described above. Without at least an elementary understanding of what it means to be anointed of God, you simply cannot "get" who my father was, or rather, who he became after he was saved and healed as I described above.

From being the one who did everything in his power to avoid attending church services, Dad was now attending every revival meeting he could find, often preaching himself. It was at one of these revivals that he

first met my mother, although she definitely made very little impression upon him that evening. A later chapter of this book will detail how the two met and later married. Suffice it to say for now, however, that Dad understood he must have a wife beside him to help support him in the ministry to which God had called him.

Perhaps this would be the appropriate point, then, to explain what I mean by saying that God spoke to my father. I would be the first to admit that many such claims these days often appear to be disingenuous. Unquestionably, claiming to hear the voice of God in our day can be used as a method for manipulating others. After all, when someone says, "God told me to do it," your options as to a response are quite limited. You can either go along with the plan saying: "Who am I to argue with God?" or insinuate that the minister did not hear from God, thereby totally impugning his character.

By the previous sentences, you should have an idea of the skepticism of this author as to ministers' claims of hearing God's voice in general, especially when they claim to hear God's voice several times in one week.

I remember Dad saying toward the end of his life that God had spoken to him approximately 40 times. By this time he was 91 years old. Therefore, on the average, he heard from God less than once every six months. So how do I know that these were not just manipulative boasts made by Oral Roberts?

People who claim to have heard from God every other day must be considered under a Matthew 7:20 analysis: "...[Y]ou will know them by their fruits." (NASB) While Scripture states specifically that we are not to judge others, we are in fact to evaluate what is produced as a result of their lives and ministries. Having said that, all of us make mistakes from time to time, no matter how well-meaning. In the main, if a person's "words from God" are real:

- What is heard from God will never be in contradiction to Scripture. Scripture always trumps "*words* from God."

- In my mind, it would be unusual for the frequency of the "words from God" to far exceed the frequency of words from God received by Bible prophets such as Ezekiel, Daniel, Moses, David, Paul, and etc.

- Evidence that the minister truly heard from God will be revealed at some future time. (1 Samuel 3:19b "[A]nd the LORD was with him, and did let none of his words fall to the ground.")

- There will be real fruit as a result of that minister's life, fruit that cannot be reasonably denied.

Did my father always hear perfectly from God? I will leave that judgment to the reader, however, it is undeniable that the man had fruit—real fruit—which is still being harvested even today. Therefore, in my estimation, he should not be categorized with those who currently claim to receive "words from God" so much more often. Additionally, we forego an entire dimension when, because of one of these misguided folks, we assume that God no longer speaks to human beings. God does not change. (Malachi 3:6) If He ever spoke to human beings, then He speaks today. He did, and He does!

*"Beloved, I wish above all things that thou mayest pros-
per and be in health, even as thy soul prospereth."*
—3 John 1:2 (KJV)

"GOD IS A GOOD GOD"
Chapter 2

Mother and Dad started their ministry together in the late 1930's by traveling to speak in various churches. Dad also pastored several churches during those days. That period of time in America is now of course referred to as "The Great Depression" and its aftermath. My parents could not afford a home of their own and were thus forced to live along with their children in the homes of other ministers. This was apparently a common practice during those times. The churches frequented by my parents certainly would not have possessed the funds to obtain a hotel room for a guest preacher nor would my parents have been able to "pay the piper" for such. However, while this may have been the norm for others, not having her own "space" weighed heavily upon my mother. She wanted a home of her own and who could have blamed her?

The couple, with babies in tow, eventually left the evangelistic trail and began to pastor in such places as Enid, Oklahoma.

But during those years they still did not own their own home, again, being paid so poorly that there was no possibility of even making a down payment on a home. This lack became a point of contention between

Mother and Dad. Finally, my mother gave Dad an ultimatum. She announced that unless she was able to move into a home of her own by the deadline, she planned to take the children and return to her mother's house. While some would be anxious to criticize my mother for this ultimatum, I suspect that her desire was God-given. After all, if God truly loved Oral and Evelyn Roberts, how could He possibly get any pleasure from His servants being so poor? Believe it or not, the church people of that day actually joked—without apology—about their poverty stricken pastors with this little ditty: "God, if you'll keep our pastor humble, we'll keep him poor!"

I see this as an important point in Dad's story. It explains, at least in part, why he was not only so deeply anxious to remove himself and his family from abject poverty, but also his gargantuan yearning to help others escape poverty's clutches as well. It explains many things about Dad's future philosophy and the direction of his ministry in the years ahead. Around our house there was much talk of a way of thinking that will continually renew poverty, a poverty-mentality if you will. I would say that Dad, with my mother by his side, spent a great deal of his Christian life fighting this attitude. He attempted to help people not only to escape poverty itself, but also to escape the thought processes that tend to perpetuate poverty.

While I would definitely agree with many of his critics that some of the methods used toward that goal were unorthodox and sometimes even hokey, at bottom I believe these things were done because of a sincere desire to help people, not to take advantage of them, as some have accused. There is no question that Dad's poverty deeply marked his psyche. He did not forget for one moment from whence he had come.

One Wednesday night in Enid, Oklahoma during the fall of 1946, having come to a "point of no return" in his own mind, fueled by my mother's ultimatum, Dad marched to the pulpit during the course of what had been a routine, midweek church service.

He told his audience of his family's need for a home of their own. He told them that he was about to take an offering. Well I do not suppose that was so unusual, but then he did something completely unprecedented. He reached into his wallet and pulled out the amount of his entire weekly salary, $55. He had apparently just been paid and my mother had carefully budgeted for that week's groceries from that amount. Dad placed the money on the altar, explaining to the people that he was unwilling to ask them to give sacrificially unless he and his family were willing to do so. My mother had—thankfully—been unable to attend that evening because one of the children had been ill (I do not know which one) and had absolutely no idea of Dad's seemingly desperate move. (Can you imagine her reaction had she been there?)

Many of the people did respond to Dad's appeal, but overall, I do not believe Dad received the response for which he had hoped. At the close of the service, he had no choice but to return to the house where the family was currently residing and tell my mother what he had done. Having been the recipient of many a baleful stare from my mother over the course of my childhood as well as my adulthood, I really cannot imagine my father having the temerity to face my mother that night, and yet he did. A courageous man was Oral Roberts! He told her exactly what he had done—without apology. My mother, always the practical one, was naturally at a loss as to how she was going to feed the children that week. I never heard Dad go into detail concerning Mother's reaction to his "sacrificial gift." I just remember Dad saying: "It was a very cold bed that night."

At approximately 4:00 a.m., Dad was awakened by a pounding on the front door. He naturally assumed that someone in the church was ill, or a similar catastrophe had occurred. However, he opened the door to one of his church members, Art Newfield, who did not seem visibly upset. Mr. Newfield was a farmer who had originally prospered from his crops, however, due to recent unwise investments in the stock market, he had lost much of what he had gained. Art Newfield had been present in the service that night but had not participated in the offering, despite the fact that He felt the Lord urging him to do so.

When Mr. Newfield arrived home, he had been unable to sleep. After an hour or two of tossing and turning, he remembered that he had buried $400 in a forgotten corner of his farm. I can imagine him there, digging up that money in the dead of night. Only he had no intention of spending it on himself or his family. He felt an even stronger urging to give it to the church—so that the nice young pastor and his family could have a home. Newfield figured the $400 would not be enough to save his farm anyway, so why not do something good with it? He handed four, crisp one hundred dollar bills to my astonished father and then he made a statement—a statement which profoundly changed my father's thinking, once again. He said: "Pastor, *this is my seed* toward your new house."

Now if you have been around the church world of today, perhaps a comparison between giving to God and planting seeds may be familiar to you. But on that night, in the late 1940's, it was a revolutionary concept. Oh yes, many later took this idea and used it for ungodly purposes.

Yes, it has certainly been contorted into all sorts of money-raising, terrible schemes that sometimes did in fact cheat people out of their hard-earned money.

But the idea that my father received from Art Newfield that night was directly from God. And I suppose it could only have started with a farmer, one who understood that you could not possibly reap a crop unless you *first* planted seed. While human beings understood the concept of the seed as it dealt with corn, wheat, barley and the like, up until that time no one had learned how to *import* the concept to the realm of finances, i.e., giving money as a seed into the Kingdom of God.

What was the result of all this? My parents along with their two older children did obtain a home of their own. The blessings of God flowed upon Art Newfield and his family and they did *not* lose their farm, as they had feared. (Of course I always wondered if that bed was warmer toward dawn, but was far too shy to ask, and, well, now it is too late.)

But as important as the event with Art Newfield's planting his "seed" was, an event occurred soon after which proved to be of even greater significance.

The Good God

Having contracted tuberculosis at seventeen, Dad's education had been interrupted. However, from the time of Dad's conversion to Christ, he had developed an urgent desire to continue his schooling. While a full-time pastor, he managed to finish high school and begin college. Whenever he believed the family would be staying in the same town over the course of a full college semester, Dad would enroll in as many classes as possible without too much interference with his pastoral duties. During this time he attended both Phillips University and Oklahoma Baptist University.

During a sociology class at Phillips, he was disconcerted when his professor made this statement: "It would have been scientifically impossible for God to have made a woman from a male rib." Before Oral Roberts had an opportunity to express his own outrage, he heard the Lord speaking in his heart: "Son, don't be like other men. Don't be like other preachers. Be like Jesus, and heal the people as He did."

Dad's commitment to reading and studying the Bible never waned. One particular morning, he had just a few minutes before the bus would arrive to transport him to his morning classes. The family had just finished breakfast and Mother was doing the dishes. He picked up his Bible hurriedly, planning to read the first thing he found, in order to reach the bus stop on time. And there in front of him was a verse he had never noticed before. By this time, he had read the entire Bible many times, but he had no memory of this particular scripture. It was 3 John 1:2: "Beloved, I wish above all things that thou mayest prosper and be in health, even as thy soul prospereth."

He started yelling for my mother to come quickly. She wiped her hands on a dishtowel and ran into the bedroom, wondering what in the world was wrong. I suppose that every generation of Christians over the centuries have emphasized only a certain part of the Bible. Today we may tend to emphasize giving and prosperity more than such things as holiness and the "weightier matters of the law." However, in my parents' day, things were quite the opposite. Therefore, when Dad read the verse out loud to my mother, she stated emphatically: "Oral, that's not in the Bible!" So Dad turned his Bible around and showed the verse to her. Perhaps this was one of the reasons why our family always joked about Mother having been born in Missouri. It is referred to as the "Show Me State" and Mother certainly fit the model. When she realized that the words Dad had been saying were in fact a part of the Holy Scriptures, she said: "Why doesn't anyone talk about this?" Dad replied, "I don't know, but *I'm* going to start talking about it!"

It was this verse that more than any other part of the Bible in itself, proved once and for all to Oral Roberts that God was not that terrible thing in the sky—waiting hopefully for people to make a mistake so that He could pounce upon them. The verse proved to Dad that "God is a Good God." I do not know whether that phrase came to him on that particular day or whether it came to him later, but I do know that the phrase became a watchword for him and determined much of what he was to do over the remaining years of his life. He later said in sermon after sermon: "God is a good God and the devil is a bad devil!" He later found John 10:10 which stated: "The thief cometh not, but for to steal, and to kill, and to destroy. I am come that they might have life, and that they might have it more abundantly." John 10:10 was another verse which Dad quoted repeatedly, and for good reason! Later, Stuart Hamblen, a famous Christian songwriter, wrote a song entitled: "God is a Good God." Dad was determined that every audience of his healing crusades from that moment on learned and sang that song! I can still hear one of Dad's crusade soloists, Bob Daniels, singing that song and oh, what an impression it made upon me:

> Every life is but a flame my Lord caused to burn,
> Every star a shining world that my Lord owns,
> Tho' He owns the Heavens,
> He still has time for you
> If in prayer you'll make your wants and wishes known.
> (For) GOD IS A GOOD GOD,
> Every heartache He understands,
> There is healing power there are miracles
> In the touch of His wonderful hands.
> What He's done for others He will do for you,
> If you'll only believe and trust Him too,
> For GOD IS A GOOD GOD,
> And His goodness He will show to you.

Now do not make the mistake as others have that because of Dad's short catchy phrases such as "God is a Good God" and others, that Oral

Roberts was merely an uneducated, country boy. Granted, the majority of Dad's education was not formal, nor was he the recipient of the many earned degrees so often touted by scholars. Having said that, however, there was no question that Dad was self-educated. While later he wished he had taken the time to complete his formal education, at the time, he believed he was studying all he possibly could while at the same time, working full-time for God's Kingdom. As the years went by, he studied on his own and later was tutored by many Oral Roberts University college professors. He also read on his own, voraciously. I remember when he even read Kant, Nietzsche, Kierkegaard, and others. I honestly do not know how he "plowed through" them.

Additionally, many folks surmised from reviewing his books that Dad was uneducated. I suspect as well that Dad enjoyed confounding some of his critics by allowing them to believe his educational level was far beneath theirs. He reminded me in a way of a pool shark who pretended to be unskilled, until later when he knocked every ball into the correct pocket. Sort of a Columbo-of-the-Christian-world. Dad was very well-read, from newspapers to news magazines to biographies, philosophical works, theological treatises and a barrage of novels. He was extremely well-informed regarding current events, coupled with what many would refer to as "street smarts" as well. While I was in law school, I often attempted to stump him with a legal term or case precedent I had recently learned; however, I was most often to be disappointed.

Over the years, our family members often attempted to best him at "Word Power" and other such games, but Dad was always the winner. I learned early on never to underestimate him. Of course, that is what he wanted!

By now you may have realized that his books (over 120 of them!) were written purposefully *for* the uneducated. They were written in an easy-to-read style so that his partners could understand and apply the principles to their lives. Dad well understood his audience. While Dad did have a few ministry donors with formal academic training, the vast majority had been trained in the "school of hard knocks" and those folks could not possibly have understood Dad's books had they been written on a higher, intellectual level. And while Dad often enjoyed keeping his own intellectual abilities to himself, he was more than anxious to share with others the principles he had discovered in the Bible. Once Oral Roberts discovered that God was indeed a good God, that God was actually interested in His people living an abundant life *on this earth*, his entire perspective was dramatically altered. And, it was a message that God wanted him to express to the world.

Jesus went through all the towns and villages, teaching in their synagogues, preaching the good news of the kingdom and healing every disease and sickness.

–Matthew 9:35 (NIV)

"THE HEALING WATERS"

Chapter 3

You will remember from an earlier chapter that when the Lord first spoke to Dad while he was riding in the back seat of a borrowed car, part of what God said involved my father praying for others to be healed—and more specifically, that Dad was to take God's healing power to *his generation*, quite an undertaking. In our day, healing services, while perhaps still considered "on the fringe" by some, are not all that unusual. And yet, when Dad left pastoring in favor of healing meetings, such events were clearly an anomaly, even for those in the Pentecostal Holiness Church, the denominational group of his childhood and in which he had pastored. And, even though Dad's memory of those words from the Lord was still keen indeed, he did not have a clue as to the when and particularly, the how.

He did, however, feel a restlessness all through his pastoral years. He later referred to his years of pastoring as his "dark" years and refused to talk much of that part of his history. This should not be seen as an indictment of his denomination or of any particular church. Rather, it would be more accurate to conclude that he did not feel fulfilled in the pastorate as that was not his true calling.

Personally, I feel that those years may have been more formative to his understanding of God than even he recognized. However, one part of Dad's nature that was immovable was that once he moved on, he never, ever looked back. To the end of his life, he always had at least some restlessness that there might perhaps be one more thing he should be doing for God. Once he made a move forward, the idea of returning to something he had done before was not worthy of consideration! Have you discerned yet that Oral Roberts was somewhat stubborn? Well, read on and I shall tell.

Honestly, I do not understand how in the world he could have had the time to be restless. During his mid-twenties, Dad was pastoring a church full-time, studying his Bible, preparing sermons and praying many hours per day. He was also attending college part-time. Anyone else would have been worn to a frazzle and ready for a vacation, but not my father. He knew there was more for him, much more.

It was during this dissatisfied period of his life, one of those many times when he had to have been feeling terribly impatient, asking God for some details that he felt impressed by God to read the four gospels, i.e., the Books of Matthew, Mark, Luke and John, along with the Book of Acts. But not only that: he was to read them three times during the next 30 days, *on his knees*. He believed that if he would do this, God would show him who Jesus REALLY was. I simply do not know how he did it. Can you imagine the discomfort of reading the Bible, or anything for that matter, on your knees? But perhaps Dad was so careful to fulfill this directive because he was so dissatisfied with his progress in the ministry by then.

During these days, Jesus' presence had become so real to Dad as he read on his knees that he actually began to wonder if Jesus were there physically. He would quickly look up, wondering if he would actually be able to see Him. Additionally, to understand the man you must understand that if he believed God had told him to do something, it would have taken Heaven and Earth to keep him from doing it. I would say that Oral Roberts was the very definition of the word "driven." I have met a lot of people over my lifetime, and yet during all of my years I have never met anyone who was so highly motivated, who was so focused, and who was so completely unchangeable, once he had made a decision.

I can visualize Dad on his knees, struggling to fully understand the miracles of Jesus, His teaching, His dealings with the Pharisees, His disciples and Roman soldiers. I suppose Mother could have rushed into the room screaming that the house was on fire and my father would have allowed the house to burn down around him. That was my father and I exaggerate not!

The Birth of a Healing Ministry

On the evening in which Dad finally completed those long hours on his knees, he got on his face before the Lord, having reached a point of no return in his own mind. He poured his heart out to God. That same evening, the Lord gave him an answer: "From this hour, you will heal the sick and cast out devils by My power."

Can you imagine the expressions on the congregation the following Sunday morning when Pastor Oral Roberts announced that on the following Sunday afternoon, he was going to have a healing crusade. Dad went home that afternoon and put out a fleece before the Lord.

You will find that "putting out a fleece" originated in the Book of Judges with a man named Gideon. (See Judges 6:37-40.) It is a method of determining God's direction in one's life. Dad told God that if He had really meant what He said about wanting Dad to pray for the sick, then He would need to show him during the course of the upcoming meeting. First, there would have to be an audience of at least 1,000 people. Dad's typical audiences in those days consisted of about 200 souls! Secondly, sufficient money would have to be collected in the offering in order to cover the costs of the meeting. Thirdly, and most importantly, at least one person would have to be healed. Actually, the final portion of the three-tiered fleece had one more qualification. The person who was healed would have to definitely know and acknowledge that he or she had experienced a true healing from God. Further, Oral Roberts would have to know it.

Never one to do things halfway, before the Sunday afternoon meeting, Dad went downtown, applied for and accepted a full-time job selling men's clothing. Apparently at this point, he was through with pastoring, no matter what! Of course you have no doubt already predicted the outcome of the fleece. When Dad arrived that Sunday afternoon, there were already 1,200 people in the audience! Once an offering was taken, the count was just a few dollars *above* the costs of the meeting. And what's more, there were many healings, starting with a woman whose hand had been unusable for more than 30 years. Dad stayed to pray for the people until early evening. More importantly, by the time the meeting was concluded, no one in the room doubted that Dad had been used of God to pray for the sick. And Dad knew, unequivocally. On the following Monday morning, Dad resigned his pastorate and that clothing store lost one who might have become its best salesman ever.

Looking back with the vantage of time, I honestly do not know how Mother and Dad had the faith to take their children, leave a steady "job" and start a new ministry in Tulsa, Oklahoma, with absolutely no earthly guarantee of success. Perhaps I am just being a proud daughter when I make an analogy to the life of Abraham: "By faith Abraham, when he was called to go out into a place which he should after receive for an inheritance, obeyed; and he went out, not knowing whither he went." (Hebrews 11:8)

In 1947, one of the few people Dad knew in Tulsa was Steve Pringle, a pastor of a small church. Rev. Pringle was having a revival about that time and asked Dad to speak one evening. Things went well so Pringle asked Dad to continue preaching for several more evenings. At some point during one of these meetings, a man took a shot at Oral Roberts. Thankfully, the shot did not get close enough to do any damage to my father.

In truth, the only reason why the incident is even worthy of recognition after all of these years is that the shooting was reported by the Associated Press. I do not know if it was an uninteresting news day or whether preachers being shot was more a novelty then. For whatever reason however, the news media reported the incident and it became the "shot heard around the world" for Dad's ministry. Overnight, Oral Roberts was front-page news, giving him name recognition when a healing crusade of his own was later announced.

It is important for me to mention as well that only the largest cities had auditoriums with enough seats to accommodate the numbers of people who flocked to Dad's crusades. So in the cities where large auditoriums were available, that is where Dad's meetings were held. He would have the main services in the main auditorium of course, but he would also have a smaller room designated for people who were called "invalids" in those days. Remember that we are talking about the late 1940's through the 1960's, long before individuals with disabilities were referred to by more positive terms.

The problem came, however, with areas in which no large auditoriums had been constructed. As the word spread, people often drove hundreds of miles to attend Dad's crusades, meaning that there always seemed to be thousands of people to accommodate without a large enough seating area in which to do so. Therefore it was not long until Dad began purchasing and transporting his own tent for the areas of the country which did not contain a sufficiently large auditorium. Dad ministered overseas as well and while I believe he at times took a tent with him, my memory is that his overseas meetings were more often in auditoriums.

By the peak of his crusades, Dad had purchased a tent that was designed to seat 10,000. However, on most evenings the tent contained standing-room-only. I remember seeing many people standing for the entire service, seemingly never getting tired. And by the way, 10,000 may not seem all that large to you, dear reader, but can you picture the sights, the sounds, and even the smell of all those people under a tent on a warm evening? Why, because of the throngs of people there was hardly room for anyone to move under that tent. But it mattered not, for very few people even wanted to move. Everyone was glued to his seat or where there was room to stand. It was that powerful!

Of course there was no question that it was the healings that were bringing the crowds. I would venture a guess that some of the vast numbers who attended those crusades came due to the novelty. But God used even those circumstances, or throughout the course of the meetings, many of the scoffers became convinced about the truth of the Gospel when they saw Dad preach and pray for the sick.

Even though it was the healings that seemed to be Dad's "claim to fame," those events were always preceded by a sermon. Oh and by the way, if you were not already aware, over the years Dad developed absolutely incredible sermons. In "The Fourth Man," he preached about the three Hebrew young men who Nebuchadnezzar threw into the fiery furnace because they refused to bow down to an idol. One of the most remembered parts of any of his sermons, I believe, was his presentation: "Christ in Every Book in the Bible."

Although I have no proof, I believe it was my father who originally came up with the terse words about each Biblical book. He would stand on the platform holding a heavy microphone and say each one of those by memory, and without hesitation. While many people can memorize long passages, few can say them from memory with such fire in their voices! Before he was even halfway through the books, the crowd would be on their feet and by the time he was through, the crowd could no longer hold back the shouts of praise to God. He not only had an incredible memory but also the power to deliver those things he had memorized (as if they were not memorized at all) as if he were saying them for the very first time. The collective thrill at the close of these presentations is simply something that cannot be reduced to words, at least not by this author. It was mind-boggling, it was inspiring, it was life-changing.

He preached a sermon called "Samson and Delilah; Battle of Champions" which dealt with the human sex drive, a subject which was typically taboo in the 1950's in America. He preached about Jesus delivering people from demon possession. He preached about the Roman centurion who understood the authority of Ceasar and therefore was willing to accept Jesus' authority to heal his sick servant. He spoke about Peter, who had been fishing all night and caught nothing, but when Jesus

climbed aboard, all of a sudden he caught a "net-breaking, boat-sinking load!" (Dad later commissioned a large painting of that scene that hung in his office at ORU. The other disciples were looking at the results, i.e., the fish, of what God can do for you, but Peter was looking at Jesus, the author of those results.)

Spellbound

During his crusades, Dad also had a crusade soloist, a man with a wonderful voice whose song would set the tone of the meeting in advance of the sermon. The first soloist I remember was a man by the name of Bob Daniels. He had a deep, resonant voice that helped to raise faith in his hearers.

Later, a man known by many as the "Christian Bing Crosby," a man named Vep Ellis, became the crusade soloist. Besides being a wonderful singer, Vep was also an accomplished songwriter. Vep often wrote songs to complement Dad's sermons. For example, one night after hearing Dad preach about Jesus calming a storm on the Sea of Galilee, Vep wrote: "I Can't Go Under for Going Over; the Master is on Board!" And when Vep sang, well, as Dad used to say: "He brought the house down!" (Interestingly, his four sons have recently sung some of their father's songs on two CD's. It is wonderful to see that Vep's great music is still making a difference.)

After Dad preached about the lepers (described in 2 Kings 7:3) who struck a blow for deliverance, despite their illness, Vep wrote: "Why Sit We Here Until we Die?" After Dad preached regarding the sufferings of the Apostle Paul, Vep wrote a song entitled: "A Prisoner of the Lord." And there were many more.

I will never forget the anointing of both Bob Daniels and Vep Ellis when they sang as the last event just before Dad's sermon. Then when the song ended, I can still hear Dad's associate evangelist, Rev. Bob DeWeese, announcing that Dad was ready to preach. In a booming voice which never really required a microphone, Brother DeWeese would say something like this: "And now, it is my happy privilege to present to you the man whom God raised up for your healing deliverance, Oral Roberts!" And my, did the people cheer. What a moment!

If you have spent much time in church, you will probably have noticed some people falling asleep during sermons, well, that is if you were able to stay awake in order to witness that boring phenomenon! But not so with Dad's sermons. Dad had a talent "on loan from God" which kept his audiences on the edge of their seats. I personally cannot imagine how anyone could have slept through an Oral Roberts sermon. First of all, he interacted with his audiences in such a way as to get and to keep their attention, from beginning to end. He would often identify and speak to certain sections of the audience. He would say things such as "You, up there. I can't see you very well. Maybe tomorrow night we can get those lights moved so I can see you better!" No matter how large the audiences became, he made each and every person feel he was speaking to them personally and individually.

I believe that part of Dad's success in keeping his audiences engaged was that he had a natural ability to tell stories from the Bible (and other stories as well). He had a way of keeping his audiences spellbound and believe me, it would have been difficult to get bored!

Once the sermon was completed, he asked if there were folks who wanted to accept Jesus Christ as their personal savior. This is what is known as an "altar call" within Christian circles and I have alluded to this experience in an earlier chapter when I spoke of Dad's own history.

I was not born until 1950, three years after Dad began healing crusades so obviously, my memories would not have begun much before the late 1950's, however I can say from my own experience that the only lull in my Dad's meetings was (to me at least!) what came next. After the altar call came testimonies of individuals who had been healed in earlier meetings. During this portion of the evening, Dad would quietly leave the platform in order to pray for those who were terribly sick, often folks with terminal diseases, who were unable to stand (or be carried and held) for long periods of time.

Back at the ranch where I was, Brother DeWeese was interviewing people who had been healed in a previous meeting. To me, this part was the "ho hum" section. By the way, if you or someone you know was one of the "testifiers," I hope you will forgive me for my lack of appreciation of those testimonies. What can I say, I was an ungrateful kid! At that point in my life, I simply had no interest in events that had already happened. I wanted to see things WHEN they happened. So imagine for a moment, this little girl fidgeting in her seat when without warning, the audience and I would hear a piercing scream! Whispers would start circulating through the tent and we would soon come to understand that someone in the invalid tent had been healed. What a thrill went up and down the spine of everyone inside that tent!

The truth is that my mother was not so keen on her husband praying for the folks in that separate area, for after all, many of them had communicable diseases and who knew what else. But her strongest objection was that Dad might be called upon to touch someone with tuberculosis. You will recall that this was not only a terminal disease in those days, but it was also the very affliction from which Dad had almost lost his own life. But my father totally ignored her, for getting sick again was the last thing on his mind. He was so anointed of the Holy Spirit, so full of the call of God on his life, so intensely concerned about the people he knew were waiting for his prayers that I cannot imagine him turning back for any reason. And while certainly all those folks did not get healed, when one did, word would quickly reach the main auditorium, and often notify us with a shout of inexpressible joy.

How do I find the words to express Dad's intensity when he laid his hands on people and prayed for them? While sometimes those prayers lasted no more than perhaps 30 seconds or a minute, during that tiny fragment of time, nothing else and no one else existed for my father. He was not thinking of the next person waiting for his prayer, he was not looking over that person's shoulder to see who else was in the room. While Oral Roberts was praying, for him that person was the only one on Earth. Never have I witnessed such intensity of purpose.

After Dad was finished praying for the invalids, he would take a tiny breather before returning to the main service. By this time, he had preached somewhere between forty minutes up to even two hours. He had conducted an altar call, then prayed for those critically ill people with heart-wrenching ailments. Is it any wonder that after the emotional and physical drain of praying for the invalids, Dad's clothing was totally soaked with perspiration?

But here is where my mother would shine! When the auditorium was chosen or the tent girded onto the earth, Mother made sure that a tiny room was provided where Dad could go between the Invalid Tent and the main service. If the crusade was being held in a tent, the "room" I speak of was no more than some irregular pieces of wood that had been temporarily nailed together into a square with no ceiling. The "room" always had a rickety door (just stable enough to give ingress and egress along with a small light bulb hanging from the ceiling, which always seemed to be swinging dangerously). The room was typically just high enough to shield most of Dad's body from inquisitive eyes.

Inside, there was a wide bowl in which Dad could "wash up" at least to some degree. There was also a clean shirt Mother provided for my father. But the crowning point of that room—well, as far as this little girl was concerned—was the cup of steaming hot chocolate, all ready for Dad to drink at just the right moment. Remember that I am speaking of Dad's meetings that were in a tent which meant that the night air could be felt just about everywhere. What happens when you perspire, then later cool down? Well, my mother was concerned that Dad would become ill under those conditions, so she would always manage to have a cup of warm cocoa waiting for him. Oh my, how I wanted to drink that cup of hot chocolate! I could just imagine how good it would have tasted! Well, I never even got one sip, but don't shed any tears for me. I drank plenty of hot chocolate elsewhere, believe me. It's just that I was absolutely convinced that the cocoa would somehow have tasted even better if it had been the cup meant for my daddy!

At any rate, after drinking his hot chocolate, Dad would return to the main tent or auditorium to begin praying for the sick. By that time, Robert Deweese had already called certain prayer cards, perhaps cards "B" and "C," for example, for that evening, and many people would have already lined up. The beginning of the line would go across a ramp that was on the front of the platform so that people could stand on a level just under where Dad would be. My recollection is of Dad praying for them while sitting in a folding chair but I believe he stood many times as well. The people would come in front of him one by one or sometimes family by family, so that everyone in the audience could see what was going to happen, if anything.

The Source of Healing

Unfortunately, many people both then and now did not understand that all healing comes from God. They expected Dad to just zap them

with a healing, regardless of their attitude. Many folks became angry because they felt they did not need to sit through a sermon first before Dad would pray for them. They did not want to hear the Word of God preached. They simply wanted what they wanted when they wanted it. They wanted to be prayed for immediately!

I remember Dad saying that no gift of healing would operate against unbelief. First of all, whatever gift Dad had came from the Lord, not from him and no one was more acutely aware of that reality than Oral Roberts. Secondly, the gift was based upon Dad's faith in part but *also* on the faith of the person for whom he was praying. Dad therefore enforced an absolute requirement that a person was not allowed into the prayer line until he or she had heard at least one sermon. Actually, as it worked out, most of them would have already heard two sermons by the time the letter on their prayer card was called.

In retrospect, I think the system was ingenious and God-inspired. In order to be prayed for, one had to be allowed into the prayer line. In order to gain entrance into the prayer line, one had to have a prayer card. In order to obtain a prayer card, one had to show up at least by the close of an afternoon meeting. Therefore, most people who were allowed in the prayer line would have first attended an afternoon meeting during which they would have heard a sermon by Dad's associate evangelist, Robert DeWeese. After the close of that meeting, they would be able to obtain a prayer card. Then they would have to return to a meeting either that evening or on a later evening, hear Dad preach, *then* Dad would pray for them.

I recently heard a television preacher blast Dad for what I suspect was the story of a person who had run afoul of Dad's system. The minister told of his wheelchair-bound friend who had apparently come to one of Dad's crusades for healing, but was turned away. After hearing the minister's account, I wonder whether perhaps the individual had been unwilling to follow the system that Dad had so carefully orchestrated. Perhaps he expected to be prayed for immediately and did not wish to sit through a sermon before receiving a prayer.

It is interesting to note as well that in most of the crusades I attended, by the time of the last meeting of a specific crusade, always on a Sunday afternoon, there were many individuals who held prayer cards but whose letter (from a prayer card) had not yet been called. The result was that at the close of the altar call of the final meeting, Brother DeWeese would ask the entire audience to fold up their chairs and hand them to ushers who came along with carts for that purpose. Then Brother DeWeese would ask the people to form long, serpentine, double lines with just enough space in between so that Dad could pass inside the lines. Then instead of the people coming to Dad at the platform, Dad would come to them. He would then proceed to pray for each and every person who still held a prayer card.

I personally witnessed this on an untold number of Sunday afternoons. I do not know how Dad was physically able to walk continually, up and down through those lines for the process took several hours, with no break for him. (I would have had to stop for a restroom break at least once!) And remember, these prayers did not start until after Dad had already preached a sermon, given an altar call and prayed for those in the invalid tent. And of course this explanation does not take into account that Dad had preached and prayed for the sick during meetings on many *preceding* nights—sometimes in five-day crusades and in earlier years, sometimes in month-long crusades. Can you imagine how fatigued he already was before he even started to reach out his hand and touch each and every person who formed those lines?

None of those prayer sessions I witnessed contained less than one thousand people. And most of the time the number was far higher— hurting people standing there, still holding a prayer card—looking to

Oral Roberts and hopefully, to God. I do not recall those Sunday afternoon meetings ever concluding before 6 p.m.

Now while it may seem that the prayer lines on Sunday afternoons contained only a sort of "leftover" prayer and were therefore ineffective, as opposed to the prayer lines that were conducted on a more individual basis on earlier evenings, I can remember many great healings that occurred on those afternoons. True, you could not see as much as you could when the people came across the platform. However, often you would hear a horrendous scream, and you knew that someone had just been healed. The few of us sitting in chairs on the sides of the huge serpentine line would hear the scream, then jump to our feet, searching for the area where Dad was. The people near to him were by that time jumping up and down with excitement, so it was difficult to see exactly what had happened—but it did not take a rocket scientist to know that a great healing had just happened in our midst!

The Finest Hours

As I write this I cannot help but cry with pride over Dad's terrible sacrifice during those crusade meetings. I would say that those hours were clearly his finest hours. There were many times I was around my father in which he was clearly *not* anointed by God. I do not mean times when he was preaching, but other times away from the pulpit or a crusade. Believe me, he had his moments in which his faults were obvious to all of those around him! But oh the times he was anointed, oh my goodness. When I saw God working through Dad, it was the most mind-boggling thing I have ever seen. And it was so real. There simply was no way for an honest person to deny what was happening before his very eyes.

Dad had nothing left when those meetings were over. I remember so many occasions flying back home with him (and of course the others in his crusade team) after those meetings. He was exceedingly quiet. I was always told to: "Let your father rest, honey." And I understood that. Many times I would come up to him, grab his hand and just smile up at him without saying a word. He would sort of smile back, but only for perhaps a second, then he would seem lost again, in another world of his own. I often wondered what was in his mind at those times. I do not remember him sleeping as others might have done during those hours. No, I would say it took him many hours to come down to earth, so to speak. Well, whatever was going through his mind, I knew better than to bother him. Though a mere child I understood that he needed time to be left alone, to return to live on earth with the rest of us earthlings! Just the normal, "it's time to eat, it's time to go to work, let's read the newspaper, or whatever."

Having said all of the above, it would be unusual if Dad's careful "prayer card system" was performed perfectly by each individual charged with that responsibility over the years. Therefore, I assume that mistakes were made. I do know that Dad's crusades were huge operations, requiring large numbers of helpers—some paid and some volunteers—to set up the tent (a gigantic undertaking!), to arrange the healing lines and etc. These meetings were attended by thousands of people and crowd control would have been a large responsibility to say the least. I also know that by the time Dad arrived, it was time for him to preach. At least during the time I remember, Dad rested during the afternoon meetings when the prayer cards were given out, then he only arrived at the evening meeting perhaps during the congregational singing, and then it was time for him to preach after one song performed by the soloist.

The point I am making is that once Dad set up the system, he would have had little to do personally with carrying it out. So I suppose it is entirely possible that mistakes were made and perhaps there were in fact people who were refused prayer when they should not have been.

The truth is that the preacher's cutting remarks about my father hurt me deeply. And yet, I do realize that no system devised by man ever works perfectly. I would just say that while mistakes were probably made over the years, I believe Dad's heart was right in the requirements set up for the healing services and that by in large, those who were willing to accept Dad's system did in fact receive prayer.

If you were healed in Dad's ministry or know someone who was, I would love hearing from you. In case you are wondering, I no longer find those testimonies boring! I can be reached at robertajpottslaw@att. net.

I said earlier that Dad's healing meetings were courageous but I really did not explain. Today, healing services, at least the ones I know about, typically have people come up to the platform after they claim to have been healed. As a member of the audience, you do not have an opportunity to actually see anyone healed. You only hear the testimony about what an individual says happened. While I have no doubt that some of these people were in fact healed, it does not take a keen observer of human nature to realize that many of these folks appear on the platform simply because they are seeking attention, not because they truly received a miracle. But with Dad's meetings, the audience saw with their own eyes when someone was healed because Dad prayed with the person right in front of him, on the platform. Again, I am not criticizing other ministers' methods of conducting healing services—truly I am not. I am just saying that when a person claims to have been healed these days, you not only have to take it by faith that the Lord heals. You also have to take it by faith that that stranger is telling the truth.

In Dad's healing meetings, however, even those who walked in with no observable faith in God at all had a difficult time leaving with the same attitude. The healings were in your face and it was difficult to deny what you had seen. What you saw was what you got!

The flip side to all of this is that the percentage of people who received a true, noticeable healing from God was far less than the percentage of people who apparently received nothing. Perhaps you will see me as a heretic for admitting this, so let me tell you a little secret. Dad admitted it as well. Well, why not? Anyone who was there would have known. And of course this is why I say that my Dad's method was so courageous, because it was undeniable when a person appeared to have no change whatsoever after Oral Roberts had prayed! Perhaps some saw Dad only as a failure, as a result. But when someone was healed, oh my. How do I put it into words? How can I explain the thrill that went not only through my little heart but which also went through every living, breathing human being in the audience?

When a visible, undeniable healing took place the audience was on its feet, shouting and giving glory to the God of Heaven. The emotion inside each of us was absolutely indescribable. It was electric! Words cannot express it for you first saw the person waiting in that long, seemingly endless line of hurting people. The expressions before people received prayer varied. Some had a look of expectation. Many did not. I think it was the children who may have received my attention more than the adults, perhaps because I was myself a child. If you, dear reader, could have seen for yourself the looks of incredible pain on the faces of the parents! Of course if their child did not get healed, it wasn't so wonderful. But when a child was healed, the look on the faces of those parents, well it was as if Heaven had come down to them. You could see excitement, their incredible relief, and often surprise that God had really met them at the point of their child's need. Some parents would scream in an expression of delight. Others would be quiet—but their faces carried a radiance like the sun.

I suppose the humorous part is that many of the children who were healed often did not show as much emotion as their parents. It was as if at their young age, they had remained so close to God that they had almost perfect faith in Him. Before Dad would pray for children, he typically spoke to them first about faith and put the explanation into a child's vernacular. Then after a child was healed, it was almost as if the child expected it. Well, Brother Roberts had said it would happen if they believed, didn't he? Perhaps this is an indication of what Jesus meant when He said: "Truly I say to you, whoever does not receive the kingdom of God like a child will not enter it at all." Mark 10:15. The children seemed to take God's healing power more as a matter of course because they had an innate understanding of spiritual things, whereas their parents had obviously been living on the earth for far too long. And perhaps this was why my mother often leaned over to whisper to my brother and I: "Now children, stretch out your hand with your daddy. He needs you to pray too." And I felt I was a part of it all.

A Vast Audience—Television!

In the days of reality television shows with which we are now so accustomed, it may not seem all that surprising that Oral Roberts began televising his crusade services. In retrospect, Dad's first one-half hour television shows that showcased a healing ministry before the world were perhaps the original reality TV shows. Certainly in the 1950's, this sort of program was far from the norm. These were the days of the situation comedies like Father Knows Best, Leave it to Beaver, Sky King, Lassie and the like, to mention some of my favorites. Only church people had ever seen a human being reach out and touch another individual believing that a terrible sickness would vamoose! That kind of thing simply was not done on television. And oh, the cost of such a thing.

Well, my father's employees, bless them, learned very quickly never to tell him that something could not be done. Dad was larger than life. He was the sort of man who simply would not accept "no" for an answer.

Of course back then, there were only three major networks. There was no cable or satellite as in our day. And the folks at the major networks were incredibly resistant to such programming. How did Dad convince them to broadcast programing that had never been done before? There is in fact no other explanation than this: it was a miracle.

Of course somewhere toward the beginning of Dad's healing ministry he had a radio program that reached throughout the country. As a little girl who missed my parents dearly as they travelled over the world in healing crusades, hearing Dad's radio program on Sunday mornings was true delight. I remember that the radio broadcasts would start with a quartet singing. Remember the voice of the famous "Tony the Tiger?" It was Thurl Arthur Ravenscroft who made more than 500 television commercials for Kellogg's Frosted Flakes, touting: "They're gggggreat!" But Ravenscroft was also the bass singer in one of the quartets on Dad's radio broadcasts—and how wonderful that music sounded to me. The song those early quartets seemed to sing most often was "The Healing Waters." Dad himself often led the audiences in singing this great song during the meetings. While the name of his magazine was later changed to "Abundant Life" (from John 10:10), the first title was "Healing Waters" after the song written by Rev. L.L. Pickett and H.H. Heimar:

> Oh the Joy of Sins Forgiven!
> Oh the Bliss the Blood-Washed Know!
> Oh the Peace Akin to Heaven,
> Where the healing waters flow!
> Where the Healing Waters Flow,
> Where the Joys Celestial Glow;
> Oh There's Peace and Rest and Love,
> Where the Healing Waters Flow!

The Best Kind of Color-Blind

The subject of Dad's crusades, however, cannot be fully told without reference to Dad's "color blindness." Actually, he was color blind in two ways, naturally and racially. Those crusades took place during the late 1940's through the 1960's in America. You will recall that the famous Civil Rights Act was not passed until 1964 and before that time, it remained legal and accepted—even for Christians—to treat African Americans as if they were somehow inferior. Whenever Dad planned a crusade in a certain town, he started with local pastors, and had at least a modicum of their cooperation. He of course had the attendance of many of their church members as well.

In the south, the locals desired to make Dad's meetings conform with other meetings held in that part of the country. Basically, only whites were to be allowed to attend the meetings, or if African Americans were allowed, the locals expected them to be separated from the whites, in their own section, of course in the back! When Dad learned of this, he was incensed. How could they possibly expect him to tolerate such? When asked about racial questions he would often quip, "I'm an Indian. I'm neither black nor white." But the truth is he was seriously opposed to the racial "norms" of that day.

Dad absolutely refused the kind of "organization" expected by the local pastors. In the towns which would not allow African Americans to attend the meetings along with the whites, Dad would insist upon one evening during the course of the crusade to be set aside for him to preach and pray for *only* African Americans. In other towns, Dad made it clear to his employees and volunteers that the African Americans could sit wherever they liked.

However as I understand it, certain towns had municipal ordinances which would allow African Americans to attend the meetings, but absolutely required them to be segregated within the audience. When police officers assured members of Dad's crusade team -- vociferously, I might add -- that they would in fact enforce those heinous regulations, Dad felt he had no viable option but to obey. Even then, however, he made an exception during the altar calls, daring anyone in the crowd to complain.

You can imagine that in those days he was highly criticized for his stand and was even threatened by some who so violently disagreed, however, Dad refused to succumb to those pressures.

As far as I know, the threats remained only that, although I assume there must have been hard feelings as a result. Be that as it may, African Americans have classically been some of Dad's most loyal supporters over the years. Many of them later sent their children to Oral Roberts University. I believe this may explain what might otherwise be seen as a disproportionate number (in comparison to Caucasian Americans) of African American students at Oral Roberts University. These folks did not forget. (By the way, if you or someone you know experienced what I have been discussing above, I would love to receive an email from you with more details.)

As a final note regarding Dad's healing campaigns, I must mention a terribly humbling experience when he attempted to hold a crusade in Melbourne, Australia. I never learned the reasons why, but understood as a child that some people had actually attempted to burn down Dad's huge crusade tent, forcing him to leave town. It was as if that entire continent became to us a symbol of terrible loss and pain for my father. The unspoken rule in our household was the conversation was not to extend to the Melbourne crusade, or if it did, it should be only in hushed tones. Dad always saw his Australia crusades as nothing but a terrible disgrace and so did I, that is, until after Dad's death. Soon after he passed away, I received a telephone call from a lady named Liz Wilson with what was a starling revelation to me. Here is the story she wrote at my urging regarding Dad's meeting that took place in Sydney before the disaster in Melbourne.

"I was about 12 years old. Sydney and surrounding places were buzzing with excitement. Oral Roberts from Tulsa, Oklahoma, America was actually coming to Sydney to set up a tent! Our church at Petersham was excited. Us kids and others from the church spent all of our Sunday afternoons and some Saturdays going to places close to where the tent would be—to give out pamphlets and information about the meetings. Some materials were not so gracefully accepted—but we didn't care. We considered it a challenge!

"It took a 25-minute bus ride (sixpence each) for the ride to Burwood. Then a train and then a tram ride which took us fairly close to the tent. God provided our fares. We sold pop bottles and saved the money to go to the crusade. The churches were praying, especially my mom. Russian Christians came to our house to join in prayer with her for the meetings.

"Then WHAM! A pastor from Queensland showed up with a busload of—retarded and crippled people—which really freaked us kids out. We felt uncomfortable. They set up tents on our lawn and made sleeping quarters all over the house. Though we usually had just enough to keep our own family fed, it seemed like God made food available for all. Many church folks helped put out countless chairs. For us it was just plain exciting!

"Well, the big night finally came. Us kids were allowed to be in the back part of the tent where your dad would come in. He took time to pat the boys on the back and give the girls a hug. He said: "You've been busy. God will bless you." We were all so excited!

"Your dad did not come through the curtains until Brother DeWeese announced 'God's man for this hour…Oral Roberts.' Now I am grown and I know what anointing is, but at the time, all I knew was that something exploded and that is not an exaggeration! Everyone jumped to his feet. The air was filled with such expectation. I had never felt like that before. Some of us kids even cried, kids that never cry! The Holy Spirit was in that place. And then came the song: 'Where the Healing Waters Flow.' The pastors on the platform and the whole tent congregation stood to their feet. Then he preached—like nothing we had ever heard—different. Local drunks who often like to rest on the brick front fence; some of them came and got saved.

"The people confined to wheelchairs and invalids on beds…what a sight. He would go down to them with such a gentle spirit, such love. We were there. We saw it. Some later said: 'He had the humble spirit of God as he tended to the sick and lame first—he didn't make a big deal.' It seemed that he related most to the hurting.

"We witnessed the most miraculous healings take place, especially those that had been camped and in our home in wheelchairs, crippled beyond belief. And the way some of their faces had been so distorted and so scary to us kids, GONE! And that is how it went, night after night.

"It was later in Melbourne where some people tried and almost burned the tent down—but it was not that way in Sydney. In Sydney, all but one of the many people who had been brought to our house went home healed!

"Even though I had grown up in the church, I had never made a public decision for the Lord. I heard your dad say: 'You may have been raised in a godly home, but have you accepted the Lord by saying the sinner's prayer?' And there I was. I felt like someone had told him exactly who I was and what I was thinking. Your dad said: 'If you are ashamed tonight to come forward and accept him, do you know that Jesus will be ashamed of you before His father in Heaven?' I felt chill bumps all over me. I knew it had to be now or never…but still hesitated. Suddenly two massive wings appeared behind your father. He said: 'Do you know if you make this decision, all the angels in Heaven will rejoice with you?' I could not wait to go down! My big sister, Tamara, was an altar worker and she led me to Christ! Oh what a night! It changed my life and the lives of so many others, forever!"

For Dad, the catastrophe which was Melbourne had so overshadowed his memories of Sydney that it was as if the former had been no more than a dream. And yet, even the latter humiliation could not invalidate the wonder working power of God in the mind of Liz Wilson, and most likely, many others!

But when Jesus heard this, He answered him, "Do not be afraid any longer; only believe....

–Luke 8:50 (NASB)

"ONLY BELIEVE"

Chapter 4

The bedrock of Dad's preaching in his crusades could be defined with one word: "faith." But how was he to get that concept across to the people who attended his meetings? First of all, it was through his sermons. Most if not all of them were designed to teach people what was necessary in order for them to actually receive a healing from God. Dad preached that healing starts with an individual believing that God will do *now* what Jesus did when He walked the earth. After all, for years, the media labeled Dad as a "faith healer." While that term brought pain in his younger daughter's heart, for it was intended largely as a pejorative term, in its purest form I must reluctantly admit that it was correct.

Dad also spoke of a "point of contact." This concept came after Dad prayed for a lady by the name of Gladys Hanson. Before Gladys stepped into the prayer line at one of Dad's earlier crusades, she began praying: "Oh Lord, let his hand be as thy hand and I will be healed!" She continued to quietly repeat this entreaty to the Lord, even as Dad put his hands on her to pray. She was instantly healed, but Dad stopped after his prayer to inquire as to what she had been saying over and over. "Oh

Lord, let his hand be as thy hand and I will be healed!" Gladys' prayer made a deep impression upon Oral Roberts because he well knew that his hand had no power! He understood that the power came from God, not from him. And yet, something had happened to Gladys when Dad had reached out his hand.

Dad later compared it to turning on a light in your home. A lamp is plugged into an electrical outlet that is connected to the power plant. On its own, the lamp has no power, but when it is hooked into the power source, light results. In the same way, Dad began to understand that while his hand had no power in itself, if he *and* the person for whom he was praying would believe as Gladys had, then Dad's hand could be used as an extension of God's hand. Dad began calling it a "point of contact," When his hand touched the body of a sick person who believed in this manner, contact would be made between God and man. A point of contact is something you do, and when you do it, you release your faith.

A point of contact also sets the time. Consider this. Chad and Phil discuss having a meeting. Chad asks Phil "When?" Phil answers: "Oh, anytime." Chad asks "Where?" Phil replies, "Oh anywhere." Obviously, the two will never meet! Now if they had decided to meet the following Monday evening at seven in a particular restaurant in a particular town, they would most likely meet. The point is, you have to set the time. I have known people who have said for years, "Well, God can heal me anytime He wants to." Never once have I known such a person to be healed. You must set the time to release your faith, just as with Chad and Phil's meeting above.

Making Beautiful Music

Dad also used music as a vehicle to help people believe that God could heal them. Of course music speaks of different things to different people. Many of us enjoy listening to music for its own sake. We may enjoy the rhythm, the harmony, the words, or perhaps its effect as a whole. Of course lots of people enjoy sitting for hours at a symphony or other concert, simply for the sake of the music in itself. Not so Oral Roberts. Yes, toward the end of his life when he was too old to do anything else, he may have sat around and listened to a Patsy Cline CD for a few minutes, but when he was young and vigorous, on fire with God's calling on his life, I cannot imagine him spending even five minutes simply listening to music. No way, wrong number.

Rather, for Dad, music was something that should be used to inspire action. Music was worthwhile only if it could be used to help people. It must have a purpose and was never to be enjoyed simply for its own sake. Of course that goes right along with Dad's psyche in so many other ways. With one exception before I was born, our family never took a vacation. Our family never sat around and talked about the price of hamburger meat at the grocery store and certainly not the weather or how Aunt Effie might be getting along. There was no such thing as relaxation or "shooting the breeze." Everything was done for a purpose. While it is true that Dad became quite a golfer, and did on occasion spend hours discussing basketball, even those things were for a purpose—never for the joy of the game alone.

In Dad's crusades, music had a specific purpose, again, to help increase the level of an individual's belief that right then, *in the now*, as he liked to say, God would deliver what the Bible promised. Not only did the attendees hear a faith-building song before the sermon, but while Dad was praying for the people, they also heard a song. And when I say "a song," I mean one song and one song only! The song was called "Only Believe" and the chorus (the only part Dad used) contains merely two lines (which are repeated!):

Only Believe, Only Believe;
All Things Are Possible, Only Believe;
Only Believe, Only Believe;
All Things Are Possible, Only Believe.

During the opening years of the Oral Roberts crusades, the music was generally accompanied with a Steinway piano played by Roberta Millard (now Page) and on a Hammond organ, played by Geneva Millard. Roberta was Jeaneva's aunt. (I was later named for those two ladies, although my parents shortened my middle name to "Jean.")

As tent gatherings are comparatively rare in our day, we tend to forget the potential danger of inclement weather as we now so often enjoy the new posh arenas such as the newly constructed Bank of Oklahoma Center here in Tulsa. But in 1950, it was a tornado that literally ripped that canvas tent away, leaving 7,000 people exposed to the winds and pouring rain. Although almost all the crowd escaped, mercifully without injury, the Steinway was destroyed. Dad later used a Hammond organ alone. A wonderful organist, Bob Fulton, played the organ for many years while I was growing up. Later when I was a teenager I played the organ in a few of Dad's meetings and it was not until then that I learned how fundamentally important the song "Only Believe" was to Dad.

I had been instructed that while Dad was praying for the sick—a process that generally lasted at least one hour and sometimes two or more—I was to play "Only Believe" and only that song. Well again, the chorus contained two lines and two lines only. I now have a version of a quartet singing the song on my I-Tunes. The track is 40 seconds long. Does that give you an idea of how many times I was expected to play that song and only that song over the course of several hours?

Now it's not that I don't really love the song. I do. And even then I understood that it was important for people to hear a song full of faith while they were waiting for a prayer from Oral Roberts. It was just that, well, after playing it twenty times or so, I was thoroughly bored. I did manage to play it in several different keys and attempted to change it somewhat every time I played it, but after about ten minutes, I was more than ready for a different song!

As Dad was so incredibly intense, I assumed he would never notice if I added another song or two here and there. I thought he would be so focused upon praying for the people that the song being played in the background would not even reach his consciousness. I soon learned the fallacy of my assumptions, however, when Dad suddenly stopped praying, turned around and spoke to me, in front of all those people. He said: "Roberta, would you please play "Only Believe?" Being terribly shy to begin with, his "request" given publicly was more than a little embarrassing! Thank God my only punishment (well-deserved, I might add) was that humiliation, but believe me, that was enough. I learned from that experience, however. I realized that "Only Believe" was far more than just a two-line chorus to Oral Roberts. In retrospect, I think he felt that God required that song, and only that song, in order to use His servant, Oral Roberts to be an instrument of healing during those crusades.

I do not mean to imply that there was something magical about that song or about anything else that Dad did, for that matter. On the contrary, the song pointed Dad and the people to the One who has power, real power, not magic. It points out the fact that all healing exists in God, and never in people. Unfortunately, there were some, particularly individuals in the media, who believed that Dad was simply a fake. Dad told me near the time of his death about a certain town where the authorities required that a district judge sit on the platform on the first night of a crusade. The judge was there to certify that no trickery was involved during the healing line. That particular judge did in fact certify to the city leadership that there was no fraud involved in the meetings and that crusade was allowed to continue.

God Will Not Share His Glory

While there were many skeptics, there were also those at the other end of the spectrum. They believed that Dad had some power *in himself.* Dad's meetings unfortunately drew such people, in inordinate numbers. I remember one lady who would show up at a crusade and manage to be a part of the healing line over and over in many different states, usually because of an unsuspecting volunteer. Once she got near to Dad, she would bow down to him as if he were a king. I can still see the look on Dad's face one night when this occurred. It was not at all pleasant. Some people get fascinated by God's power, but not by God Himself. After a minister would usher the lady out of the immediate area of the platform, I remember Dad explaining to the audience once again that he in himself had nothing—that any healings that had occurred that evening had been brought about by God, and not by Oral Roberts.

When I was little, we lived on what we called "the farm," although it would have been more accurately described as a ranch. One afternoon the doorbell rang and I ran to answer the door before my mother could get there. I do not remember if Mother and Dad simply forgot to tell me about the lady I described above or whether I did not recognize her name. When the lady stated that she wanted to see my father, I readily invited her into the living room, assuming that such was the polite action to take.

My mother was aghast when she saw the woman "innocently" sitting in her living room. I do not remember what words were exchanged in order for Mother to usher the woman out of our house, but I do remember the expression on my mother's face. I learned from that experience that all people could not be trusted and I never made such a mistake again.

There is a reason, however, why I mention those strange individuals who seemed to imagine that Dad had some sort of power. The truth is that as much as God was using Dad, it would have been easy for Dad to start believing that he did have something other than a gift, placed upon him temporarily by God. I suspect that "Only Believe" was an anchor for Dad to hear over and over while God was using him so mightily. You have to understand that many people were healed before everyone's eyes, night after night. If one did not consciously focus upon Jesus as the true healer, it would have been tempting to see things another way.

There is no question that Dad had a huge ego. No one could have accomplished what he accomplished without such. But despite that ego, I know Dad fought the natural inclination to begin believing he was anything special in himself. I believe the song was a continual reminder to Dad that the events taking place before his eyes and seemingly through his hands were brought by the God of Heaven, and not by Oral Roberts. I suppose it will be obvious from the above that the healing ministry that I personally witnessed had a gigantic influence upon my life. It gave me a concern for hurting people that I seem to feel more than many others. But it was an incident witnessed by only three souls that may actually detail the essence of the healing story, as it were.

There always came a time during any given healing line (other than the ones on Sunday afternoons which I described previously) in which Dad knew he could no longer continue for that evening. His strength had flagged and for that evening at least, he simply had nothing more to give. By this time he was soaked with perspiration, again, and could think of very little but getting back to his motel room to go to bed. I do not ever remember him going out to eat with friends or family after a healing crusade. Most ministers enjoy going out to eat after preaching or having any sort of church service. It is "the rule" in a sense.

Dad is in fact the only minister in my experience who did *not* typically socialize after his meetings. As a child I certainly did not understand that. Why couldn't we go somewhere? As a child growing up in church, the only time I was allowed to stay up late in the first place was if I was in a church or evangelistic meeting of some sort. The only way to legitimately expand upon that time was to go out to eat after such a service! Who wants to go right back to the motel? How boring. But my father ALWAYS went straight back to the motel. He generally would have room service bring him perhaps a sandwich, or a bowl of hot soup if one were available (for his throat was always sore after speaking). Or sometimes, one of his evangelistic team would drive to a nearby snack bar and bring him a sandwich and potato chips. There were few fast food places in those days and those which were in existence had typically closed by the time the meeting had concluded for the evening.

I never knew if Dad gave a signal to Brother DeWeese or how the others in his crusade team knew when Dad came to the point when the meeting had to be concluded, but they always seemed to know. And it certainly was not the time when there were no more people waiting in the line. Looking back, I suppose the people still waiting must have been terribly disappointed. Maybe some of them were even angry. I honestly do not know. All I know is that there came a time when Dad knew that even had he continued to pray for the sick, absolutely nothing would happen. He knew that his prayers at that point would be useless.

Perseverance

It was on one of these nights when Dad had concluded the meeting. He intended to make a beeline for the car. Collins Steele or perhaps another in his crusade team would be waiting in the car with the heat at full blast to prevent Dad from getting so chilled. Dad could not wait to jump in the car and wend his way back to rest and solitude. But on this particular occasion, he was waylaid by a mother with her little boy. "Brother Roberts, I have my prayer card. I have my little boy. You have to pray for him. You have to pray for him!" Knowing my father I can see the look that must have crossed his eyes toward that woman and it would not have been friendly! Once he had something in his mind, once his direction was set, don't dare interrupt him! As his daughter I knew better than to interrupt him at such a time. It simply was not worth the consequences, believe me!

But this little lady was undaunted by my father's demeanor. Her determination was not at all quelled by Dad's seeming reluctance to notice her. She kept insisting that he pray for her little boy, but that was not all. She hung on him telling him that he must put his hand on her little boy's hip. "Brother Roberts, he was born without a hip socket. Touch his hip. Touch his hip!" She was just as focused upon her son's healing as Dad was on getting out of there! Goliath had finally met Hercules! There came a moment when Dad realized he could not simply ignore the woman. He was going to have to deal with her.

He responded: "Ma'am, I've been preaching and praying for the sick for several hours now. I'm bone tired. I have nothing left to give to your boy or to anyone else." But that little mother simply refused to give up. She absolutely refused to leave until Dad reached down his hand and touched the little boy's hip. When Dad finally relented, he learned that the mother was telling the truth. The little boy indeed had no hip socket. Dad could feel the place where everything went in instead of being filled out.

He said something like: "Ma'am, you have no idea what you are asking of me. I have never seen God perform a creative miracle. I have no faith to believe your little boy can be healed. I'm sorry. I can't help you." With that, he started to get into the car. But the little lady was not about to be ignored. She said: "Brother Roberts, you do the praying and I'll do the believing!" Mainly to get rid of the relentless woman, Dad laid his hands upon the little boy, but only in a perfunctory manner. He knew nothing would happen. He said a short prayer (perhaps with anger in his heart!) and the lady finally allowed him to get in the car and leave for what he saw as a well-earned night of rest.

As was typical of my father he gave no further thought to the incident. His mind soon leapt ahead to his sermon for the following evening. My father rarely looked back. He always looked forward.

On the following evening, the crusade was conducted in a similar fashion to that which I have related earlier. Dad preached, prayed for the sick, gave the signal the meeting was over for the evening and attempted to arrive at the car unmolested, in order to rest so he could start the process all over again on the following evening. But just when he thought he was safe, just when his eyes caught sight of the vehicle, ready and waiting to take him to his rest if he could just reach the door, there she was again with her boy in tow.

Being well-acquainted with my father's moods and temperament, his youngest daughter would never have dreamed of accosting him at such a moment. That took real courage—something I had not yet discovered at that point in my life. And yet, nothing was going to deter that mother. "Brother Roberts, Brother Roberts, put your hand on my little boy's hip." Can you imagine the look in my father's eyes? I don't even want to go there. Without having seen it, I *know* what his face looked like. Angry, frustrated, tired, and holding on to his tongue until it contained track marks! How had she gotten past his crusade team and the volunteers, again? They were supposed to keep a clear path between the back of the platform and the car!

Why was he being confronted again, two nights in a row! Those thoughts must have been racing through his mind in that moment. However, in order to stave off another barrage of demands upon his tired body, Dad reached down his hand to again place it upon the little boy's hip. And he felt a hip socket. The hip no longer went in where it was supposed to go out. Assuming he had simply grabbed the wrong hip, Dad felt the other hip. But both hips felt exactly the same.

Okay. I know what you are thinking. And if *you* are skeptical, imagine how Dad felt. He did not believe it either. Perhaps he did not even want to believe it. He later stated that he would never have believed it at all—except that he simply could not deny what he felt with his own hands as he touched the little boy.

As far as I know, such was the only time my father ever experienced what he referred to as a "creative miracle." I do not remember Dad telling that story very often. It was not exactly a story that touted his kindness and certainly would not have impressed the hearer with the high level of patience possessed by Oral Roberts! And yet that story, more than any other I know, allows us to grasp my Dad's healing ministry, at its most basic level. It was never my Dad. It was faith in God and in Him alone. That little lady somehow understood. "Brother Roberts, you do the praying and I'll do the believing!" Yes, the song was correct. "Only Believe." And God's power is the same today as it ever was. His power is not dependent upon a person. God's power is dependent on the *faith* of a person, faith in the God of the universe. He is God and there is none other!

Give, and it shall be given unto you; good measure,
pressed down, and shaken together, and running over,
shall men give into your bosom. For with the same mea-
sure that ye mete withal it shall be measured to you again.
                                                    –Luke 6:38 (KJV)

"THERE SHALL BE SHOWERS OF BLESSING"
Chapter 5

I suppose the most vitriolic criticism heaped upon Oral Roberts was his method of fundraising. And perhaps he may have deserved at least a portion of that criticism. On the other hand, dear reader, if you reject the concepts Dad preached because they may not always have been carried out perfectly, you will cheat yourself out of good things which God has for you.

Before collecting an offering in the crusades, I remember Dad talking about making a "Blessing Pact with God." It was basically an agreement that one could make with God Himself that if an individual gave of their financial resources into ministries that were carrying out the scriptures, the gift would be multiplied then returned to the individual through others. Dad asked people to become his "partners." And the truth is that those who believed in Dad's ministry took this term very seriously. Many of them continued to give and to otherwise be a part of Dad's ministry for many years after he was no longer conducting crusades. Similar to the poor widow who cast her two mites into the collection box all those many centuries ago, these precious people gave, not out of their surplus, but out of their want as Jesus described in Luke 21:4. Here is a picture of one of Dad's many meetings with his partners.

Seed Faith

This method of supporting his ministry, while at the same time showing the giver a Biblical way to being blessed themselves, was later developed into what Dad referred to as "Seed Faith." If you have been exposed to evangelistic ministries, churches or the like for any time at all, you have probably heard these things so often that they are now strictly a repeat. What you may not understand, however, is that these concepts came from the Bible and that Dad is the one who exhibited them for his world to see. In my experience at least, most of us would be hard-pressed these days to sit in very many churches or hear evangelists take an offering *without* at least obliquely referring to "planting a seed" or praying that God will bless people for giving to His Kingdom. But in the 1950's when Dad first began talking about such things, the concept was totally new. No one seemed to even be aware of the verses Dad discovered, much less preach about them!

Dad wrote several books regarding the concept of Seed Faith so I will admit to having oversimplified it, however, it can basically be reduced to three components: (1) God is your Source—from Philippians 4:19: "But my God shall supply all your need according to his riches in glory by Christ Jesus." (KJV) (2) Give to God and His work—from Luke 6:38: "Give, and it shall be given unto you; good measure, pressed down, and shaken together, and running over, shall men give into your bosom. For with the same measure that ye mete withal it shall be measured to you again." (KJV) and (3) Expect a Miracle—from Galatians 6:7: "Be not deceived; God is not mocked: for whatsoever a man soweth, that shall he also reap." (KJV)

Sadly, from the beginning, the seed faith concept was fraught with terrible controversy and disagreement. It was because of Dad's Seed Faith teaching that one particular Pentecostal denomination came against Dad's ministry, very strongly. While I would not have wanted to be in the room with Dad and those church leaders on that fateful day, I now wish I could have seen the looks on everyone's face—from a distance of course! Such was anything but amicable. Dad's short description to me was that these folks "called him on the carpet," saying that he was not preaching the Bible. The basis for the accusation was the concept of Seed Faith. Dad's response was to lay his Bible on the table and say to that august group: "Show me!" According to Dad, they could not point to any scriptures they believed he was violating in his sermons.

At the time, Dad believed that the recriminations came at least in part because of jealousy. Dad's meetings were very successful at that time and drew large crowds. Concomitantly, the crowds of that particular denomination had decreased. I could not possibly claim to know the motives of those men that day, although perhaps jealousy could have been part of the scenario. However, there is another reason that may have driven the accusations at that point. Of course this happened years ago, so why bother to mention it now?

My reasoning is that the arguments of these men went to the very heart of a controversy, which still rages today. The issue is this: Is it wrong to expect to be blessed when we give? People in general feel guilty giving to God THEN expecting a return. In their heart of hearts, they think it's a good thing to give. Nobody seriously argues that point. But what comes next? Does it just end there? While their words say "no, no", the actions of many people prove their *belief* that it is somehow evil to expect God to do anything for them *in return* for their giving. No one blames the farmer for planting a field with wheat, expecting to get a good wheat crop in return. It's just that we cannot seem to transfer that principle into a different realm—giving to God. And yet the Bible speaks over and over about planting seeds, giving and receiving, expecting harvests, and so forth.

I believe that the Seed Faith concept came squarely against this feeling that many have, particularly—okay, I'm going to say it—church people. They could handle the giving part, but asking for God to do something for them in return was somehow... wrong. Receiving back from God in return seemed to make them feel dirty or wicked. The only giving which was "good" was *when* you expected nothing in return. Otherwise, they assumed there must be a greedy, grasping motive lurking in the very heart of the giver.

Having said all of the above, the concept of Seed Faith can be and has been bastardized by some over the years. The concept can be twisted into "Giving to Get." Similar things were already happening in Bible days and because of that, Paul the Apostle actually had to defend *himself*: "Unlike so many, we do not peddle the word of God for profit. On the contrary, in Christ we speak before God with sincerity, like men sent from God." (NIV) So there is nothing new about this controversy.

I would state unequivocally that in its purest form, the concept of Seed Faith is Biblical, it is good and it works. Of course it does not apply to money alone but to the giving of our time, our talents, and, in an even greater way, ourselves. Moreover, by listening to the critics, we can miss something wonderful God has for every human being. If we allow Satan to somehow distort this Biblical concept in our minds, he will have succeeded in removing the breath and the fire out of it and we will lose the blessing God intends for us.

I, for one, have decided to grab onto the good principles which Jesus, Paul the Apostle, and others left on the earth for my benefit. I have no control over others who choose to cheapen those principles, but I do have control over my own actions. I have seen Seed Faith work in my life—over and over—and over and over—and over and over again. I simply will not allow anyone to steal that from me. Reminiscent of the cowardly lion: "not no way, not no how!"

The truth is that while some years later, new leaders of that particular denominational group sincerely apologized to Dad, he really never got over the hurt of that time. Their criticism affected his psyche for the rest of his life. From that time on, Dad felt isolated from the entire Pentecostal movement. In some ways, though, the censure of the others in the room that day may have provided a positive influence in Dad's life because it opened up his mind to the entire body of Christ, rather than only those denominations in which he had grown up. As a result, the concept has been disseminated around the world and, despite its misuse at times, there is no question in my mind that more people than we can know have been incredibly blessed because of it.

As simply one of the vast examples of good results, the reader might find it enlightening to learn of comments I heard recently from men and women who formerly served on the Board of Regents at Oral Roberts University. The new leadership of the University (which will be more fully described in a later chapter) invited the former leadership for a private meeting. These individuals spent perhaps two hours reminiscing about their times on the Board—tough times when the necessary funds did not appear to be forthcoming.

Many of them described moments in those meetings in which Dad asked them to donate rather large sums of money. Almost every one of them had a particular story of their own about those "moments," but each of these stories had one point of commonality. They were each asked to give an amount that was for them a little beyond anything they had planned, and yet they had given the specific amounts asked of them because Dad convinced them that they would in fact be blessed as a result. Sounds just like a typical fund-raising scheme, does it not? So far, their stories were not so different from what some of us may have heard about—and possibly shuddered about!—on numerous past occasions.

As I sat there listening, I was waiting for the ax to fall. I was certain one of them was going to say something like: "I lost my house over that stupid donation Oral Roberts talked me into that day"—or perhaps something worse! But I was dead wrong. One by one, they began describing in detail the wonderful things that had occurred in their lives—events which seemed to have begun soon after they made that specific donation.

To a man (well, I think some of them might have been women!) they said that even though it was somewhat scary at the time, they were so incredibly glad they had given those amounts to God. They talked of how they later sat back and watched miracle after miracle in their lives, things for which there was simply no other explanation. It was absolutely amazing to hear.

Let the reader understand that in no way do I give my father the credit for the concept of Seed Faith. After all, these principles had been resting securely, dormant in the Bible for centuries, just waiting to be discovered. They were not Dad's ideas—they were God's method of giving His people increase. It is just that Dad is the human being who brought them out of obscurity and offered them to the world, despite the fact that he knew in advance he would get clobbered for it!

Ever since people began to apply these principles to their lives "Showers of Blessing" have been brought down from above—but only for the brave souls who were willing to receive what God had to give them. I remember so often singing this song during Dad's crusades:

> There shall be showers of blessing."
> This is the promise of love;
> There shall be seasons refreshing,
> Sent from the Savior above.
> Showers of blessing,
> Showers of blessing we need;
> Mercy drops round us are falling,
> But for the showers we plead.

And dear reader, the world needs these blessings now much more than it ever did.

And these signs shall follow them that believe, ... they
shall lay hands on the sick, and they shall recover.
—Mark 16:17-18 (KJV)

"EXPECT A MIRACLE!"

Chapter 6

I wish I had a dollar for every basketball court my husband and my father viewed while attending a myriad number of NCAA games together—virtually all over the country. I never made an effort to count all the NCAA Tournaments, the NIT Invitationals and so many basketball games in between. But there is only *one* basketball court in the world that contains the snappy phrase: "Expect A Miracle!" In case you are wondering, those words are painted in bold letters on the

MY DAD, ORAL ROBERTS

basketball floor at the Mabee Center in Tulsa, Oklahoma at Oral Roberts University.

So where did that now rather famous saying get its origin in my father's ministry? By Dad's own admission, the phrase was born out of panic, panic originating from threats against his life by a man who did not believe in God. The gentleman was angry because of the wonderful works of God which were happening during an Oral Roberts crusade during the early 1960's. Actually, such opposition should have been expected to one as familiar with scripture as Oral Roberts. Jesus warned his followers in advance that "[s]ince they persecuted me, naturally they will persecute you." (John 15:20 NLT)

And yet, until it happens to YOU, well, one would almost have to be superhuman not to feel at least some degree of trepidation after a death threat. There was one particular crusade wherein Dad had started to wonder if he could force himself to even leave his hotel room—knowing that once he arrived at the tent he would be expected to preach a stirring message. You try it sometime.

But Dad's attitude changed, interestingly enough, *as he started out the door.* As he acted in faith believing that somehow, some way the Lord would protect him despite the impending danger, he heard God saying to him: "Expect a miracle. Expect a new miracle every day." He was so excited at hearing a fresh word from God that Oral Roberts forgot all about his fear and the threat of death. Once he was able to get his mind off of himself and upon God and the needs of the people, it was as if the world was his banana.

Suddenly he was in his element, preaching a rousing sermon, praying for the sick, and watching God provide the very miracles He had told Dad to be expecting. I often heard Dad quote a line from Job: "For the thing which I greatly feared is come upon me..." (Job: 3:25) It's all about what we expect. From the context, it would appear that for years Job had been expecting the worst—and he got it! So instead, why couldn't we expect miracles? Why shouldn't we expect good things?

Dad was so excited about the concept "Expect A Miracle" that he had the little phrase printed on little plaques and mailed them to his partners. Those little plaques went all over the world and were often displayed on desks and kitchen counters everywhere. More importantly though, as Dad began to preach that pithy phrase based upon the scripture I have quoted above and others, "Expect A Miracle" became the focal point for countless thousands to trust in God and look for good things, rather than the negative. The words set the stage for deliverance of multitudes of hurting people. It became an incentive for people to dare to believe God.

Okay, I simply cannot go further in this chapter without admitting that while loving Dad's ministry with all of our hearts, over the years my husband and I found it necessary to inject, well, at least a modicum of nonsense. Unfortunately, our grins were at my father's expense. At Dad's partners meetings, when people agreed to donate money to certain projects, he would ask them to come to the stage in front of the entire audience so he could thank them personally.

In the course of meeting each donor, he would ask him or her to say before the microphone: "I'll do it, and I'll expect a miracle!" It was actually a wonderful thing for them to repeat. It was just that Dad's pronunciation of the word "miracle" on those occasions was funny to us, for rather than the first syllable sounding like the word "mere," when pronounced by my father it sounded more like "mar." We were not really being rude when one of us would mimic his pronunciation, we were just lightening things up a bit, right? You're right, it was rather tacky, but sometimes Dad could be so intense!

Despite our silly jokes we well understood that "Expect A Miracle!" is far more than a pleasant phrase—or at least it can be. It can become a mindset. It can become a modus operandi. If you truly adopt "Expect A Miracle" as a way of life, it will be a game changer! How many times do I remember hearing the telephone ring and my mother saying: "Oh Lord! Is that my miracle?" Dad so often reminded his partners to have a lifestyle of expectation, and my mother lived it.

There was (and is), however, a caveat that Oral Roberts took pains to describe as well. Expect miracles from God, never from people. If you were to expect a miracle, i.e., that your banker friend would give you a loan tomorrow, such expectation could lead you down the primrose path. It is only when we look to God and see people merely as *instruments* through whom God can work that the "Expect A Miracle" concept will work in your life.

Imagine. What if tomorrow you made a decision before you dragged yourself out of bed? What if you said to yourself, "Today, I am going to expect a miracle!" What if you did that—and meant it—every day for the rest of your life. Is that manipulating God? Let us pretend for a moment that 10-year old Billy expects his daddy to come home from work tonight with a new pair of shoes for him. All day long he has said to himself: "I just know my daddy's going to bring me those shoes. He loves me and he knows how much I need them. I can't wait until he gets home! I know I can trust my daddy because he loves me so much and he knows just what I need!"

But if you went next door, you would meet Danny, another 10-year old boy who also needs a new pair of shoes. All day long Danny says: "Well I know my daddy could bring me a new pair of shoes if he wanted to. I sure do need a new pair of shoes but I don't know if Daddy would have time to do something for me. He's so busy! He's so very important. But, what am I gonna do if I don't get new shoes?"

Now for one tiny moment, become God in your own mind. Which child would get your attention? Which child would captivate your heart?

No, Billy's expectations are not manipulating his father. It is just that he expects his father to do good things for him. He's not looking for bad things. He is expecting good things. So who do *you* think will get those new shoes?

As Vep Ellis' great song urges:

EXPECT A MIRACLE every day,
EXPECT A MIRACLE when you pray;

If you expect it God will find a way,
To perform a miracle for you each day."

"LET'S BUILD A BRIDGE"

Chapter 7

On that fateful night in 1935 when God first promised to heal Dad of tuberculosis, God also spoke to him, albeit briefly, about someday building God a university. However, there were no details, and particularly no time frame. After all, without a miracle, my father would not have lived long enough anyway.

I was a young girl in the 1960's and cannot claim to know all that was happening in the colleges and universities of that day. I do remember, however, hearing of the terrible unrest within student bodies on so many college campuses in America. I remember seeing news stories of college students actually trying to burn down administration buildings and otherwise deface other campus buildings. And, while there were many Bible schools at the time, the liberal arts universities in this country were almost all secular institutions. Parents had virtually nowhere to send their children for a liberal arts education without the concern that their children would be met at the door either by a non-Christian or often, anti-Christian faculty.

Take for example, my oldest brother Ronnie. Ronnie excelled in foreign languages and wanted very much to study languages in college. He chose a university well-known for its high standards of scholarship, but oh, what a terrible price he and each of us in our family paid for that choice. Sometimes I feel we continue to suffer for his decision, for he is gone from us now.

Ronnie was so terribly bright and at that time, his life was so incredibly promising. As he was the son of an evangelist, he grew up immersed in the things of God and in the Bible. Ronnie was well-versed in scripture and had an amazingly analytical mind. In comparison to his, I would say that my academic potential was, well, approximately at the kindergarten level, if it reached that high. And yet at the same time, Ronnie did not see himself on a plane above others.

I do not know how the faculty at his chosen university learned that Ronnie was the son of a famous preacher, but once they knew, several of his professors delighted in questioning everything he believed—everything which he had been taught at home—and everything that a large part of his world rested upon. At first Ronnie made a valiant effort to counter the comments made to him, in an open classroom, in derogation of Christianity.

And, perhaps these professors sincerely believed it was for "his own good." Granted, perhaps other young men would have shrugged off the embarrassing and belittling comments which were directed so pointedly at Ronnie, day after day, but not so my brother. I do not know how Dad and Mother learned of Ronnie's predicament, but once they did, Dad immediately traveled to visit Ronnie in his dormitory. I suspect however that by that time, the damage had already been done.

Ronnie was never the same after that semester. I know what you are thinking. Perhaps Ronnie's life would have taken a negative turn at that point no matter what, but personally, I doubt it. To me, it is fatuous to

assume that the repeated comments of those professors had no affect on Ronnie's young, malleable mind.

Consider it for a moment, in terms of our own times. I well remember hearing the remarks of faculty members at state universities on recent national newscasts. Their views are often scary, in my view. Of course those universities cannot fire these folks because of how most universities define such things as "tenure" and "academic freedom." At most universities, academic freedom appears to mean that these professors are free to inculcate our children with all kinds of disgusting ideas and viewpoints. Consider the giant investment of time, love, money, and so forth which each parent has made into their children over the course of seventeen or eighteen years. Do you really want to entrust your son or daughter to one of those radical professors?

While Ronnie's early collegiate experience was certainly not the only factor which influenced my father to commence planning a Christian university in the early 1960's, it greatly influenced the timing and provided an almost indefatigable impetus which burned within Oral Roberts for the remainder of his life.

It was somewhere within this timeframe that Dad heard the voice of God speaking to him:

Build Me a University.
Build it on My authority, and on the Holy Spirit.
Raise up your students to hear my voice,
To go where My light is dim, where My voice is heard small,
And My healing power is not known,
Even to the uttermost bounds of the earth.
Their work will exceed yours, and in this I am well pleased.

In the Sky

At this time, my parents had two children who were not yet college age (my brother, Richard and me) but who were growing fast. It was not until a few months before Dad's passing that I learned the following. When the time came for Dad to begin building a university, he and Mother had a college savings plan. I have no idea how much money was contained in that fund but I can tell you that in our family, it was my father who was the "spender" and my mother who was the "saver." Despite the fact that Dad was larger than life and a man with incredibly persuasive powers, in our household there were no large plans that could be made without getting past my mother. It seemed, at least during my lifetime—that Dad was always in the sky—dreaming, believing God, coming up with all sorts of ideas. Some were great, and some rather off-the-wall. Mother, on the other hand, kept both feet squarely on the ground. She was clearly the practical one of the two.

Mother pulled Dad down from the sky, somewhere underneath the moon, at least, and Dad pulled Mother up just far enough to meet him somewhere in the middle. I can picture Dad going to Mother and excitedly telling her that God wanted him to build a university. I can see the wheels turning in her mind, thinking: "Let's get this straight. You have no Ph.D. You have no faculty. You have no students. You have no buildings. You don't even have any property on which to build. But you're telling me you are going to build a four-year, liberal arts university that will some day be fully accredited, correct?"

And perhaps it is a good thing that I was not in the room when he first related to my mother the above words from God. I suspect she said the same thing to him on that occasion as I had heard her say many times over the years, "Oral, are you sure this is what God is telling you?" Even though my mother was physically quite small in comparison to Dad's large frame, it would have been a mistake to assume she was the sweet little wife who stayed only in the background.

Yes, she was that homemaker who cooked the meals, did the dishes and raised the children. But on those few occasions when she questioned my father, she seemed more closely related to Mighty Mouse, one of my favorite cartoon characters! And yet, in the course of that conversation my father apparently convinced his parsimonious "Miss Evie" to withdraw the entire contents of that college savings account and make that amount of money a portion of the initial seed in order to begin a university.

That little college fund was similar to the mustard seed Jesus described as the "smallest of all the seeds on earth." And yet, it eventually became that plant which had such large branches that the birds (ORU students?!) did and are continuing to "nest under its shade." (Mark 4:31-32)

So how did Oral Roberts do it, or rather, how did God build a Christian university? God did it, using Dad as his instrument, through Dad's faithful partners. The gifts received from Dad's partners seemed to come in all sizes, but for the most part, Dad's partners were anything but well-to-do. I would just say that if the large donors were the pinnacle, those partners who regularly gave small amounts were the bedrock of the gifts which built a major university. If the large donors could be said to have built the buildings, it was the partners who enabled the University to keep afloat on a month to month basis.

And who were those courageous people to whom Dad referred to as his "partners?" First of all, with notable exceptions most of them had no college education themselves. Many of them did not "care a fig" about education, but they trusted Oral Roberts. Many of them had been healed in his crusade meetings, or perhaps a family member had been healed, or perhaps they had witnessed healings while attending the crusades. And, the fact that Dad's partners contributed so much to Oral Roberts University is testimony *in itself* that the healings actually occurred. Had the healings in Dad's crusades just been faked as some have suggested, there would not have been a body of people who so believed in God's power and so believed that He had called my Dad, that they would have given of their limited financial resources—and continued to give for the rest of their lives.

Perhaps this is the biggest miracle of all in reference to the life of Oral Roberts. Even today, I am confronted by total strangers, who have never stopped talking of their experiences while attending Dad's crusades. The people never forgot and they sent both their money and many of them, their children, nieces and nephews, and grandchildren to Oral Roberts University.

The Start of ORU

So how did a healing evangelist start a university? Of course one of the first things on the agenda was to secure property. When I was a little girl in the 1950's I remember Dad often driving our family to a farm that was located at 81st and Lewis in Tulsa. Interesting how smell can be such a time machine, for the strongest impression that continues to remain in my thoughts even today was the smell of the alfalfa that had apparently just been cut. I loved that smell! Dad would tell his wife and children: "Someday, God is going to build a University here!" Then we would pray. I am not sure I even knew the meaning of the word "university" in those days, but I did understand how real the dream was in my father's heart.

I did not know until later that Dad had been badgering his attorney, Saul Yager, to somehow purchase that farm. Poor Saul. As a lawyer, I have also felt the vexation of a client who simply will not give up. Saul patiently explained, over and over, to my father that the property was owned by a wealthy oil family and that although they had been approached by several others, the family had decided not to sell! However, at one point Dad prevailed upon the hapless Saul to make an offer to purchase the property notwithstanding the seeming impossibility of acceptance. When Saul approached the family, he was astounded to learn that they had decided to sell the day before.

Once the property was secured, Dad invited his partners to come to Tulsa to see what God was doing, or rather, what He was getting ready to do. These meetings were originally called partners' meetings but the name was later changed to "Laymen's Seminars" for they continued on over the years in order to maintain the funding of the University as well as minister to those partners who attended. By the time of the first partner's meetings, Dad had completed the original three buildings, two to house the partners and later to be used as dormitories for the students— Shakarian and Braxton Halls, and the other, Timko-Barton, to serve as a meeting place and cafeteria.

Imagine yourself as a minimum wage earner who had been healed in one of Dad's crusades or had attended one of those crusades many years before, and out of your grateful heart, you had been sending $10 per month, without fail, to Oral Roberts' ministry ever since. Now you come home from work one afternoon and spy a letter from Oral Roberts waiting for you in your mailbox. The letter says that if you could just get to Tulsa, Oral would pick you up on a city bus, put you up in a hotel room, feed you over several days, and show you what had been built at 7777 South Lewis—to a plot of ground which would one day be a university. Those folks got their letters, and they came, believe me, they came.

Notice that Dad practiced what he preached. He preached that receiving was always preceded by giving. And that is exactly what he did with his partners. These days, such a seminar would have cost *them* money to attend. But Dad started by planting a seed. While those seminars were not as exciting as the crusades I had witnessed in the 1950's, the seminars had their own special charm as well. The people enjoyed good music, wonderful preaching and wonderful healings (organized in a manner similar to what had been done on the last day of each crusade in which people would line up and Dad would go to them, rather than them lining up as on the earlier evenings.)

Then during one of the sessions, and only one, Dad would present a specific project. How does one raise the money to build a university? How does one keep from being overwhelmed by such a gargantuan task? By dividing it into specific projects, and each project into bite-size pieces. Dad had small models made of each building that he proposed to build. Once a person had determined to give the money for his little bite-size piece, perhaps a dormitory room or the like, he would walk to the model, then remove the front piece which would light up that little section. As I told you in an earlier chapter, these folks would go by to shake Dad's hand and he would have them say: "I'll do it, and I'll expect a miracle."

And it is another amazing testimony of God's faithfulness that so many of these people wrote back to my father's ministry office months after they had arrived home, to tell Dad of the miracles God had brought to them after they gave their hard-earned money in one of those seminars. It was Seed Faith in action. When people criticize such things it makes only a small impression on me, because I saw it work, time and time again, in the lives of the partners and in my own life as well.

I have mentioned Vep Ellis before, one of the men who sang in Dad's crusades. When Dad started talking about building God a university, Vep wrote a song that had originally been inspired by Lee Braxton, the Chairman of the Founding Board of Regents. Vep wrote a song he called: "Let's Build a Bridge." It told the story:

> An old man toiled thru the heat of the day to cross a chasm wide.
> His hands torn and soiled, he could now go his way
> He'd passed to the other side;
> But yet he toiled 'til his day was done
> and while he labored, he prayed.
> To build a bridge for others to come and follow the path he'd made.
> Let's build a bridge for those who will follow,
> Give them a span to worlds yet unknown;
> Rich our reward today and tomorrow,
> Then we shall live after we're gone.

Vep also wrote "ORU Saved," after hearing Dad preach at one of the Laymen's Seminars as I discussed above. But it was the original fight song that Vep wrote which became more well-known, at least to ORU graduates like this writer:

"Oh O-R-U, Oh O-R-U, Oh O-R-University!
Holy Spirit blessed, seeking out the best of the human trinity.
Oh O-R-U, Oh O-R-U, ordained of holy destiny.
May her torch still burn at the Lord's return and count for
eternity!"

I was perhaps eleven or twelve years old when I first remember Dad announcing that he would build a university. A fire was begun in my "little girl heart" that day and I shall never forget it. I do not know if Mother and Dad would have agreed to send me to any other university when I reached the appropriate age. I just know that I never once considered going anywhere else. I was much too shy to tell my parents or anyone else for that matter, but I was the most loyal Oral Roberts University adherent, from the day it was first mentioned in my presence. ORU was not just my Dad's dream. It became my dream as well, a huge, overriding force in my life from that day forward.

And what was it that called to my shy, immature little heart? I suppose to begin with, it was the idea that every person was important, individually—that each of us consisted of three parts: mind, spirit and body. I remember Dad saying that at other universities, man was considered little more than a head walking around on two toothpicks. Other schools concentrated on the mental alone. It was academics, which were primary and nothing else really mattered. But Oral Roberts University would teach its students to develop *all* of ourselves. Not only our mental capabilities but also we would learn to exercise and keep our physical bodies in good condition. And just as critical was our spirit—that man's spirit could only be satisfied and excel if it was in close touch with its Creator. If all three of those dimensions were developed, with excellence, we could become the whole person and carry out the dreams and visions for which we were created.

A Big Vision!

Who could seriously argue with the purposes of a Bible school? In such institutions, individuals were taught to preach the gospel, all over the world. What's wrong with that? Well absolutely nothing, as far as it goes. It's a wonderful thing. But there were so many places where the message of Bible school graduates would never be welcome. Few preachers will be invited to preach to a group of engineers, for example.

Oral Roberts University promised to teach us not to go to the "uttermost bounds of the world" merely in a physical sense but also into every person's own, individual world. Let's face it. Most of us live in our own little world and we rarely leave it, because that has become our comfort zone. Our world may consist primarily of our home and our workplace. To the sports enthusiast, add the world of perhaps several basketball courts within a 50-mile radius. To a music lover, it might be the nearest concert halls. The idea was that the ORU graduates would not only become preachers and/or missionaries in the classical sense, but they would also carry the gospel message into the various worlds of their specific academic disciplines. An individual with a Masters of Business Administration, for example, would have a platform. Not to preach, but to *be* a Christian in every phase of the business world. The ORU graduates would have the credentials to go into the respective worlds of many different academic disciplines—places where a preacher would never be heard. A degree from Oral Roberts University was more than a degree. It was your ticket, your union card to bring the gospel into a different world in a different way on a different plane in a different dimension than had ever been done before.

I suppose to the skeptic, all of this may sound like stuff and nonsense. And nonsense it would have been if it had remained words only. Granted, it started out with words and words alone. But those words expressed an idea, one which not only grabbed at my heart but which also captured the hearts of intellectuals who were also Christians all over the country. Those people came, anxious to teach on the faculty of the new university, wanting to assist in the development of the dream that Dad had expressed.

Looking back, it is miraculous that these people could possibly have trusted an evangelist to do what Dad had promised to do. And yet they believed God and they believed Oral Roberts. They resigned their current teaching positions, accepted ORU's low pay scale, packed-up their families and all they owned then came to Tulsa. And the same force drew parents to send their children to the fledgling university. They too sensed that God was doing something that had simply not been done before.

The church had heretofore been quite distrustful of the intellect and particularly higher education. Bible schools were acceptable of course, but there was a fear that if you fully developed the intellect of an impressionable young person, he might be drawn away from the things of God. And certainly, that danger was and is very real. Could young people be educated and strive for excellence on an academic scale while developing their spirits with a love for the things of God?

Yes, it was in fact incredibly dangerous. It was for this reason that many church people had previously been so fearful of academic learning that they had contented themselves with substandard education, just so long as they could "keep the kids holy and in church." But Dad was not to be satisfied with anything substandard. It had to be excellent in order to satisfy Oral Roberts. The dream God had for ORU met the danger head on and by in large, slew the dragon.

Dad's insatiable desire for excellence would explain his reasoning for asking Rev. Billy Graham to dedicate Oral Roberts University. What a great day that was! How could I forget sitting outside that afternoon in 1967 in the space between the three buildings I mentioned previously. How stunning when Billy Graham said something like the following: "If Oral Roberts University ever departs from its founding vision, let it be accursed!"

For me, the years seemed to drag and I began to wonder if Junior High School and High School would EVER end—so I could move into the dormitory and finally become an Oral Roberts University student.

Whether or not Dad mentioned Ronnie's experience in college to his donors has long since escaped my memory, but I can tell you that Ronnie's experience remained sadly fresh in my own mind. Therefore I had no difficulty at all understanding ORU's *raison d'être*. I was one of the few, though, who had even an inkling. It was not until years afterwards when I learned that Dad had faced terrible opposition with his proposal to build a university, even from his own ministry associates. The truth is, however, that if I had known, I would have seen it similarly as one sees a gnat—just something to be swatted away. My Dad said he was going to build a university, and so in my mind it would be built, without question. Oh, the faith of the young! But while I had never had the opportunity to be truly close to my father, I knew him from my quiet observations. I knew ORU would happen, just as he said.

But lest I portray myself as a hyper-spiritual individual, I should point out that my overwhelming interest in ORU did not relate solely to matters of faith. At that time we lived in a house on campus not too terribly far from the dormitories. I knew that once ORU opened, there would be BOYS inhabiting one of those dormitories. While I really did love the Lord as a young teenager, I was also boy crazy. The thought of associating with and perhaps even dating college men was a thrill beyond anything I could have imagined.

And when those young men started showing up on campus, I did manage to go out on dates with some of them. One wonders why my parents would have allowed their young impressionable daughter to date those "older" men. The good news for me was that Mother and Dad were very busy and they were also often out of town. Dad continued to have crusades during many of those first years of the University. Additionally, I had almost without fail been an obedient daughter while growing up. I suppose my parents either trusted me or were simply too pre-occupied to realize how much time I was spending with those good-looking, brilliant freshmen and sophomores. On the other hand, perhaps those young men were much too concerned with retribution for having been caught doing anything "unseemly" with the daughter of the President. For whatever reason, God protected me and I had a great time getting to know the students.

After what seemed like centuries to me, 1969 finally came. I was 18 years old, a recent high school graduate and at last qualified to become an ORU student. The University had been operating about four years by that time, but it was still quite new and in many ways revolutionary.

So was Oral Roberts University what it had promised to be? Oh yes. All that, and more. The academics were daunting I must say. The volume of the assignments for each class was beyond anything I had ever experienced. And yet the challenge motivated me to begin studying almost immediately.

Of course high school had conditioned me to understand that in order to succeed in school, studying was anything but optional. And, while my heart was prepared to be a whole person—body, mind and spirit, I was unprepared *physically* for the aerobics requirement, i.e, the part of ORU designed to develop our bodies. While Dad spoke of such things when he described ORU, it apparently had never dawned upon him to ensure that his own daughter was exercising and preparing for this eventuality. Therefore, when during my first semester I was required to jog for an entire mile and a half, I was shocked! Were they kidding? No, they were not!

I remember barely passing on that particular requirement. However, as painful as that original mile and a half was, the desire to keep fit, which I still carry within me now that I am "an old lady," was birthed all those years ago at Oral Roberts University. Attending Oral Roberts University began a pattern of exercising which has never left me, thereby helping me to escape many health conditions experienced by some of my not so fit, similarly aged friends. Certainly, such would *never* have happened in the life of this former couch potato, but for ORU. My life patterns were changed at ORU and college set the tone, from an exercise standpoint, which has endured throughout my life.

A " Spiritual Being"

And what about my spirit? Now I know what you are thinking. No one needed to develop my "spiritual being." After all, I was the daughter of a famous evangelist and spiritually speaking, already light years ahead of the other freshmen who landed at ORU that fall, correct? Well, certainly my father had been preaching and praying for the sick all over America and all over the world. But remember that most of those years I had been in Tulsa, Oklahoma going to school. Yes, I was able to attend many of the crusades, but the bulk of my existence had been at home, with my father preaching to others far away.

Most folks fail to realize as well that just because you are related to an evangelist means little if you fail to reach out for the things of God *on your own*. After all, developing your spirit toward the things of the Bible does not happen through osmosis. As some of the other members of the Roberts family have unfortunately proven, every individual has to *decide* whether they are going to serve God. God is a gentleman. He never forces people to serve Him. And, as Dad used to say: "God has no grandchildren. He only has sons and daughters!" We each must make a choice. God created each of us with a will of our own.

So how did ORU develop and increase the spiritual component in my young heart?

In a million different ways.

There was a sense of community and caring at ORU that I have never again experienced following that time. Similar to Dad's models of the buildings, the real-life dormitories had also been split into bite-sized pieces. The individual unit was known as a "wing." My memory is that there were about 30 of us girls per wing.

Eventually, a new program was begun wherein each wing of girls was matched to a wing of boys, for the purpose of social activities. These "brother/sister wings" enjoyed joint activities such as barbeques and the like. In case you were wondering, ORU did NOT nor does it now have coeducational dorms. While I would have been a most eager participant of the brother/sister wing program, I must sadly report that this concept was not conceived until *after* my graduation. More's the pity.

During my dormitory years, however, we had devotions, prayer, Bible studies, and so forth, according to the wing where we lived. There were wing-backers made available to us, i.e., Tulsa families who brought us goodies and treated us similarly to their own children. We had chapel services which contained wonderful preaching and teaching. While there admittedly were some professors who simply "didn't get it," the vast majority of the faculty were individuals who truly wanted to inspire us toward the things of God while at the same time assist us in gaining a strong, academic underpinning. I will never forget the sacrifices made by our professors.

They were some of the most loving, caring people I have ever known. Each of us were special to them. Later, when during the summer following my freshman year I enrolled in a class not offered at ORU at a different university, I was shocked! That secular university I attended had absolutely no sense of community. The professors did not even know their students. After class, the teacher would leave the classroom immediately, never speaking to anyone.

It was obvious that there was a giant separation between the student body and the faculty. Having no other collegiate experience, I had had nothing to compare with my school until that time, but I quickly realized how blessed I had been at ORU. We were like a family and there were no strangers.

Toward the beginning of my sophomore year, I became ill and was rushed to the hospital. Thankfully the problem was solved with a fairly minor surgery, however, in the meantime, I became hopelessly behind in my math class. While I excelled in History, English, French and other "fuzzy" subjects, for me, both mathematics and science could be compared to hieroglyphics for which no Rosetta Stone had ever been discovered. A "techie" I was not, so even though it was only a basic mathematics course, for me it represented a giant hurdle.

However, without anyone asking him, my math professor, Dr. Lavoy Hatchett, showed up in my hospital room, textbook in hand. He went over the assignments with me and would not leave until satisfied that I understood them, well, to the best of my limited capacity would allow anyway. I cannot express what anxiety his unpaid tutoring resolved during his visit to my hospital room. And lest you assume such sacrifice was made only because I was the President's daughter, think again. ORU's faculty members did such things routinely. It was their modus operandi with their students, again and again and again.

And then there were those who inspired us to create, like Dr. Alice Rasmussen, one of the few women of her day with an earned doctorate who was also a Christian. I suppose Dr. Rasmussen was about the tiniest woman I have ever seen, and yet, she walked as if she owned the world. She was like a Chihuahua, who saw herself as a German Shepherd. Since she was a Spanish teacher and I was a French minor, I never enrolled in one of Dr. Rasmussen's classes, an eventuality for which I cannot claim to have been totally disappointed at the time.

Many years after having graduated from ORU, Tulsans began hearing of a pantomime entitled "A Toymaker's Dream" conceived by an ORU graduate, Tom Newman. It was being performed all over the world and was causing quite a stir. Soon after, Newman formed a company called Impact Productions. Of course such is in itself a long story. Suffice it to say, however, that Impact Productions has had an incredible effect on Christians and non-Christians alike with its feature-length films including "End of the Spear," several television series, and animated projects designed for children. It was perhaps ten years ago when I first had the opportunity to interview Newman on a radio program. When asked what had inspired him, Newman spoke of a tiny little woman who had "built a fire under him" at Oral Roberts University. Her name was Dr. Alice Rasmussen.

A list of well-known graduates of ORU would include individuals such as Michele Bachmann, United States Congresswoman from Minnesota, a graduate from the ORU law school. Bachmann (whom I knew only tangentially) has been a frequent guest on Fox News for several years and is now expected to run for president. And speaking of Fox News, their reporter, Kelly Wright was able to wrangle an exclusive interview with O.J. Simpson following his criminal trial. He is an Oral Roberts University graduate. Of course David Barton of Wallbuilders, another graduate of my alma mater has made many appearances on national news programs.

And there is simply no time to mention such distinguished graduates as Stephen Mansfield who wrote the famous tome: "The Faith of George W. Bush," and Cliff Taulbert, of "Once Upon a Time When We Were Colored" fame.

Kathie Lee Gifford attended ORU. Her sister and I played tennis, but I have to honestly tell you that both Kathie and Michie far excelled me athletically. (That's nothing; almost everyone did!) There is Jim Stovall of the Narrative Television Network and "The Ultimate Gift" fame. There are those like Terry Law and Ron Luce who have brought the gospel all over the world.

We have unfortunately lost to Heaven such graduates as Billy Joe Daugherty, founder of a very large church and ministry in Tulsa, Victory Christian Center. You may remember when Billy Joe made the national news with his forgiving spirit a

Here's a picture of Dad and Billy Joe just months before both he and Dad passed away.

few short years ago after an attendee actually socked him in the mouth during a church service!

There were other pastors and evangelists such as Ken Copeland, Myles Munroe, Bill Shuler and Daniel King, and many, many more who attended Oral Roberts University.

Sadly, we lost Larry Dalton whose musical talents as a Steinway Artist were almost unparalleled, in so many distinctive ways. Thank God, Don Ryan, an ORU graduate and current faculty member is now a Steinway Artist. There is Don Moen of Integrity Music and Larry Wayne Morbitt of Phantom of the Opera fame. Unfortunately though, we lost the first judge produced by our law school, the Honorable Ozella Willis.

Accredidation and Beyond

By the spring of my junior year at ORU, I had already met and become engaged to a fellow student, Ron Potts. On March 31, 1971 Ron and I attended chapel, as was our normal custom. What can I say—it was required of all students! We saw that morning as no different than any other school day. Little did we know, however, that Dad was getting ready to make an announcement to the entire University community that morning.

Just short of six years from enrollment of ORU's first class, the school had received FULL accreditation by North Central Association of Colleges and Secondary Schools. I never saw my father as excited as he was on that day. It was pandemonium in the auditorium.

Everyone was on his feet and Dad was standing before us with unabashed tears in his eyes. But before the tears could advance into full-blown weeping, some of the students could no longer contain their exhilaration. It was an un-staged forerunner of what is known today as a flash mob. The students went wild!

Of course I have to admit that as much as Ron and I understood the implications of full accreditation—our degrees would mean something! We were even more excited because Dad dismissed classes for the rest of the day. That is the only time either during my four years of under-graduate classes coupled with my law school years when I ever remember classes being dismissed on a regular school day. It was amazingly, incredibly wonderful!

Unfortunately however, all the years since the founding of Oral Roberts University were not sweetness and light. "Sweetness and Light," by the way, was a term Dad used often. Knowing him as I did, while he would have wanted me to be as positive as possible in my account, he would not have wanted me to gloss over the truth. He never liked syrupy accounts which contained very little reality. There were tortuous times when the funds to maintain the University did not seem to be forthcoming. It seemed that the school was a greedy animal—making payroll, maintaining the buildings, keeping the library current and on and on the list goes.

The needs of the University brought stresses that could never have been envisioned by a mere mortal like my father. And yet, Dad remained the president of the University until 1993 when he was 75 years old.

For several years before that time, he struggled arduously with the question of a successor to the presidency. The obvious choice to Oral Roberts was his son and my brother, Richard. But his anxiety concerned whether Richard would be accepted as deserving of that role. Would the current administration yield to Richard's newly granted authority? Could Dad stay in town, or must he leave so that folks would look to Richard and not to the founder? I suspect these thoughts and many more were rolling around in Dad's head for several years before 1993.

Over the perhaps five years before Richard was named as Dad's successor at ORU, Dad commenced a litmus testing process of the current ORU administration as to their eventual loyalty to Richard. Those who did not readily show a deep loyalty to his son were quietly moved out. There were some wonderful people who were mistreated in those years. It would give me great pleasure to tell you the names of some of these individuals, individuals who had been so intensely loyal to Dad, sacrificing readily for the cause of Christ, many of whom would have given their very lives for the University and for Dad's ministry.

These individuals certainly did not fall into the category of others who were hurt, then later publicly disgorged their hatred by writing a "tell-all" book. No, these folks lived upon a much higher plane. They quietly folded up their tents and went elsewhere, trusting the Lord to make things right in the future. How many people have been hurt at ORU over the years? I cannot say it is a short list.

And lest you believe I am including the author in the above group of scarred saints, I am not. I will describe in a later chapter more of my own history. All that is necessary to say at this juncture, therefore, is the following. While many have assumed that it was my goal to be

President of ORU, such was never the case. I will admit a desire as a member of ORU's administration to be academic dean at some future point—years down the road. However, I had absolutely no inclination to be president of a university.

First of all, I knew I was unqualified. But I suppose the main thing that caused my disdain for such a post—not that it was ever offered to me!—was that it carried expectations of fund-raising skills, certainly not my cup of tea at least in those days. My desires were to be a part of ORU's academic world and to leave the fundraising to whomever God would call for that purpose. But I digress.

To Dad's credit, I must tell you that he later bitterly regretted many of the measures designed to clear the way for his son. However, at the time, I know he felt these things were necessary. Dad used to say, "You don't know you're making a mistake when you're making it." While at first blush that may sound simplistic, the wisdom therein cannot be belied. Even the greatest person makes terrible mistakes, and that was certainly true of Oral Roberts.

Did things work out with Richard as President of ORU? No, they did not. Does Richard deserve all the blame? I doubt it. You will remember from my narrative that early on, a great deal of the faithful, month to month donations to ORU came from Dad's partners, who had come alongside to help as an outgrowth of his crusades. Many of these people were older than Dad, hence by the 1990's, they were in their 70's, 80's and even 90's. Obviously, their ability to continue giving to the University was more than limited.

And for a tiny moment, put yourself in Richard's shoes. Do you think Oral Roberts might have been a tough act to follow?

Of course by the time my brother became ORU's president, I was no longer a part of the University, so I was not privy to all of the details of the actual events during the years in which Richard was president.

Regretfully, the relationship between Dad's two youngest children had and continues to be rocky, to say the least, so I obtained very little inside information from those quarters.

One would have to be blind, however, to have missed some of the things that occurred over the years after my "departure" from the school of my dreams. How can I say that there were no excesses, when there were? How can I defend some of the events that occurred? I cannot. Over the years I heard many accusations of wrongdoing. I even received many telephone calls at my law office asking that I file lawsuits on behalf of individuals who claimed terrible mistreatment under Richard's regime. As if I would have ever considered filing a lawsuit against the University founded by my own father! Having said that, however, I could not help but wonder what was happening at 7777 South Lewis. Were things as terrible as some claimed?

The first news that ORU was in deep trouble came when a lawsuit was filed here in Tulsa. That lawsuit was fraught with such serious implications that I received a telephone call from a fellow attorney only hours after it had been filed. The lawyer stated: "Roberta, the lawsuit is shattering because the allegations themselves are so serious."

It was just under three months from that telephone call before Richard had resigned as ORU's second president. During that time, he had solicited Dad's help to retain his position at ORU. By then, Dad was a few months short of becoming 90 years old. While being amazingly sharp for his advanced age, no one would seriously contend that Oral Roberts was at his optimum intellectual level at that point in time. I would say that Dad's first reaction to all the hullabaloo, and hullabaloo there was, consisted almost purely of an emotional response.

He saw an attack upon Richard perhaps as an attack upon him and upon his entire ministry. He certainly had that proclivity in years past. And once Dad allowed himself to assume a defensive posture, just about anyone's attempts to help him veer in another direction were most often doomed to failure.

The bright spot in this scenario, however, was Billy Joe Daugherty. I cannot name another graduate of Oral Roberts University who pulled at Dad's heart more than Billy Joe Daugherty. Over time, Dad learned the details and realized that Richard's resignation was for the best.

What Was God Thinking?

How can I describe those times? I lost track of how many days, day after day after day, in which the major newspaper in Tulsa, the Tulsa World, contained a front-page article about the ORU debacle. My husband and I had recently moved to the shores of a nearby lake and I was driving in to my law office in Tulsa every day (or most days) during those times. Every morning my husband would carry in the newspaper before breakfast and I would shudder to imagine what dastardly words had been written for that day. Am I exaggerating? Could it actually have been 30 days in a row with a front page article about ORU? Or was it 60 days?

The articles began to blur in my mind because of the intense pain that ripped through my heart each time one more terrible word was said about the University of my dreams. Just seeing the newspaper itself, laying on the kitchen counter still bound by its rubber band like a snake preparing to strike, daring me to read it. How could ORU survive? What was God thinking?

And yet God proved once again that while we may feel like Isaac—tied up and seeing nothing more than the blade of a sharp knife above our heads—God always has a ram in the bushes. God was not finished with ORU. In 2007, exactly 44 years after the school received its official charter, God's faithfulness to *His* University became perfectly clear. He began speaking once again. Only this time it was not my father who heard that clear definitive voice of God. This time God's voice was heard by a family, veritable strangers to what God had been doing over all those years in a town on the other side of Oklahoma.

As far as I know, the Green family had no ties to the campus, spiritual or otherwise, and could not claim any true involvement with Dad's ministry over past years. And yet, God chose them to be the catalysts for a new day at Oral Roberts University. The Greens began hearing of the troubles at the University. While others were furiously blogging on the internet, spreading rumor upon rumor about the scandal, the Green family were quietly and steadfastly listening for God's voice. And they heard.

While they did not know that much about Oral Roberts University, they were acquainted with some of those they referred to as "the fruit," i.e., the good things which had been produced because of the school. Having seen and known for themselves some of ORU's graduates, the state of affairs at the University pulled at their hearts and, thankfully, would not let them go. One of those individuals whom the Greens so lovingly referred to as the good fruit which God had produced through ORU was Billy Joe Daugherty. It was the Tulsa pastor whom the Lord used to put Oral Roberts and the Greens together. It was Billy Joe who arranged for the family to travel to California to meet personally with Dad.

Was it easy for Dad to surrender the place for which he had expended blood, sweat and tears all those years, to a family of well... unknowns? Of course not. But Dad soon began to discern the direction in which God was moving. He it was who had weathered the storm all those years ago in the original transitional period of the early 1960's. There was Oral Roberts: well aware that the worldwide perception of him in the 1960's was solely as a healing evangelist. And yet, he with his inimitable confidence expected that same world to see him also as a college president, instantly! Not a small feat!

One of his sermons in those days had even inspired Vep Ellis to write a song entitled: "Move with God." The song contained these words: "So let us now determine in our hearts the way God's moving and move with God!" How could the author of that long-ago sermon refuse to move now, even in the 21st century—2007? No, change rarely comes without apprehension, and yet Dad soon began to perceive that "[t]his was the Lord's doing, and it is marvelous in our eyes." (Mark 12:11)

But as "marvelous" as it was, the school still had no head. As Dad was aging and insisted upon living in California rather than Oklahoma, the visits of my husband and I had necessarily become more and more frequent. During those visits, while Dad's physical body had aged to an extremely delicate level, his spirit and mind were still amazingly sharp. He had not changed. We used to say in our family that Dad "ate, drank and slept" ORU—that ORU was his "baby." During those latter days, the overriding concern of Dad's being remained ORU. What would be the future of the University, his baby? I would not say he feared death, but I do believe he feared he would die before ORU's future was secure.

Yes, the Greens had heard from God and things at the University were definitely in a better frame of reference than they had been in the recent past, however, without a president, well, how could Dad be happy about going home to the heaven God promises all who believe? You might say it was audacious for Dad to expect the Lord to adjust His timing schedule in accordance with his own personal expectations. And it was. However, that is in itself an apt description of my father and it was certainly not without Biblical precedent. Dad was "Expect a Miracle" personified!

Beyond Christmas

Despite numerous health issues, Dad tenaciously held on to his life. It was not until September of 2009 that the new Board of Trustees of Oral Roberts University found and inaugurated a new President, Dr. Mark Rutland. Dad was extremely happy about the choice of Dr. Rutland, having said he would have chosen the man himself.

Travel is physically excruciating for the elderly and yet at 91, Oral Roberts traveled once again for what became the last time, to Tulsa in order to see "his baby," ORU, be put officially into the hands of Dr. Mark Rutland.

On the evening after the inauguration of ORU's new president, Ron and I visited Dad's hotel room across the street from the campus. Ron said to Dad: "Oral, your daughter and I have already purchased our tickets to fly to California to be with you for Christmas." Dad answered, "Well you can come, but I won't be there!" Dad knew that ORU was in safe hands and he died ten days before Christmas.

But for the Green family's entrance upon the scene, the University which Dad had built *for* God, would be closed today. It would be a boarded-up wasteland—or perhaps leveled by some entrepreneur greedy for gain. But God had other plans. From my vantage point, one of the greatest proofs of Dad's original call from the Lord Himself to build a university is the fact that it has come through the fire and yet survived to do even greater things for God's kingdom. Of all the things

Dad did during his lifetime, it is the University that will have the greatest impact upon the world. Quoted earlier in this chapter are the words of Vep Ellis' song penned in 1963, written to encapsulate the vision of Oral Roberts University: "Let's Build a Bridge."

When I arrive in heaven, perhaps I will learn whether or not Vep was himself aware of the song's prophetic nature. As I last heard Dad's voice singing those old songs in his hospital room just before his death, however, in my mind the old man in the song had become my father:

An old man toiled thru the heat of the day to cross a chasm wide.
His hands torn and soiled, he could now go his way
He'd passed to the other side;
But yet he toiled 'til his day was done
and while he labored, he prayed.
To build a bridge for others to come and follow the path he'd made.

Let's build a bridge for those who will follow,
Give them a span to worlds yet unknown;
Rich our reward today and tomorrow,
Then we shall live after we're gone.

...Jesus of Nazareth... who went about doing good...
                                         –Acts 10:38 (KJV)

"SOMETHING GOOD IS GOING TO HAPPEN TO YOU"

Chapter 8

One of Dad's favorite sayings (and he had many) was "in the now." Keeping his ministry current and alive was of major concern to him. Continuing a project just because "we've always done it" was anathema to him. We might say today that he wanted his ministry to be "on the cutting edge" but in the 1970's, his terminology was "in the now." And this phraseology was heard often at his ministry headquarters (which by then had been moved from downtown Tulsa to just across the street from the ORU campus) and at Oral Roberts University. His crusades seemed to be winding down although Dad was still having a few of them, particularly in the New York area where he had large numbers of partners. He understood that it was time to change the format of the presentation. How often did I hear him say: "We never change the message, but we are always ready to change the *method* of getting it across to the people."

A Broadcast Innovator

You will recall that Dad had televised part of his crusades and was a true pioneer in putting evangelism and particularly the healing ministry onto television sets, and thus into people's living rooms. By this time Dad also had been producing a half-hour television show that was seen in many areas of the United States, but not on a national basis. While these programs were continuing to be produced, they were carried on Sunday mornings and were not all that different than other Christian programming at the time. But while Dad continued the Sunday morning programs, by the 1970's, Dad's approach with television was about to widen exponentially. In addition to the more standard Sunday morning programs, he was about to make television specials that would be aired nationally including top stars and personalities.

How can I explain those times? Basically, there were only three channels (besides the educational channel which had few viewers, as far as I am aware). There was ABC, NBC and CBS. There was no HBO, no movies on television, and no DVD's. There was no capability as now to "DVR" a television program. If you missed a program you had wanted to see, it was just too bad. There were no video recorders, at least not in the homes of regular folks. And what was worse, you had to *GET UP from your chair* to change the channel! There were no remote controls for your television set. Imagine that!

One afternoon in the early 1970's, my husband and I drove to my sister, Rebecca's house. (There were automobiles back then, just in case you were wondering.) Rebecca and her husband, Marshall, always seemed to have the latest in the new technology of the day. When we arrived, they could not wait to show us that their television set had what was referred to as "cable." And it certainly had not been misnamed because there was in fact a cable right in front of our eyes.

It was a long, thick cord that stretched between their television and a plastic looking box-like contraption about the size of a novel when turned to the side. With the addition of cable television, they now had access to watch a few more channels than just the three major networks. We thought it was amazing! My brother-in-law, Marshall, could actually change the channel without leaving the couch! Oh, did I mention that if someone went to the kitchen to get a snack, he was seemingly duty-bound to trip over that horribly inconvenient cord?

Well, the point of that story is to tell you that during those days, people had very little in the way of choices regarding which television show to watch and yet television was still new enough that people spent the majority of their evenings "glued" to their television sets anyway. Remember, there was no Internet! People did not have laptop computers on which to sit and surf the Internet. There were not even any personal computers!

So it was in this scenario when Dad started making television specials on NBC in Burbank, California. It was apparently the same studio where the hit television show, "Rowan & Martin's Laugh-In" was made for that show's comics often joked about "Beautiful Downtown Burbank." This was of course a euphemism as that area of Los Angeles was anything but beautiful! And I suppose Dad's decision to produce television specials to be shown nationally shows Dad's pioneering spirit perhaps even more than televising his crusades years before because the major networks—with their clear monopolies on American viewers—had no interest in what they referred to as "religious programming" on days other than Sunday.

A television show that featured a sermon? On a weeknight?

After all, Dad's primary purpose was to spread the good news of Jesus Christ to the world. Well that was not all that different in itself, but asking the network to put that show on *prime time*? Such was simply not done in those days! But wait, he was asking for even more than that. He also wanted these specials to include big name television and movie stars. He wanted to feature groups of students from what was at that time merely a fledgling little college in Tulsa, Oklahoma. Besides spreading the gospel, Dad's purpose was to recruit more ORU students and showcase what the University had to offer to young people and their families. If you ask for the moon, you might as well attach the sun to your request as well—since there is little hope of obtaining either.

While I was not privy to the details of how Dad's dream actually became a reality, I can tell you that it was a huge miracle that a major network ever allowed an evangelist to do such things as I have described on prime time television. And how in the world did Dad get such top-name stars as Jerry Lewis, Johnny Cash and June Carter, Gladys Knight, Jimmy Durante, Roy Clark, Johnny Mathis, Skeeter Davis, Roy Rogers and Dale Evans, Louise Mandrell, Pat Boone, Tennessee Ernie Ford, Lou Rawls, Natalie Cole, Burl Ives, the Lennon Sisters, Shari Lewis, Anita Bryant and many others? Many of these programs were also done on location, including Alaska, of all places. It was an absolute miracle, perhaps even more than what Oral Roberts could have imagined, and folks, if you have not already figured it out, he could imagine a lot!

You might be interested to know that while Dad did his best to convince Elvis Presley to appear in one of his specials, he was unsuccessful. As a part of that effort, my husband was privileged to spend some time with Elvis and to hear him sing into the morning hours with great singers like J.D. Sumner, the Imperials and many others.

Dad chose such men as Dick Ross and Ralph Carmichael to produce the television specials. While I have no idea what the cost of those specials were in today's dollars, I know the cost was so astronomical that Dad spent many hours arguing about that particular issue with both Dick and Ralph. He also argued with them vociferously, as he wanted much more up front, blatant spirituality than was offered to him. I hasten to point out, however, that these were men who were true professionals in their area. I suspect that their reasoning was most likely more related to fear of the network being unwilling to run the programs than to a lack of "God-friendliness" on their part.

It was somewhere during this time that Ralph Carmichael, who had done work previously with such greats as Bing Crosby, Ella Fitzgerald, Rosemary Clooney and Nat King Cole, wrote a beautiful song which became Dad's theme song for television over the years: "Something Good is Going to Happen to You."

> Right there in the dust, he sat by the gate,
> To listen to footsteps and patiently wait.
> The blind man just didn't dream that this was the day
> That Jesus of Nazareth would pass by his way.
> Something good is going to happen to you
> Happen to you, this very day.
> Something good is going to happen to you
> Jesus of Nazareth is passing your way.

More than any other song, I would say Dad is known for Ralph's beautiful song that proved that despite the new format, the message was entirely the same as what Dad had preached in the 1940's and 1950's in his crusades.

Unfortunately, Dad endured great reproach among some in the Christian church due to these nationally televised "Contact" specials. The "regulars" on the program were a group consisting of Oral Roberts University students called the "World Action Singers." The regular soloists on the program, my brother, Richard and his first wife, Patti, along with the World Action Singers produced some incredibly beautiful music.

I will never forget the thrill of these programs and the voices of Richard and Patti along with those singers. There was incredible talent among those singers (especially when their voices were enhanced by a few "ghost" singers!) The programs perhaps might be called variety shows in that they had a guest star, musical numbers, then perhaps a little comedy, typically followed by Dad preaching a short sermon. But those were not the things with which some found fault. Now that all the years have passed, shall I call the movements made by the singers "choreography?" Dare I now finally refer to it as dancing?

Unless you are familiar with Christianity, you may be unaware that in the 1970's, many Christians were dead set against any form of dancing. Of course if any of us were to review those programs now after we have seen current television programs, we would be aghast that anyone thought the "choreography" was anything but chaste. However in those days, this sort of thing, call it what you will, was absolutely unacceptable to some. And yet despite the disapproval of some churchgoers, the bulk of American viewers saw the specials for what they were—clean, wholesome programming which talked about Jesus.

The movement of the World Action Singers, while not particularly sexy in my view, was one of the things that drew the viewer and kept the viewer from changing the channel. I suspect Dad felt that if he could just get people to keep watching until he had a chance to preach, then he would get an opportunity to give them the Gospel message. Millions did stay tuned in and while there is no earthly way to place numbers on such things, I can tell you that many, many lives were changed as a result of those specials.

The specials were more successful than Dad could have ever dreamed and the success was on many levels. One of the specials, the Valentine's program aired in 1971 even received a nomination for an Emmy award. I doubt Dad ever imagined that one day he would actually be known around the world *more* for those television specials than he had been known for his healing crusades, but that is what happened. On the other hand, he did understand in advance that any preaching he could wrangle onto prime time television would reach far more people as a whole than traveling in crusades could have ever done.

And in addition to the direct influence these shows had upon people's lives, they did in fact bring students to Oral Roberts University. While I have said earlier that it was Dad's precious partners along with the larger donors who financed Oral Roberts University from an earthly standpoint, it was the television specials that brought the large numbers of students to the campus.

But it was only the succeeding years that have revealed to me the truly miraculous nature of the Oral Roberts television specials. Drawing the large audiences such as Dad's television specials brought would be totally impossible today. Nowadays, I doubt there are ever such vast numbers of people watching one particular television program at any given time. It just does not happen anymore. There are too many choices with the advent of satellite television, the Internet, and such sites as

Facebook and Twitter. Additionally, engineering such productions today would be so costly as to be outside of any evangelist's reach. And finally, I cannot imagine any secular network accepting an evangelist's money to carry those programs, even if he had the funds in the first place. It just could not happen now.

But at that time, who knew that the 70's would have contained that short window of time? Who could have known? Only God knew that the 1970's would provide that small time period before people had a choice of several hundred channels at once, before they could be on cell phones, before they could surf the internet, before costs rose so astronomically and before preachers no longer had the clout to be allowed on prime time TV on a secular network. God knew, and He showed one man, Oral Roberts. As a result, something good really did happen, not just to Dad, but to the nation.

These all died in faith, not having received the promises,
but having seen them afar off, and were persuaded of
them, and embraced them...

–Hebrews 11:13

"WILT THOU BE MADE WHOLE?"

Chapter 9

And now I am compelled to describe to you what was to become and remains today as a true enigma to this author. The City of Faith was, I suppose, my father's largest undertaking as to pure scope. Curiously enough, the news media love to tell the story of how that project almost led Oral Roberts to the undertaker!

Personally, I felt that opening a hospital where patients could be treated using standard medical procedures, while at the same time receiving prayer was an absolutely marvelous concept. So many people I knew were patients in the City of Faith hospital over the years of the early 1980's and had such incredible experiences that perhaps I never truly understood what all the fuss was about.

But I suppose anyone reading this book will have heard of what the world referred to as the "900-hundred foot Jesus" episode. When you read the following paragraphs you may ask yourself, "Where was she? Why doesn't she know more?" The answer is: Colorado. By the time the idea of building the giant complex called the "City of Faith" was put into motion, my husband and I were no longer living in Oklahoma. Therefore some of my descriptions below are from a distance. On the other hand, I wonder if this distance could possibly provide a more insightful analysis. That, dear reader, is for you to decide.

A Regret?

Although I never heard him say it, I strongly suspect that Dad deeply regretted "sharing" the dream he had about the City of Faith. Must I discuss this chapter of Dad's life? It is so terribly painful even now, for while the dream clearly came from God Almighty, perhaps God only gave the "900-foot Jesus" dream to Dad as a personal encouragement when he was struggling with building the City of Faith. Perhaps the dream was not necessarily intended for Dad to share with the world?

Of course the truth is, when Dad perceived God as having done something good in his life, he could not resist telling others. He always had great difficulty in keeping secrets! That was without question a huge part of his psyche. You may remember Joseph in the Bible. His brothers were so angered by his dream that they actually sold him into slavery. Perhaps in a sense Dad felt that he himself had been sold into slavery after announcing his dream! But I am getting ahead of myself.

Thus far, I have basically described only successes, which my father had enjoyed during his lifetime and those were many. But he clearly had what the world (and certainly the news media) would describe as failures. Undoubtedly, the City of Faith was perceived as a failure by all but the most ardent of Oral Roberts supporters. I firmly believe that Dad heard from God when he built a medical clinic and a hospital, a vast complex referred to as the "City of Faith." It was a gargantuan facility containing over two million square feet and reaching 60 stories above the ground of south Tulsa, just on the south side of the Oral Roberts University campus. But from the beginning there were problems.

Was it the fault of the doctors, administrators, nurses, and others who answered Dad's call? I cannot honestly say that it was—although clearly there were a few "bad eggs" in that august group. Was it Dad's partners? Clearly not, because those precious people sent their hard-earned money, over 100 million dollars, to build it in the first place. Thus one cannot by any stretch of the imagination blame it on the partners. And who could possibly blame it on the patients who came? No, that would make absolutely no sense.

Can the debacle be blamed upon the other hospitals in town that fought the City of Faith's opening "tooth and nail," who would not allow ORU medical school students to observe and learn in their hospitals? Certainly, a part of the problem was that many of the folks who gave of their resources to the place did not come as patients after having given of their financial resources to build it.

But who is to blame them when most people would prefer to be in their own home town surrounded by family and friends while an in-patient at a hospital. Of course there is the factor of health insurance—not always covering the medical bills when partners did venture to Tulsa. And what about the Tulsa community? Why did they continue going to the older hospitals rather than the new, bright and shining City of Faith? Perhaps that is easy to explain as well: their doctors already had relationships with those existing hospitals and few were willing to change those relationships. Tulsa is a very traditional town and while such certainly accounts for much of its charm in the eyes of this author, such conservatism in that particular instance wreaked havoc on the patient load at the City of Faith Hospital.

It was while all of these things (and many more I suppose) were in process when Dad began to suffer heartbreaking discouragement. Dad had always been prone to emotional "ups and downs" as is typical for many preachers. They have such great highs, but what goes up, must come down. On one of those painstaking evenings when he was no doubt questioning his ability to hear and understand God's voice, Oral Roberts had a dream. When I first heard my father describe the dream, it was so encouraging.

A Daughter's Perspective

Now I know what you must be thinking. Oral Roberts was my father and he could do no wrong according to his loving daughter, correct? Actually, during those particular years, I felt myself in a deep morass based upon my feelings of having been ignored most of my life. Thus at that time, it was difficult for me to conceptualize my father having done anything right! And yet none of my emotional turmoil and negative feelings toward my father could prevent me from grasping the absolute perfection of his dream of merging medicine with prayer.

As I have told you, the complex itself was enormous by anyone's calculations. Dad was deeply concerned as to whether it would fail to carry out the goals he believed the Lord had had in telling him to build it in the first place. He felt under the burden of the finances of keeping the building project going. The place seemed so "heavy" to him. It was one of those terribly long evenings when he had a dream in which God showed him a picture of the entire complex.

Of course it was the kind of picture that is seen only in dreams. Basically, in the dream Dad saw the Lord pick up the entire complex in his hands, then look to Dad saying something like: "Look, Oral. It's not so heavy. I'm holding it in my hands." In the mind of this author, it was a dream that said nothing about Jesus' true height. It was simply meant to be an encouragement perhaps to Dad alone—that when we feel our burdens are too heavy to bear, as we so often do, the Lord will carry them on our behalf.

I am told that Dad first made a public announcement of this dream in a letter to his partners. Somewhere in that letter, he apparently stated that if he were truly unable to finish the City of Faith, the Lord would take him "home." If you are a Christian, you see your true home as Heaven. Death is no threat to a true Christian. Heaven is in fact God's ultimate promise to those who believe. However, to a reporter (whose name has long-since been forgotten by this author) it sounded as though Dad were saying that he had actually seen Jesus—outside of a dream—and that he could estimate Jesus' exact height, i.e., 900 feet.

I do not remember if Dad actually used that number but perhaps in his discussion he attached some sort of dimensions to God in his dream. Looking back it absolutely astounds me that I simply cannot remember these details. Was it the pain that has truly blocked the details from my mind or perhaps I chose not to think of such things, then later forgot them? I do not know the answer.

Of course the reporter's most damaging assumption was what Dad meant by all of these things. The report quoted Dad as having said something to the effect that if Dad failed in this, his latest project, God would kill him. Did Dad mean it in such a way? Absolutely not! However, dare I say it? Dad did have a tendency to exaggerate for effect. He also had a tendency to feel sorry for himself when things were not going his way. Perhaps you can claim never to have done either of the above, but I simply cannot. It is clearly a widespread human tendency and never let it be said that Oral Roberts was immune.

The "crowning" part of this story however was when a man who was apparently known for dog racing heard the news account and gave over a million dollars to the City of Faith. And get this, so that God wouldn't kill Oral Roberts. Oh my.

As anyone would expect, the report of that gift was carried nationwide and caught the attention of vast numbers of people. It was obviously anything but a positive report and made my father appear to be nothing more than a buffoon. The history of the City of Faith remains as one of those unfortunate news stories which never seems to have lost its impact even all these years later. While we routinely throw our newspapers into the trash after having read them, stories that vast numbers of people found exciting at one time or another seem to continually "pop up" in the future.

Even now it seems that if Dad's name is mentioned by the secular news media, the "900-foot Jesus" story is massaged again, and again and again. I suppose it is our basic human nature that we prefer to discuss what we see as failures rather than the successes of others. All the better for us to deal with our own failures I suppose.

How did this debacle occur? Why did it occur? How could it have occurred? I am at a loss to answer those questions but as my father struggled to reinstate what was lost due to those terribly negative reports, my own personal humiliation was and remains intense. Of course many people blame the devil when bad things happen to them. And clearly there is Biblical precedent for that assumption (see John 10:10 and other passages). However, I cannot honestly contend that it was merely an attack of Satan. Unquestionably, blaming our failures on Satan has become an easy, convenient cop out for some. No, it was more than that alone.

I have no doubt that the dream—including both the merging medicine with prayer and of the Lord holding the complex itself in His hands—was from God Himself and Dad wanted it perhaps more than he had ever wanted anything in his life up until that time. He was not a man who easily faced failure. The more things went wrong, the harder he fought. Just as ORU had been and still is today, to Dad, the City of Faith was an extension of his healing ministry. Dad had a driving desire to help those who were hurting. He wanted a hospital so much. He wanted the doctors of the ORU medical school to be the best they could be and learn everything they could learn in order to help their patients.

Hearing God

Some have believed that in his bulldogged struggle, Oral Roberts did not hear the voice of God accurately. I will let God be the judge of that. However I can tell you that my father was a real, honest-to-goodness human being with faults and failures like the rest of us. I would say that whatever mistakes and errors in judgment he made, the plain truth is that he heard and obeyed the voice of God abundantly more than most.

While the complex itself is no longer open solely for its original purposes, let the reader understand that there have been many medical practitioners who "caught" the original vision of the place. For example, there is a group of doctors here in Tulsa who are providing free medical care along with prayer, to the poor of our community. Their sister organization is training resident physicians in a Tulsa hospital, then sending them worldwide to provide aid—and prayer—during severe health crises. Both Good Samaritan Health Services and In His Image are outgrowths of the City of Faith, begun by a former physician there, Dr. John Crouch. There is also Blessings International founded by a pharmacologist (also a former professor in ORU's medical school) whose organization provides prescription drugs to sick folks all over the globe, handed out with prayer.

Of course it is easy to judge Oral Roberts. With the help of the media, America has become in some senses a society of judgment. We seem to be so hard on others and so easy on ourselves. We place people on impossible pedestals then are "shocked" when they fail to perform to the level of our expectations. Was Dad perfect in this debacle? Perhaps not. In later years he was not open to discuss this issue—even with my husband who typically found a willingness in my father to hash out difficult issues.

Whatever Dad's faults or failures may have been, I think the more important question to be posed at this juncture is whether our world would have been a better place today had merging prayer with medicine—as proposed by Oral Roberts—happened and continued to happen. Can anyone seriously question my assertion that since that time, the health of Americans has gone south? Is there any reason to remind you of the healthcare crisis which continues to elude our politicians even today? Must I discuss the unresolved cancer, diabetes, heart disease and the like which we see and experience all too often in this country? I think not. Is the world correct when it pretends the answer is stem cell research or cloning? I think not.

I would just say that the idea, combining the best which medicine has to offer with God's healing power, remains a gleaming concept, an idea waiting to be discovered, or I should say rediscovered—on behalf of the masses of hurting people around the world.

It is as if Man O'War had been locked into a stall—impatient, straining to escape—waiting, waiting to be released, chomping at the bit to storm out onto the racetrack, to race with the wind, carrying with him the health which only God could have envisioned for His people. Not health based upon all kinds of life-sustaining drugs which often bring a sort of "living death," but a health which gives us life to our years, happy, productive, Godly living until the day we reach the appointment which each of us has with our Creator.

When I picture that horse in my mind, I can hear Dad preaching during my childhood about a man at the Pool of Bethesda described in the Gospel of John. He had been waiting there for 38 years—waiting to be healed. There were many others there, others to whom scripture refers as "sick, blind, lame and withered." And they were waiting as well.

That man told Jesus, "I have no one to help me" (John 5:7) into the healing waters. Jesus first asked him: "Wilt thou be made whole?" then He told him to "rise, take up your bed, and walk." Like the race-horse, the concept of the City of Faith (a promise from God) is still waiting. Reminiscent of the man at the Pool of Bethesda, millions of sick people are waiting desperately for help. Thus perhaps the crucial inquiry in our day has not changed: Perhaps Jesus is asking *each of us*: "Wilt thou be made whole?"

I spoke recently to a lady now living in Kansas. When she was fourteen years old, she had a life expectancy of two months, having been diagnosed with lymphoma and Chron's disease. She related that she was one of the first patients at the City of Faith. She remembers very well the prayers said for her and the surgery that took place in the hospital there. As a result of her experience at the City of Faith, she was totally healed, then lived to marry and have children. She and her husband became missionaries and, by the way, sent their daughter to Oral Roberts University. So was the City of Faith worth it? Just ask Janice Stubbs.

Here are the words of a song written by the great Vep Ellis:

> Wilt thou be made whole?"
> Body, mind and soul,
> Rise, take up your bed and walk,
> Rise take up your bed and walk.
> Loose every shackle, break every chain;
> Rise, new life to gain
> Rise, in Jesus' name.

*He that believeth on me, as the scripture hath said, out of
his belly shall flow rivers of living water.*

–John 7:38

"OH, BLESSED HOLY SPIRIT"

Chapter 10

How can I articulate the pressures and hurts Dad experienced during his life? Even growing up in the home of Oral Roberts, I have no hope of a complete understanding of these things. But more importantly, how did Dad deal with it all? Consider the following:

Many pastors criticized Dad for his healing crusades. He said that on many evenings as he preached under that tent, he felt daggers coming at him from behind. Why? Because while many church people were very excited about the preaching and praying for the sick which occurred during Dad's crusades, some of their pastors were not. I hasten to tell you that many pastors loved Dad's ministry but I would be less than truthful if I allowed the reader to believe that all pastors accepted Dad's ministry with open arms. They did not.

On the Edge of Their Seats

While Dad did not plan crusades in a town unless there were pastors who were willing to "sponsor" him, some of those pastors were only involved because their members gave them no graceful way of escape. I suppose those particular pastors felt pressure to at least give lip service to Dad's ministry, as so many of their members were carried away by the events of which they had heard. And by the way, when I use the term "sponsoring" pastor, I surround the word with quotation marks because the pastors sponsored the meetings only in that they were willing to sit on the platform during the meetings and attend a pastor's meeting in advance of the crusade. It does not mean they sponsored the crusades from a financial standpoint!

So picture it. The pastors sat on the platform behind Dad while he was preaching. Some were happy to be there; others were not. Few men could have walked onto that platform without feeling a measure of intimidation. And yet, on that very platform Dad preached the most stunning sermons you can imagine. His audiences were literally sitting on the edge of their chairs, fearing that they might miss one word.

Then there were the imprecations Dad received due to the Seed Faith concept, which I discussed earlier. There was the night in Amarillo when a tornado totally destroyed the tent Dad had used for his crusade meetings. As wonderful as it was that virtually all of the 7,000 strong inside that tent escaped without injury, how was Oral Roberts going to raise the funds to purchase yet another tent? In that bitter moment, he wondered whether his ministry was finished right along with his tent.

A Terrible Blow

The reader may already be aware that my older sister, Rebecca and her husband, Marshall Nash were killed in a plane crash in 1977. A short five years later, in 1982, my brother, Ronnie, committed suicide. Some parents never seem to recover from losing one child, much less two. In 1979, Dad was forced to face the divorce of my brother, Richard, and his wife Patti. After Richard's remarriage to Lindsay Salem, their first child, named "Richard Oral," lived merely a few days after his birth.

There were the terrible slings and arrows Dad experienced as a result of building the City of Faith and the dream previously discussed.

There was my Mother's fall, which brought on her death in 2005. Her passing left Dad with feelings of heartrending loneliness. They had been married 66 years.

And lastly was the resignation under pressure and serious accusations against my brother, Richard, as President of the University that Dad had founded. And what I have mentioned were only some of the major difficulties experienced by my father.

So how did Oral Roberts survive the misunderstandings, the censure and even hatred when many would have simply given up and long ago sailed off into the sunset? "Not by might, nor by power, but by my spirit, saith the LORD of hosts." (Zechariah 4:6) Jesus referred to the Holy Spirit of God as a Comforter, and He surely was that to my father.

But how did Dad get through the hours, the long nights—losing sleep time and time again due to the problems, the challenges, the terrible pressures of his life? Through the baptism of the Holy Spirit. Through speaking in tongues.

By expressing to God "groanings which cannot be uttered." (See Romans 8:26) Dad would not have wished this part of his story to be told while he was living, but now that he has gone to Heaven, I believe it is important for me to tell you that he was prone to depression. I spoke in an earlier chapter of the anointing that can come upon an individual temporarily. As wonderful as that is, it comes with a price tag.

First of all, true anointing from God does not come without a preparation of one's heart. Oh I realize the term "anointing" is thrown around quite liberally these days by lots of preachers, but how many of them arrive at the platform and just "shoot from the hip?" My Dad paid the price! I witnessed the hours Dad spent before God. I saw the sheets and sheets of notes he took and the marked-up Bibles. I had to be quiet all those hours and come up with silent games along with my brother—just to survive all those hours! I know the price he paid. I lived it and I paid it too! I do not tell you that as a complaint. I boast in that because I knew my daddy was real!

Once it comes, the anointing lifts you high, and oh, how wonderful it is. Needs are met. People are changed and healed and inspired! But when it is over, you come down again, back to the earth. Dad used to say: "The problem with life is... it's so daily!" Similar to the experiences of Elijah, Dad came down from those beautiful moments of anointing, and had to be a normal person again—like the rest of us! Under those circumstances I suppose a sense of depression would have been inevitable. And yet, Dad learned to rely on praying in the Holy Spirit during those times—upon that heavenly language sent from God Himself.

Oh, I am well aware that many people scoff at speaking in tongues. So what else is new? Even many Christians believe that speaking in tongues was for Bible days only and has no practical use for today. And yet when we forbid the help of the language of the Holy Spirit in our lives, we rob ourselves of the very power that can help us to survive. There is little to be gained by arguing with the detractors or with those who do not believe speaking in tongues can be helpful today. I am simply glad to have had a father who showed me—by his example—the reality of the Baptism of the Holy Spirit as described in the Book of Acts.

How many times I remember Dad discussing Jesus' comment made at the Feast of Tabernacles: "He that believeth on me... out of his belly shall flow rivers of living water." (John 7:38) While Ezekiel 47:9 tells us that where the river flows, everything will live, perhaps one must actually reside in the desert to truly grasp the imagery of that verse. Most of us are so spoiled either by irrigation or plenty of rain that when we hear these scriptures, no picture of a lush riverbank flashes in our minds.

Nor do we consider the opposite: dry, cracked soil, brown and lifeless. But those two examples are accurate descriptions of our lives—both with and, however sadly, without the Holy Spirit. The only river that can flow through our lives through that cracked, depressed soil of our being is the river of the Holy Spirit. Nothing else will do.

A Girl's First Adventure

When I was nine years old, in the summer of 1960, I begged Mother to let me travel to Houston with Dad. He was getting ready to conduct a tent crusade there and for a reason that now escapes me, Mother was unable to accompany him. Like most girls my age, I so wanted to be treated as a grown up and realized that if I were allowed to go, without Mother being there, I would be on my own, so to speak. Oh, it was not that I wanted to do anything against the wishes of my parents.

On the contrary, I was very close to Jesus at that point in my life and the last thing I wanted to do was to violate the principles of right and wrong which had been painstakingly ingrained in me by my mother. No, it was just that I longed to feel more like an adult rather than a helpless infant. At any rate, perhaps my potential to make good arguments as a future attorney came to the forefront, for I was successful in convincing my parents to allow me to go to Houston with my father. Unfortunately as circumstances developed, I learned that I was not quite as prepared for adulthood as I had hoped.

Dad and I had connecting rooms in the motel. On the evening of the first meeting, I was ready to go ahead of time with Bible in hand—excited about getting to ride in the car with Dad and Collins Steele. We would be without anyone else—alone. It made me feel so very important just to think of it! I kept waiting for Dad to open the connecting door and tell me it was time to go. I kept knocking on his door, with no response. I finally gathered the courage to open the door and realized that...Dad was already gone!

He had left for the meeting and totally forgotten about taking me with him. Didn't I tell you he was focused? Once he had his mind on his sermon, there was no room for anything else in his brain, certainly not a snot-nosed kid like me. Thinking back, that must have been the very reason for my mother's reluctance in allowing me to go without her. She knew what would happen!

At first I panicked, wondering what in the world I was going to do. The thought of missing that meeting was a tragedy of epic proportions in my little mind. Not only would I get into trouble with my mother, but more importantly, I would miss the first meeting of the very thing I had fought so valiantly to attend! At least Mother had possessed the presence of mind to ensure that her little nine-year old girl had some money in her wallet. After a few minutes of immense frustration, a terrible sense of abandonment and a giant foreboding of severe disciplinary action in the future, I eventually thought of calling a taxicab.

Thank God, I finally did manage to arrive at the crusade unscathed. I was late of course, but at least I was able to get there on my own. I do not think Dad ever realized that he had forgotten me or that I had arrived late that evening. The truth is that I could have walked into the tent and sat down in a chair with a bag over my head and Dad would never have had an inkling of anything amiss. Would you say he was single-minded? Slightly!

And yet as disconcerted as I had been due to preceding events, I was immediately captivated by the service, as was everyone else. I quickly forgot the entire scenario that had led to my arrival in a taxicab, being immediately caught up in the spirit of the meeting. That crusade, along with many others, had a huge impact on my life and was very formative in my thinking.

It was not until later, though, when I learned of something with which Dad was already well-acquainted—something which may have eclipsed the "daggers" he felt from some of the disapproving pastors behind him on that raised platform. What was it? It was an exposé published by the now defunct Life Magazine. While it was suggested by some that it was the dreadful article about Oral Roberts that brought about the demise of the famous magazine, I make no such claim. All I can say is that the anguish due to the assertions made in the magazine article were so horrendous that Dad could hardly speak of it.

It is common among Christians to raise our hands to the Lord when we meet together. The practice was common when I was a little girl and it is common currently. And yet as normal as that simple activity seems to me, having grown up in church and assembled with other Christians as a matter of custom during all of my years, such behavior was beyond the ken of the publishers of Life Magazine. The magazine had blown up a picture of crusade attendees, each with their hands raised high, and used the picture to cover most of the left and right side of the article's first two pages. In my mind's eye I can still see the huge caption, which said: "Mass Hysteria!" and "Frenzy!"

As horribly painful as that article was for me, I cannot imagine how much more it had to have bruised my father. The picture, coupled with the tenor of the article, made raising your hands to God seem beyond bizarre. It made such a course of action seem extreme and aberrational. The point is, hearing Dad preach during each meeting of that Houston crusade, I had absolutely no idea that such an article had ever been published. He never said a word. He acted no differently than he ever had. His sermons were no less powerful. In fact, I never heard him even broach the subject until that crusade came to an end.

Even when he and I had our picture taken for a Houston newspaper, my childish mind did not grasp the subject of that interview. It was

SOMETIMES PUBLICITY HURTS
Rev. Oral Roberts and Daughter Roberta

not until after that trip when I heard Dad speak of how the Holy Spirit had bathed his wounds during the upsetting aftermath of that deplorable magazine article.

You can tell yourself over and over, "It's just words" when the press characterizes you as a fool from Mars. You can do your best to dismiss the negative innuendoes, but no matter what you tell yourself, the simple truth is that IT HURTS!

It was by spending time with the Lord, speaking in tongues—in a language only God understood—that gradually gave Dad the strength and fortitude to continue with what he believed God had told him to do. He often compared speaking in tongues with exercising a muscle. That as you continued to do it, you would gain more expertise, in the sense that it would help you to deal with the inevitable onslaughts which each of us face as a part of daily living. Dad well understood that it was no accident when Jesus chose to speak of those rivers of living water *during* the Feast of Tabernacles. The Feast of Tabernacles itself stands for the proposition that God wants to "tabernacle" or pitch his tent with us. It is speaking in tongues that allows that communion, that incredible fellowship with our Creator, on this earth.

You may have some familiarity with what Ephesians 6 refers to as the "full armor of God," but many of us, even committed Christians, totally disregard the portion of the armor listed in verse 18 which gives us the most power! "Praying always with all prayer and supplication

IN THE SPIRIT..." (emphasis added). To many faithful Bible readers, it is as if the verse simply does not exist. To many, that verse wallows in the miasma of total disregard, even to some noted Bible scholars. It may as well have been written in Sanskrit! And yet it is the very heart of the armor and would explain how the apostle Paul himself survived the shipwrecks, the imprecations, being beaten with rods, the threats, the danger, the imprisonment, the thorn in the flesh, and everything else which he endured.

Of course Dad may have felt like he had been boiled in oil simply for accentuating the Baptism of the Holy Spirit. Undaunted however, to the end of his life he spoke of it, and urged others to engage in speaking in tongues. Some have said that Dad was the founder of what is now referred to as the "Charismatic Movement." That claim is for others to make, not his loving daughter. I will admit, however, that Dad's emphasis on a phenomenon predicted by the prophet Joel, anticipated by Jesus Himself, and experienced by the 120 in the Upper Room, did expose those rivers of living water to large numbers of people all over the world.

Not surprisingly, it was the Holy Spirit who inspired Vep Ellis to write the words sung often in Dad's crusades:

> *Oh, Blessed Holy Spirit*
> ... Now when you need an answer
> from Heaven right away,
> and after all your trying,
> You don't know how to pray;
> 'Tis then the Holy Spirit,
> Makes inner conflict cease.
> Intercession, Heaven's blessing,
> Brings a sweet relief.

Oh blessed Holy Spirit;
Cleansing through and through;
O'er my tongue it's flooding,
Like a river ever new;
A language Heaven heareth,
Tho' to earth unknown,
Sweet communion, holy union,
God and His own.

... like a person building a house, who dug a deep hole to lay the foundation on rock. When a flood came, the floodwaters pushed against that house but couldn't shake it, because it had been founded on the rock.

—Luke 6:48 (ISV)

"THE SOLID ROCK"

Chapter 11

I have known a lot of people over the years, but never have I been acquainted with someone so focused as my father. He was the most driven person I have ever known. You could almost say that his entire life was his work. For him, very little else existed. Unlike most men, he never wrote a check, he never knew how much money he had in the bank at any given time, he never bought toothpaste, razor blades or new shoelaces. The only gift he ever bought was once a year on Christmas Eve. He would go to a store, buy a black nightgown, have it gift-wrapped, then put it under the tree for my mother. That was the extent of his gift buying for anyone,

all year long. He was color-blind and could not pick out his own clothes, even had he been so inclined.

The Strength Behind the Man

So how was it possible for Dad to exist without doing those daily tasks that almost all of us do? Well actually, the question should be WHO made it possible for him to accomplish so much in his lifetime without lifting a finger outside his ministry? The answer: my mother, Evelyn Roberts.

Our house was an environment my mother created where my father was king. In our house, the world revolved around him, in every respect. She never asked him what he wanted for dinner. He walked in, sat down, and ate what had been placed on the table for him. He never had to say: "I need this, or I need that" because it was always there for him. He did not ever have to ask for anything. He never had to check to see if he was running out of something. Mother had already checked to see what he needed, then made sure it was there for him when he might need it. She took on every practical need he had and made sure it was available at any given moment.

I do remember him negotiating to purchase a new car, but the only reason I remember that was because it was so unusual. And even then, Mother wrote and signed the check, not my father. Mother made sure the cars had plenty of gas and oil and that they were properly maintained. She did not necessarily do all of those things herself of course, but she made sure they were done. Mother herself made sure that all the bills were paid, the checkbook was balanced, and so on, and so forth, not Dad.

I cannot count the times when I would be playing as a child—or being a noisy teenager—when Mother would whisper: "Be quiet, honey. Your father is studying." That meant he was reading his Bible or perhaps preparing a sermon or the like. As mentioned previously, when we were children, my brother and I devised all sorts of "quiet games" so we would not disturb Dad. Again, our entire household revolved around our father.

Creating the world I have described above would be out of the question for any other woman I have ever met, including this author. Clearly, my mother's generation (she was born in 1917) was taught to do much more for their husbands than the women of our world today. However, I suspect that even then, there might have been a few limits. I suspect that few women even of my Mother's generation did as many things for their husbands as my mother did for hers.

So why did she do this? Why was she willing to make herself a virtual slave on my father's behalf? I believe this was her way of saying: "You go out there and be a success. I will take care of everything else." Both my parents were driven. The difference was that Dad was driven regarding his ministry and Mother was driven to make sure he was a success in his ministry. The atmosphere Mother created allowed Dad to do his work. No other pressures, just work. Because of her, all Dad had to think about was his work. She took care of everything else. I would not say that Mother helped Dad much with his sermons, at least not typically. She just created a setting which freed him so that he could *create* those incredible sermons.

And my mother never criticized Dad for not helping at home. In fact, I honestly do not remember my mother ever criticizing him for anything. Not once. She never made him feel guilty, not about anything. She never made him feel less of a man, ever. He was top dog. She believed that if she gave him what he wanted and needed at home, he would succeed outside the home. Are you beginning to understand why he felt so special and why he was able to do so many special things for the Kingdom of God? It was in large part because of my mother.

As a little girl, Evelyn Lutman lived in an unhappy home. Neither of her parents served the Lord or knew much about Jesus or Christianity. Her parents were not happy with each other—not at all. Despite all my efforts, I was never successful in learning much regarding Mother's early childhood. The most Mother ever told me was that when she was still a little girl, there was a heated custody battle between her parents over her and her younger sister, Ruth.

Apparently, the court refused to grant custody of little Evelyn to either of her parents and Mother was taken to Texas to live with her grandparents, the Wingates. Mother did tell me, however, that her father was a heavy drinker. She had such terrible memories, whatever they were, that she would not allow a drop of alcohol in our house for any reason, for any purpose. Whatever her memories were, they must have been grievous indeed.

The good news is that her grandparents were very well acquainted with the things of God and they were very good to my mother. She was apparently able to relax and enjoy life for the first time. It was her grandparents who taught her what you might refer to as refinement and the niceties of life. She learned from them that it was important for your speech to be grammatically correct, that your table manners were of supreme importance, and that you were to act "like a lady."

Soon after, however, her mother became living proof that Jesus Christ can change lives, because once Edna met Jesus everything changed. After Edna divorced Edgar Lutman, she married Ira Fahnestock. When speaking to me, Mother never referred to Ira as her stepfather. She always referred to him as her dad, for her stepfather was very good to her and apparently treated her far better than had her own father.

When her mother and new "father" were first married however, they apparently did not live all that differently from the atmosphere Mother had experienced with her own father in residence. However, Edna and Ira soon learned of a "brush arbor" meeting and that a lady referred to merely as "Granny Hubbs" was always there and was always shouting. They thought it would be funny to hear that little granny shout. God's sense of humor never ceases to amaze me. I do not know whether they actually heard the old lady shout, but everything changed. Both Edna and Ira had been soundly converted to Christ by the conclusion of that brush arbor meeting. Everything was different and Evelyn soon came home.

You will remember from an earlier chapter that Dad was saved, changed by Jesus, when he was 17 years old. The following year, in 1936, he had just begun preaching. He was no longer living in Westville, Oklahoma where his father was currently pastoring, but between preaching assignments, he stayed with his parents. On one of those visits, he attended a camp meeting there in Westville. This particular camp meeting would probably be more accurately understood today as a business meeting, for it was where pastors gave reports and obtained their assignments for the coming year.

Both Evelyn Lutman and Oral Roberts had agreed to play their guitars for these meetings, although the reason why guitars were necessary given the purpose of the meeting has always eluded me. At any rate, the two were strangers, Dad having no way of knowing that my mother's family, the Fahnestocks, had been attending his father's church.

On one of those evenings, Dad rushed into the camp meeting, his guitar in tow, and realized that he had forgotten to check his appearance before entering. There was an empty seat beside a young girl. He hurriedly sat down by her and turning to the girl, said: "Is my hair combed?" While Evelyn responded diplomatically, she said to herself: "When I get you, you won't have to ask. You'll never leave the house again until you *know* you look your best!"

After the short conversation, Dad promptly forgot the girl named Evelyn. For Dad, it was not until later when he was looking for a wife that he deigned to notice her. (Men! The little dears!) However, he made quite an impression on her, for before climbing into bed that night, Evelyn wrote in her diary: "I met my future husband tonight."

It must have been sometime afterward when Evelyn Lutman secured a teaching job near Corpus Christi, Texas, would you believe, in a one-room schoolhouse. She actually taught children from kindergarten all the way through high school. I doubt there would have been more than perhaps 15 or 20 students over one school year, but can you imagine having to teach all the subjects to all the various age groups? Yet, my mother loved teaching and may have been content to stay there for awhile, had it not been for a letter she received from (guess who) that young preacher who had recently been healed of tuberculosis.

So how did Oral Roberts come to write such a letter to the girl he had "chanced" to sit beside in a camp meeting and promptly forgotten? Well, I will just tell you that God's promise to order our steps was truly carried out in the lives of my parents. If it had not been for a man named Frank Moss, I suppose my parents might have forever remained little more than strangers. Although Dad was obviously not acquainted with all of the families who attended his father's church, he was acquainted with Frank Moss.

"It's Time to Get Married"

Frank, the owner of a trucking line, often asked Dad to ride with him on various trips. During one of those otherwise uneventful trips, he made the statement to Dad: "Oral, it's time for you to get married." While Dad readily agreed, that comment inspired a long description of what Dad required in a wife. There were no less than ten things on his list! Of course the first requirement was that she be a Christian, she had to love children, etc., etc. etc.

Poor Frank patiently and kindly listened to each of Dad's qualifications regarding what he considered was necessary for his ideal wife. During a long road trip, what else were they going to do but talk anyway? Obviously, no music CD's were available at that time and otherwise, the hours would have passed so slowly. (By the way, each of Dad's qualifications had sub-parts, one of which was that the lady must be able to play the piano!)

Once Dad recited each necessary attribute, Frank thought a moment, then asked Dad if he had any candidates in mind. "Not a one," Dad replied. Undaunted, Frank said: "Well, let me tell you who she is!" He apparently went through each item of Dad's list, one by one, and advised him that Evelyn Lutman fit the bill—perfectly. Most men, at least the ones I know, would have run in the opposite direction, but not my father. He actually began writing Mother in Texas, based upon Frank's suggestions, again, having totally forgotten that he was already acquainted with her from that previous camp meeting.

I mentioned earlier that Mother already believed in her heart that Oral Roberts was to be her husband. Unlike many women of today, however, she did nothing about it, except in her prayers. By the time she started receiving letters from Dad, she had already told the Lord: "Okay, I thought this was who you wanted me to marry. If it is, you will have to put us together." She made a decision to live for God and not to chase Dad, or any other man, for that matter. I know this part of the story quite well because it was drilled into my head on many occasions!

Actually, this was some of the best advice my mother ever gave me. Don't ever look for a man. Don't ever plan to "accidentally on purpose" show up where you know a certain man will be—as some women do. Let God send him to you. Mother always said: "If you have to chase him, you might catch him, but you won't like what you've caught!"

At any rate, Oral and Evelyn began corresponding. While some had telephones in those days, neither Mother nor Dad could have afforded such an extravagance. And of course this was long before emailing was possible so snail mail would have to do. In my parents' lives, however, I believe the lack of more modern technology may have been God-ordained. Dad said later that he fell in love with Mother through the letters they wrote back and forth to each other. Years later I remember him telling his partners, "There's just something about a letter." I have often wondered if he was remembering his correspondence with my mother.

After several months of communicating by letter, Dad decided to travel southward to Texas to see his "pen pal" face to face. His mother, however, quick to sense the innermost workings of her youngest son's mind, was determined not to let him make that particular journey unaccompanied. No, she would ride along with him, and that was that. Claudius Priscilla Roberts, my grandmother, refused to allow Dad to travel that far to see a woman without her coming along. How exciting that must have been! Give me a break!

It would be much more romantic if I could tell you that when he arrived, Dad and Mother went out for a fancy dinner, but no, they went fishing! They always said the only thing they caught that day was each other.

Oral Roberts actually proposed on that very day, however, his proposal was rather unusual. He actually said these words to poor Evelyn: "My huge, happy, hilarious heart is throbbing tumultuously, tremendously, triumphantly with a lingering, lasting, long-lived love for you. As I gaze in your bewildering, beauteous, bounteous, beaming eyes, I am literally lonesomely lost in a dazzling, daring, delightful dream in which your fair, felicitous, fanciful face is ever present like a colossal, comprehensive constellation. Will you be my sweet, smiling, soulful, satisfied spouse?" Now it was Evelyn's turn to run in the opposite direction. Instead she replied: "Look here, Oral Roberts. If you're trying to propose to me, you will have to say it in English!" He apparently did, and they were married the following Christmas, December 25, 1938.

Once they were married, she began to put into motion her plan to "refine" him a little, well actually, a lot. Mother had received that intense training from her grandparents, and she had progressed from there to become a teacher. But if she was a fine teacher to the children in that one-room schoolhouse, she was an even better teacher to my father. She required him to "work on" his grammar. Her famous statement, repeated so often, was: "Say your words plainly!"

She made him practice before a mirror. She required perfect manners at the dinner table and helped him to "clean up a little" as she would have said, in his personal grooming and deportment. Dad had had very little opportunity to go to school, having to leave on too many days to pick cotton as a child. You might say that a good part of Dad's training was from my mother, for she was determined that he would be able to go anywhere without embarrassing himself. Evelyn Roberts had no way of knowing that her husband—that little boy who had stuttered and stammered—would one day have the opportunity to meet and talk with such people as John F. Kennedy, Richard Nixon, George H.W. Bush, Jimmy Carter, David Ben Gurion, Billy Graham, and oh, so many others. She only knew that he must be prepared for whatever the Lord had in store for him.

While she could be a zealot in her expectations, my mother was a gentle taskmaster. As rigorous as were her demands, she had the unique ability to make her pupil *want* to meet her expectations. She was an individual you simply did not want to disappoint.

Having told you about the atmosphere Mother created for Dad in our home, I do not mean to leave the impression that she was simply "the little woman" who kept house for him. Such would be a gross misrepresentation of my mother. For me to provide an honest view of Evelyn Roberts, then, I must contrast that sincere support with

Mother's reaction when, on occasion, she felt Dad might be getting onto the wrong track.

Oral Roberts was a dreamer—a true visionary—always in the clouds with new ideas. Conversely, the feet of Evelyn Roberts were squarely on the ground. Incredibly practical. There were times when she would sit him down and question him quite severely. "Now Oral, are you *sure* you heard from God?" Having witnessed a few such occasions, it did not require a nuclear physicist's mind to grasp the necessity of keeping quiet.

I suppose no one enjoys being questioned, least of all, my father. So given his temperament (and believe me, he had a hot temper and a large ego) it is amazing that he tolerated the rather severe questioning as well as he did. But I suspect he was as accepting as he was because Mother had the wisdom to limit such questioning to those rare occasions when she was genuinely concerned that something could be seriously wrong. I think this is a good lesson for all of us, to keep our complaints to a bare minimum. Then on those few occasions when we do speak, the other party will (hopefully) believe we have earned the right to ask the hard, pointed questions. Again, these times in my parents' lives were rare. But I will tell you that when Mother did choose to speak, she did not mince her words. She had a way of getting to the heart of an issue very quickly. And believe me, he paid attention.

Of course Dad also understood her intense love for him. He knew that once the decision was made, she would defend him with all that was within her. While she was willing to listen to those who might disagree with her husband, her forbearance had its limits. There was a line that must not be crossed, for once she perceived someone to be "against" her husband, she could become a fierce tigress. She passionately believed in Dad and his ministry. She was his greatest support and ally and was always there for him, always. My mother did not have an easy time as Dad's wife. Before he started a healing ministry, when she was still a pastor's wife, she was often desperately hurt as a result of comments made by other women in the church.

Feeling Slighted

If she had a fault, I suppose it would be an inability to forget insults. She related to me more than once an incident having to do with a new dress she had purchased while Dad was a pastor of a small church. While his salary was nothing to write home about, my mother always knew how to budget what little moneys were available to her, and had thus managed to save just enough to buy a new dress which she had admired for quite some time. The front of the dress contained beads and Mother was so eager to wear her new dress to church the following Sunday.

At that time, my sister Rebecca was a baby and thus small enough to be placed in a cradle. Mother played the piano for the service but the church apparently had no nursery as you would expect in a church today. At any rate, Mother would play the piano and keep Rebecca in her cradle just near her foot. If Rebecca started to cry, Mother would remove her foot from the piano pedals and carefully rock the cradle with her foot. Well, the gentle gyrations were apparently successful that Sunday morning, but Evelyn Roberts' new dress did not exactly garner appreciation from the other women in the church. The ladies apparently made unkind remarks about the ungodliness of wearing a dress which actually contained colored beads! I suppose they would have fainted dead away had they foreseen what some ladies wear to church in our day.

Suffice it to say, however, that Mother was shocked and stung by the remarks of those "pillars of decency" that morning. While the reader must not forget that this was 1940—a time of far different expectations within Pentecostal churches in Oklahoma than our day—even so, I think it was the tone and the disdain which my mother felt so acutely on that Sunday morning. Unfortunately, Mother had purchased the dress on sale, so she could not return it. Nor were my parents on an economic level that would have allowed her to simply hang the dress in the closet and wear something else! She realized that she had no choice but to wear that dress because she had little else which was suitable.

Mother went home that afternoon and cut off every bead from that dress. The truth is that she was never quite able to totally dismiss the incident from her mind. I think this incident explains at least to some degree why Mother and Dad felt they should be role models for their church people. They wanted to help people understand that you did not necessarily have to be poor to be a good Christian.

A Godly Mother

Despite the fact that Dad was her absolute priority, Evelyn Roberts was also a good mother. Possibly one of her greatest contributions in my own life was the Bible stories she told us, often on the way to church. While we regularly attended Sunday School and church, my mother was never willing to entrust her children's Biblical education to Sunday School teachers alone. On the way to church (it was at least a thirty minute drive in those days before the expressway was built), she told the most wonderful stories of the people described in the Bible. She had a way of making the characters come alive. Those teaching sessions birthed in me a love affair with the Bible that has never faded, for over 60 years now.

Mother was also there for us if someone was ill. My sister Rebecca often remarked: "Mother always comes through!" And, along with all the things she did for my father, and the hours she spent with her children, she somehow found time to help others outside of our family

when they were hurting. When the first class of students arrived on the Oral Roberts University campus, I remember that one of the women arrived—but her belongings did not. Of course the girl was traumatized. She had no clothes to wear to school—nothing but what she had worn on the bus! When Mother learned of the situation, she came straight home, went through her closet and asked me to go through mine. Together, we were able to find enough clothing to get the student through for a few days until her own things arrived on campus.

And perhaps it was that small event which began a life-long love affair between my mother and the ORU students. There is a small pond on campus the students named "Evelyn Pond." I also remember Dad raising the funds to buy a very expensive television camera so that he could eventually begin televising programs from the ORU campus rather than always having to travel to California. Once he had obtained the necessary finances, he had the camera rolled into an ORU chapel service. Of course he had to "show off" this new piece of equipment. He was so excited about the new camera that he shouted to the students: "What should we name it?" Almost with one voice they began shouting: "Evelyn II."

While I doubt Mother always dreamed of being the namesake for a camera, she certainly basked in the love she received from not only

An Oral Roberts television program featuring all of his children along with his darling wife, Evelyn.

students but also faculty members, Dad's partners and, well, just about everybody else. In fact, my only concern in writing this chapter is that I may say something—anything—that could be construed negatively against my mother. For if I had the audacity to do so, there would be such a storm of protest from her fans that I might be tarred and feathered. Certainly, some of my friendships would cease immediately. All right, I admit to slight exaggeration here, but suffice it to say that I have never known a person so loved in all of my years.

What is actually so amazing, however, is that Mother was loved despite her propensity to say exactly what she felt, without sparing the feelings of the hearer. She was very much a straight shooter. While others might have "hemmed and hawed around," when you came to Mother, you got an answer. It may not have been the answer you wanted, but you got an answer. On many occasions Mother responded in a way only she could to people who—for some foolish reason—asked her how they looked. She would say things like: "Did you forget to look in the mirror when you bought that outfit?"

You never had to be concerned about what Mother was really thinking. She would tell you. What was so striking, however, was that no matter how harsh the pronouncement in itself, her stern appraisal somehow endeared her to others. Most somehow sensed that my mother simply did not have a catty bone in her body and was so matter of fact when speaking that, well, it was difficult to be offended, or at least to remain offended! I never once heard her make one such comment in anger. These things were always spoken from an obviously sincere desire to help the other person—and the other person could somehow sense that.

Perhaps this is why Mother was able to withstand my Dad's occasional caustic comments she heard at times when he was tired, angry or discouraged. I heard him say things to my mother that would have crushed me. I do not refer here to profanities. I never once heard a profane word from the lips of either of my parents. Rather, Dad's words to Mother were simply harsh, impatient or perhaps ungrateful words which could pour out of his mouth before he had a chance to place a lock upon them. (Perhaps I am more understanding here as unfortunately, his younger daughter has a similarly dangerous propensity.)

If in fact Dad had a thorn in the flesh, perhaps it was that quick anger which invariably was accompanied by a look in his eyes, a look that could be almost overwhelming to the recipient. On the several occasions when I discussed a spate of Dad's unkind words with Mother, after Dad had left the room, of course, she would say something like: "Oh honey, I don't wear my feelings on my sleeve. He needed to get that out. He's just tired!" Now this is not to say that she could totally gloss over his thoughtless words. On the contrary, his words could cut like a knife. However, I believe Mother made a conscious decision NOT to allow Dad's quick, thoughtless temper to invade the sense of peace and well-being which came from the Jesus who was inside her.

With all of Dad's amazing abilities and gifts, *his* "harsh pronouncements" were not always so endearing as those that could come from my mother's lips. His words, admittedly said out of anger or frustration were rough for his children, his employees, and others to endure. Over the years, Mother became a sort of buffer between Dad and the rest of his world. She always seemed to have the correct words to "smooth over the ruffled feathers" while never once disparaging her husband. And I would contend that her ability to soften my father was in itself a gift from God.

I hasten to point out here that it is outrageously unfair for the reader to judge and convict my father too harshly for this fault. When one views his accomplishments, well, we should make allowances. Some individuals spew incredible amounts of anger while having few, if any accomplishments with which to balance their faults! Our society comes close to worshipping many in the film industry when we are well aware of their horrendously sick lifestyles. Yes, Dad clearly had faults but despite his weaknesses, he changed his world for the better. And if we refuse to balance his faults with his amazing strengths and abilities, we miss the forest for the trees.

But back to my Mother, "The Solid Rock," as I have called her in this chapter. When the world observes a Christian having problems, they habitually respond with: "See, his faith got him nowhere. What good did it do to be a Christian? His problems are just as difficult as ours!" Those thoughts may be helpful in the process of assuaging the guilt individuals often feel while running from God as fast as their little feet can carry them.

And yet God never promised a hardship-free existence. On the contrary, Psalm 34:19 predicts that we will have many afflictions when we serve the Lord. An apostle named Paul was told specifically—up front and without apology—of the things he would suffer if He followed the call of Jesus on his life. As to adversity, I suppose we are in fact in the same boat with the rest of the world. It is after that point, however, in our response to the difficulty where the two paths are to diverge.

It is in fact in the season of calamity when God stands in the heavens looking down at us, as He did Job, saying, in effect: "Will you trust me—even when you do not understand? Or were you serving me simply for the blessings you have been receiving?"

A Great Test

And perhaps those questions were going through the Lord's mind when my sister, Rebecca and her husband died in a plane crash over Kansas—and when, a few years later, my brother, Ronnie committed suicide. As harrowing as these events were for the rest of her family, I believe they tested the endurance level of Evelyn Roberts to an even greater degree. After her unhappy family beginnings, she so wanted her own family to be, well, oh so different.

She had named the house built for the original president and his family on the campus of Oral Roberts University: "La Casa de la Paz," i.e., House of Peace. Before Rebecca and Marshall died, Mother had always insisted on family dinners and other activities designed to promote a close-knit family, even after all of her children were grown and had left home. It was my mother who made sure that all of us spent time together. But after the death of her older daughter and husband, followed by Ronnie's untimely departure, rather than the family growing closer due to tragedy, I would say that we became more segmented.

Dad was a person who refused to dwell on past events, even the loss of two of his children. I do not mean to say that he did not care, for such would be a gross misrepresentation. Rather, Oral Roberts had, as it were a built-in capacity to move on, not allowing himself to be overly affected by painful events. Mother, on the other hand, suffered intensely over the loss of two of her four children. While she bravely continued with all the things I have told you about her, they seemed more taxing than before. She lost some of the "joie de vivre" she had enjoyed in her years before this time.

Then there was the divorce of my brother, Richard from his first wife, Patti, in 1979. I simply cannot compose an account of Dad's life without speaking of that event, for it had such a great impact in so many ways. To set the stage, you must first understand that within Christian circles in 1979, divorce may have been an option, but never an acceptable one, particularly for a minister. Oh they happened, but they were rare and if a minister divorced his wife, well, that could potentially bring about the end of his entire ministry. Additionally, up until Richard's divorce, neither Dad's ministry nor the University hired divorcees.

However, when Richard and Patti divorced, Dad continued to insist that Richard should eventually become his successor, both in his ministry and at Oral Roberts University. Many of Dad's loyal supporters disagreed…vehemently. Few would contest my assertion that the break-up of Richard's marriage came with a huge cost to Dad's ministry. Additionally, at that point in time, Dad's ministry and the University were "one and the same," in a legal sense, and in many other ways as well. Whatever happened to one typically had a ripple effect on the other. The fact that Richard was allowed to retain his position, both in the ministry and at the school, was quite an exception to former policy. After Richard's divorce, donations to Dad's ministry were impacted in no small way.

Like my father, Mother also remained Richard's staunch adherent after his divorce and with regard to his remarriage ten months later. Still, these events when taken together seemed to take a far greater toll upon her life than upon Dad's, at least at that time. You will recall her experiences growing up in an unhappy home, which resulted in a divorce and a terrible custody battle, over her. Mother had, as a result, taught all of her children that divorces did not happen in the Roberts family. Absolutely not. No way, no-how.

I know of no one who was more bitterly opposed to divorce than my mother. It was anathema to her, with a capital "A" and no one understood that better than this author. And yet, when it happened to her son, she simply could not bring herself to blame him or see him any differently than she had all of his life. Yes, she supported him in every way. However, this turnabout could not have helped but affect her innermost self, given her lifelong opposition to the dissolution of a marriage. It brought a conflict within her which weighed upon her narrow shoulders. She had many nightmares over Richard's divorce. Knowing her, I can tell you that she did what she truly believed to be the right thing to do.

Whether it was the correct decision, I will leave to you, dear reader, to decide.

Despite having endured all of the above, Mother had the stamina within her to continue being there for Dad. She helped him answer some of the correspondence which he received, continued taking care of the house and spending time with hurting individuals within her purview—giving them counseling, and perhaps more importantly, paying attention to them and showing them love. People were forever coming to her, telling her of their problems and concerns. She listened intently and did everything she could to be of assistance. And yet, if Dad needed her, she dropped everything in order to ensure that her husband had absolutely everything he needed.

I told you in a previous chapter that in 1993 when Dad was 75, my parents moved from Oklahoma to California. While they moved there ostensibly to "retire," I must put quotation marks around the term because for my father, "retire" meant only that he was no longer in full-time ministry. Even then, Dad spent many hours and days mentoring younger ministers and writing several more books.

Bacon and Eggs

As long as she was physically able, Evelyn Roberts continued to be a willing servant to her family and to so many others. About two or three years before her death in 2005, when Mother was already in her eighties, Dad was hospitalized for a problem with his heart. While I do not remember Dad having heart problems until his latter years, by this time, his heart was far from perfect. At any rate, by the time my brother, Richard, and I were able to fly from Oklahoma and arrive in Dad's hospital room, our father was already feeling better and joking around with the nurses. But my mother, almost one year older than my father, had had a very long, trying day.

It was perhaps 9 p.m. by the time we left Dad's hospital room to drive to the condominium in which Mother and Dad lived at the end of their lives on Earth. As Richard and I had not had an opportunity to eat dinner, I had planned to find something in the refrigerator or pantry that would hold us over until breakfast. But my mother would have none of that. She said: "Children, you haven't had any dinner. How about bacon and eggs?" We both well realized that more than anything, our mother needed to seek her bed. However, despite all of our protests, she absolutely refused to leave the kitchen. She insisted upon standing on her feet to fry bacon (no microwave bacon for her!), then eggs. She absolutely would not go to bed until she was satisfied that both of us had had plenty to eat.

I tell you that story because it is a picture of Evelyn Roberts. The needs of others, not her own, seemed always to be at the forefront of her mind. I could not possibly number the times she insisted on doing something for Dad despite the fact that she was ill or so tired that it was all she could do to remain standing. That was my mother. I believe her life said many things, but most of all it proclaimed to the world that successful Christianity is not for sissies. There is no easy button. "Namby pamby" Christians will not stay the course. My mother clearly did not fall into that category. Without "Miss Evie" as many called her, Dad simply would not have been able to accomplish all that God had called him to do.

And while it was the true Solid Rock, Jesus Christ Himself, who gave Mother the stamina to do all that she did, it is a mistake to assume that God sovereignly placed a gift upon her—like someone born with natural ability as an orator, for example. It was not that Mother was born with some sort of miraculous, Herculean physical strength that made it easy for her to endure the hardness in her life. On the contrary, her life was a combination of Christ working within her *together with* her own determination to be the person He had called her to be. My mother, all five feet four of her, shorter than all four of her children, went the distance, until God called her to Himself. I just hope someone is cooking FOR HER now!

> When He shall come with trumpet sound,
> Oh may I then in Him be found.
> Dressed in His righteousness alone,
> Faultless to stand before the throne.
> On Christ the Solid Rock I stand,
> All other ground is sinking sand;
> All other ground is sinking sand.

...[L]et us pursue the... things whereby one shall build up another." Romans 14:19

—Darby Bible Trans.

"If I Can Help Somebody"

Chapter 12

While I would enjoy telling you that I had the opportunity to be tremendously close to my father, I cannot honestly claim that. He was often out of town when I was growing up. While I was allowed to travel with him on some occasions, for the most part I stayed home, often because of school or school activities. You may, therefore, be wondering how I consider myself qualified to analyze the man as I have throughout this writing.

The answer is that because of my incredible desire to be close to Oral Roberts, I watched, I observed and I remembered many of the things I did see and hear. Though I was far too shy to ever fully articulate it to him, I was one of Oral Roberts' most loyal supporters, albeit one of the quietest. Although he began to have some idea by his last days on this earth, my father never knew in full the extent of my feelings toward him. In all my years, I simply was never able to adequately express myself so that Dad would truly understand. I suspect that part of the problems we had in getting along when I was his employee (during the 1980's) was because I had unconsciously built up Oral Roberts in my mind as an infallible man of God.

"Oralisms"

Of course upon closer view, he could not possibly have met all of my standards. I now return mentally to those days and wonder whether Jesus Himself could have totally met all of my expectations! But I digress.

When I was perhaps ten or eleven years old, one of my household chores was ironing. That is, I was allowed to iron handkerchiefs, doilies, pillowcases and the like. Mother, or sometimes a maid, did the ironing, which required a greater degree of skill. Remember, it was the early 1960's before permanent press had entered the scene—or at least before it arrived in our house. My mother was a stickler about cleanliness, the ironing, well, actually about everything. She would do the laundry, remove the items she felt I could be trusted to iron adequately, sprinkle them, then place them into a basket. Once I arrived after school, I began ironing. But just before I started, I went to a closet which contained a reel-to-reel tape player, accompanied by stacks and stacks of my Dad's sermon tapes. While I cannot say that my ironing chore was something I particularly enjoyed, it mattered not for I would totally lose myself while listening to Dad preaching.

So if I can help others by relaying some of what I refer to as "Oralisms," then as the song says: "My living will not be in vain."

—Expect miracles from God, not people! Trust God, and not necessarily people! You are God's property! If Jesus is the Lord of your life, your attitude should be that you belong to God, not to yourself and certainly not to the world. Many times when I saw Dad pray for a person's healing, he would say to the devil in a loud voice: "Take your hands off of God's property!"

—If you are angry, be careful what you put in writing. Before reducing your thoughts to writing (and this would now include putting things in an email or perhaps on a social networking site), first visualize how you would feel if what you wrote was enlarged, then placed on the wall of a courtroom. If that would embarrass you, don't write it.

—The Hebrew children were told, "If you don't bow, you'll burn." But God says, "If you bow, you WILL burn!" In his famous "Fourth Man" sermon, Dad quickly clarified that in stating the latter, i.e., if you bow, you will burn, he was not referring to burning in hell. His meaning was that when we compromise—when we bow down to others—we will lose that which we compromised to obtain.

—Don't tell all you know.

—Never fear demons but respect their power. There were countless occasions when individuals possessed by demons were brought to Dad for prayer. If you are one of those folks who simply do not believe in such things, I will not argue with you. I will just report what I saw and heard, then you must evaluate it for yourself. As a little girl, I witnessed these events over and over.

First of all, it was obvious to many—simply by the look of some of these individuals—that they were possessed, although that was certainly not always the case. Of course Dad was far more "up close and personal" with those people than those of us in the audience. He said that their breath would always be accompanied by a terrible stench, coupled with a dangerous glint in their eyes. At any rate, whenever Dad was asked to pray for an individual such as I have described, Mother often leaned over to me and to my brother, saying: "Children, you need to pray with your Daddy. When those demons come out, they're going to be looking for a place to go!" Well she did not have to tell me twice! Believe me, I prayed!

The power of God always trumps any satanic power for "...greater is He who is in you than he who is in the world." (1 John 4:4). However, we must not look to ourselves to overcome any satanic power, but only to God. Without the Lord, we are in fact more than vulnerable to Satan and his host of fallen angels.

And while we are on the subject of demonic power, I remember one evening after dinner asking Dad: "Why does it seem that the devil attacks me so much, but leaves so many others alone?" His response was something like this: "He attacks you because you are a potential threat to his kingdom. He doesn't work on unbelievers. He already has them."

—Don't hire your friends. Don't do business with your friends. If it doesn't work out, you will have nowhere to go. End of friendship.

—As far as I know, Dad never allowed his relatives or even his friends to borrow money from him, nor did he ever agree to co-sign the loan of another. Many times, Dad gave money to friends or relatives, but he refused to ever lend them money. He gave them money, expecting a return only from God, but never from them. His rule protected his friendships as well as some family relationships.

One of the largest themes of Dad's life was his desire for excellence. When he started the University, he was advised by many to just "throw up" temporary buildings or use prefab buildings, and the like. He thanked them for their advice, then totally ignored it. No! God had called him to build Oral Roberts University, not El Cheapo University. The University and its programs would be built with excellence or they would not be built at all.

—Dad was offered many gifts over the years, some which would have been quite valuable. I remember one particular time in which a business offered to put a swimming pool into our back yard. There was to be no cost to us whatsoever. I was wild with joy for I had always wanted a swimming pool more than anything. However, he politely thanked the people and refused their gift! I was totally in the doldrums for simply weeks. How could he do such a thing? His explanation at the time meant nothing to me, partially due to my immaturity but also because of my giant disappointment. He said that he would owe them something in return if he were to receive their gift. Yes, I now understand that he was absolutely correct. There is no free lunch.

—Dad talked often of "divine/human reciprocity." Without God, I cannot; but without me, He WILL not! Humanism teaches that *man* is the measure of all things. The people at the Tower of Babel—and current New Agers—look only to themselves. Admonitions to "get in touch with the child within" or to "develop your feminine side" are current admonitions which fall into the category. The truth is though, that the complete answer to the problem will never be found inside of us. We must look to God, not within, if we want meaningful help with our problems.

On the other hand, looking to God for a miracle for, say, diabetes, while at the same time refusing to discipline ourselves as to our diet will not always solve the problem either. The little boy had to offer his lunch *before* Jesus was willing to feed the 5,000; Naaman had to wash in the Jordan before he was healed of leprosy. Dad used to say: "Do something!" The solution begins when we do our part, no matter how small. Once we have contributed our "little bit," *that* is when we see the miracle.

In Matthew 12:13 when Jesus told the man to stretch forth his hand, He was saying in effect: "You have to *do* something." Things have to be made to happen!

—Be aggressive—not in a physical sense, but spiritually. Be aggressive about getting your needs met. Be aggressive about praying and adding to the Kingdom of God. Be aggressive about getting your healing.

—On the evening Dad had the dedication service for the City of Faith, Tulsa experienced a rainstorm which drenched each of us who braved the elements to attend that celebration. Despite the rain, the press showed up along with thousands of others, but the top item of discussion before the beginning of the program was the rain. The first thing I remember Dad doing at the service was grabbing the microphone and saying to that vast crowd: "You are all wondering how God could let it rain when Oral Roberts was planning on a big turnout for a large event. Well keep in mind, I'm in sales, not management!" Of course his comment brought the house down with hoots of laughter, but there was a serious truth in that quip. God's ways are not our ways. He is not a steak. We cannot order Him. He is God and He has not placed us on His management team!

—Money is not the root of all evil. Money is simply an instrument— an inanimate object. It is the *love* of money that is the root of all evil (1 Timothy 6:10). You have to have money. You have to pay your bills. The question is, do you have money or does money *have you?*

—You can't please people. You need to do what God wants and let the chips fall where they may.

—Don't strike back. Dad used to say, "When I die, no one will need to preach my funeral. The media has already done that!" The criticism he received over the years would have crushed some men, but not Dad. I think one of the reasons he was able to live so long was because he made a determination as a young man not to strike back. Of course this decision was based upon scripture. We had a conversation once about Moses' statement (Deuteronomy 32:35) that vengeance belonged to God, not to us. I was railing about that scripture to Dad. I wanted to take vengeance myself. Why should the Lord have all the fun?! (Oops, you are now fully aware, dear reader, of my terrible side!) Dad's quick response was: "Oh no, honey. You can't handle the result of the vengeance. There is a terrible cost that accompanies vengeance and only God can endure it. Your shoulders are not wide enough. That's why He reserves vengeance to Himself." Dad's habit of living seemed to be to deal with the pain of the criticism, then to go on with what He was called to do.

—Pick your battles. Don't fight unless you have a good chance of winning. If you are faced with a battle in which you have no reasonable chance to prevail, let it go and give it to God. Then ask Him to restore what the locust has destroyed. (Joel 2:25) This lesson has been invaluable to me—both personally and in the practice of law.

—Keep your word. Do what you say you will do. I can remember our house almost always being cluttered with long lists of things. Most of them seemed to be suspiciously near my father's chair in the den. The only time I remember walking into the house without the clutter of those lists was when guests were expected. Printouts and other long lists of things could be found in the den, in Dad's bedroom and often in the kitchen. They were everywhere! I would walk in the room and Dad's lap would be covered with those lists. I think I may have had some vague understanding of what they were, but I confess that at the time, they did not mean much to me. They just always seemed to be in the way.

Soon after Dad passed away, I heard from a lady who had worked in his evangelistic office many years before. One of her job tasks had been to type the prayer requests which had arrived within letters addressed to Oral Roberts. Her supervisor told her that Dad wanted the requests typed onto calculator tape (later, the format was changed to computer print-outs) so it would be easier for him to hold the prayer requests in his hands and to pray over them.

Although I have to admit that at the time I had no real concept of the significance of what to me was—well, just a lot of clutter—this sweet lady caused me to *realize and appreciate for the first time* what I had actually witnessed, albeit unknowingly, all those years while growing up in Oral Roberts' home. How many times had I heard my father either on a radio or television broadcast asking people to send in their prayer requests so that he could pray over them? Are there ministers who ask people to submit prayer requests, just hoping for a donation, without having any intention to truly pray over those requests? I cannot answer that, but I do know that my father meant it when he said he would pray. I saw him do it time after time. He really *did* pray over those prayer requests. My father was exhibiting his faithfulness to God before my very eyes—without saying a word.

—Don't talk just to hear your head rattle!

—Think big! One thing certain to irritate my father was conversation he considered "small talk." While he would consent to talk about the more mundane things of life for a few, short minutes, the only subjects on which he enjoyed dwelling had to be important ones—the world situation, politics, the economy, or etc. He loved discussing Oral Roberts University (does that surprise you?), what others were doing for the Lord, plans for future ministry, and the like. For years, he kept a sign on his desk that read: "Make no little plans here." He never thought small. He always thought big.

If I wanted to irritate him, I could simply ask him: "How are you feeling?" That was simply not an acceptable question. I finally began to learn that if I wanted to have a conversation with him which we both enjoyed, the best way to start was by reporting something good that I knew about, perhaps a church which was in the process of building a new building or a minister who was having wonderful results while praying for people.

—Remember when Satan suggested that Jesus jump off the roof of the temple? In Dad's experience it seemed that some folks were constantly doing crazy things, almost to see if God would "bail them out." You know the kind of thing I mean. These folks go around boasting of their great faith. Dad's response to such antics, however, was to say: "That's not faith, that's presumption." Obviously, God would not have honored Jesus if He had thrown Himself off a cliff. Faith has to do with believing God with regard to what He promised, not deciding what God should do just because that is what we want.

Additionally, Dad pointed out something in that scripture which few have realized. Psalms 91:11 promises that God "shall give his angels charge over thee, to keep thee in all thy ways. They shall bear thee up in their hands, lest thou dash thy foot against a stone." Under the guise of "quoting" that scripture, Satan later said to Jesus in Luke 4:10-11: "For it is written: 'He shall give his angels charge over thee, to keep thee. And in their hands they shall bear thee up, lest **at any time** thou dash thy foot against a stone." Not only did Satan have the audacity to quote scripture to the Son of God Himself, but he also had the audacity to misquote and twist it. He added: "**at any time**," a phrase which does *not* appear in Psalms 91. With just those three little words, Satan twisted the entire meaning of the Psalm and made it appear as if God were simply a puppet on a string. Of course Jesus knew the scriptures far better than Satan and did not fall for the ploy. Again, it would have been presumption, not faith for Jesus to have thrown Himself over that cliff! If God has a principle, you can be sure that Satan will twist it. And it only takes a few cleverly placed words to do so.

—It is impossible to understand the New Testament without studying and understanding the Old Testament. Sometimes Christians "pooh-pooh" a quote from the Old Testament, assuming that it no longer has any use for us since Jesus' death and resurrection. Dad disagreed with this…strenuously!

Jesus referred to such Old Testament characters as Moses, David, Elijah, Daniel, Isaiah and etc. How can we possibly understand Jesus' comment regarding the Queen of Sheba without some knowledge of her from 1 Kings? And the list of such allusions goes on and on. Granted, we must "rightly divide the word of truth" when we study the Old

Testament, however, simply ignoring it will turn a large portion of the New Testament into an unfathomable mystery.

—People often said to Dad: "I wish I had your faith" or, "I just don't have the faith to believe that." I can still see Dad standing on the platform, holding that giant microphone and declaring to that vast crusade audience: "You have faith or you wouldn't be sitting in that chair!" He would quote Romans 12:3 which states that God has given a certain amount of faith, i.e., a measure, to each of us. He would say: "Turn your faith loose!" Dad made Jesus' comments about faith come alive, for example:

- When He asked His disciples: "Where is your *faith*?" (Luke 8:25)

- After his conversation with the Centurion, He said: "I have not found such great *faith...* (Luke 7:9)

- When He told the woman who brought the alabaster box, "your *faith* has saved you." (Luke 7:50)

- When the woman with the issue of blood was healed, He said "your *faith* has made you whole." (Luke 8:48)

—As a child, there was a very large list of words I was not allowed to say: not once, not ever. And most of those words were said often by other girls, even some of my teachers! Of course all profanities were out of bounds, however, the forbidden words were much more expansive. For example, I was not to say "gee" or "golly" or any words my mother saw as "slang" and believe me, the list was quite extensive, or so it appeared to me.

Thank God my mother always answered when I asked her "why." She never once said: "Because I said so!" Sorry, parents, but you have a reason. Tell your child what it is! Nor did Mother use the reason that the profanities were evil or non-Christian. Certain words were not allowed because "that is not how ladies talk." "Ladies" did not use such words— ever. My but our generation could have learned something from my mother's admonitions! I literally brought a brand new bar of soap to an insurance adjuster once. I told him that if he insisted on continuing to use profanity in our telephone conversations, he could at least wash his mouth with soap afterwards!

—Learn to focus. In these days of multi-tasking, we often forget to focus on one thing at a time. When Dad prayed for someone, in that moment nothing else existed for him. He was not looking over that person's shoulder in order to see who might have just walked into the room. He was not texting, he was not answering his cell phone, nor was his mind on the sermon he had just preached nor on the one he might be preaching on the following evening. He had one thing and one thing only on his mind. It was that one person and that one person's need. He had piercing blue eyes and when he looked at you—really looked at you—you could not help but feel an incredible impact from that intensity emanating from his very soul. While I understand to some extent the reasoning behind the multi-tasking which happens so often in our world today, if you want to really help people, there is no substitute for focusing your entire energies on one thing at a time.

—If you are being too hard on yourself or if others are assuming that role, Dad used to say: "Remember, there was only one perfect man, and they killed Him!"

For Public Speakers, especially Pastors

—I cannot tell you how many times I was told at the dinner table, "Say your words plainly!" This was drilled into me from the time I understood what Mother and Dad meant by those words. At the time,

I found it all tremendously boring and useless. However, after having lived on the earth a little longer now, I realize that my parents were correct. It is our speech, our accent, our diction, our grammar, and our inflection which truly does categorize us to the hearer. No matter how great the message, poor grammar and speech patterns will demote us or possibly even disqualify us in many circles. Conversely, good elocution will strengthen the impact of our message exponentially. Dad and Mother were sticklers in this regard and now that I practice law, I perceive—finally!—that they were correct.

—Did you know that former President Nixon sought the assistance of Oral Roberts in order to be a more effective speaker on television? Here is one of the things Dad told him: "When you look into the camera, imagine Sister Jones sitting out there, maybe in her home all alone, with a terrible need. You're the only one who can help her. Talk to her and only to her. Concentrate your mind on her needs and her needs alone." I have no idea whether such was helpful to Mr. Nixon, but this mindset has certainly been helpful to me on those occasions I was called upon to appear on television.

—Dad found it frustrating when church folks planned large extravaganzas for the unsaved and "un-churched," expecting those folks to show up at the church building—while having little or no outreach *outside* the four walls of their church. Dad believed it was more successful for us to go to those who needed the Lord, rather than to expect them to come to us. He believed that the church building should be similar to a filling station. People who already knew the Lord were to go there to get filled up with Jesus, so they would be prepared to go and tell others outside the church. His "Oralism" was: "The church says 'Come!' but Jesus said to *GO*!"

—I learned by observing my father that a true anointing of God comes with a terrible price. The process always started with studying the scriptures, and studying and studying, then studying some more. Dad would write copious notes on yellow pads when he studied. Once he left to preach, all the notes would be left behind, but while he was preparing, he wrote and wrote and wrote—pages and pages of yellow pad after yellow pad.

Mr. Grumpy!

Of course the studying was accompanied by much prayer, and sometimes fasting, although not always. When Dad was particularly quiet, I knew he was thinking about his forthcoming message. Growing up I would often ask: "What are you going to preach about tonight?" I do not ever remember receiving a real answer. He would hem and haw around as if he did not know what he was going to preach about—but I knew better! He knew all right, but he preferred not to discuss it until after his message. (Why did I keep asking the question? The perversity of youth? I honestly do not know!)

Then there would be the ride in the car to the meeting as I have described earlier, when I was instructed to be very quiet. The look on his face was so intense you could almost see the wheels turning in Dad's brain and the steam coming out of his ears!

In his own meetings such as his crusades, Dad could arrange the schedule so he would not have to sit and wait very long before beginning his sermon. However, when asked to preach in other venues, Dad had no choice but to wait until called. And, services held by other ministries or churches always seemed to have much longer time periods between the opening of the service and the time when Dad was asked to begin his message. When speaking of Dad being forced to sit so long on another preacher's platform—waiting to preach, my Mother compared him to a woman waiting to give birth. The waiting was excruciating for him!

Of course the best part for Dad was when he was preaching. Once he was able to get in front of the people—once he had prepared himself to the max—he was completely comfortable and definitely in his element.

Interestingly enough, as Dad aged, when he was preaching he had absolutely no aches and no pains. It was astonishing to observe. When he arrived at the breakfast table on the morning of a day he was scheduled to preach, he could be in terrible pain. He did not have to say anything as such was obvious to any who observed him. For the sake of younger readers, I should explain that Dad did not have any terrible disease; he was just achy and sore—from old age as well as from shoulder problems caused by having reached out his hands to pray for what must have felt like the whole world.

He would usually be grumpy while getting ready to go, then extremely quiet in the car, but once he was called to the microphone, it was as if he came alive! He would preach—sometimes for an hour—even in his late 80's! He had amazing vitality and animation. Then once he finished preaching, all the "amens" had been said, and we were on our way home, he would become an old man again. I asked him once how he had been able to force himself to preach when he obviously had felt so awful that day. His quick reply was that he had no pain when he was preaching, none whatsoever!

Well, the above sounds wonderful, but here comes the rest of the price of the anointing of God. The aftermath. A devastating weariness, not curable by merely seeking his bed. A weariness that would last for many days. Still, perhaps the most dangerous cost of the anointing of God is what other, often well-meaning folks say to someone who has obviously had the anointing of God upon them, if only temporarily. Too many compliments can be much more perilous to the vulnerable preacher than harsh criticism. It sounds so good when people tell you how wonderful you are! It brings such joy and feels so gratifying. After all, you are the one who did all the preparing. That great move of God came because of you, right? Ah, and that is where the devil takes pleasure in destroying that beautiful anointing—by making you believe it was you and not God. It can often be the aftermath that is in fact the most precarious time for a preacher.

Yes, the anointing of God comes at a high cost, but oh, it is so worth it! The lives that are changed, the people who are healed, well, I sometimes wonder if there are days in Heaven when Dad asks God: "Can't I go back to earth and just preach one more sermon? Can't I just build one more building on the ORU campus?"

If you are a pastor or an evangelist, you may wish to re-read the chapter entitled "The Healing Waters" which described Dad's quest for Jesus to become real to him. Dad related many years later that those days, while he was reading the Gospels and Acts three times on his knees, provided a sense of what Jesus had really spent His time doing while He was on the earth. Dad saw that his own ministry must parallel Jesus' ministry in its focus. Dad was to preach the Gospel and to heal the sick, as Jesus had. He wanted his ministry to come against the same four things Jesus' ministry was against—sin, demons, disease and fear. He wanted his ministry to emphasize the same power that Jesus' ministry had. Dad often pointed out that Jesus spent most of his time teaching, preaching and healing (see Matthew 9:35).

—Be prepared before you speak in front of an audience. While Dad may not have possessed the academic credentials proudly touted by other university presidents, his love of learning was evident in everything he did. Everything he did, he studied first. I have no idea how many hours he spent in preparing his sermons—God knows—but he never once "shot from the hip" as seems to be the case far too often in these times. Use someone else's sermon? Repeat a sermon found on the

Internet? Surely you jest! Such would have been anathema to him. I can imagine the look on his face had he known of the speakers who so often use another's material. It would have been a thunder-cloud indeed!

My father was often (privately!) contemptuous of speakers who were obviously unprepared, and that is putting it nicely. Dad was also critical of speakers who stood up before people with notes in hand. He would say: "If you need notes, it's not in your heart! If it's not in your heart, sit down!"

While admittedly my speaking abilities are at the elementary level in comparison to those of Oral Roberts, I did learn how to speak in front of groups generally without having to resort to notes. I mean, who wants to incur the wrath of Oral? I understood though, that he was correct in his contention that your message must be in your heart. As Jesus advised: "...[O]ut of the abundance of the heart, the mouth speaketh." (Matthew 12:34 KJV)

I was a witness to the fact that he never went before the people unless "he knew, that he knew that he knew," that he was anointed of God. There were some crusade services in which poor Brother DeWeese was forced to keep the people singing, because Dad did not yet feel the anointing of God. This was a huge issue to him and there is no question that it accounts greatly for his success as a minister of the Gospel.

—Dad much preferred to preach in a 500-seat auditorium "full to the rafters" than a 1,000-seat auditorium, only half-full. He often said: "An empty seat never gets saved."

—Be eclectic. Dad was a voracious reader and he was always learning. Besides the Bible and Bible commentaries, he also read westerns, biographies, spy novels, mysteries, and even a little romance. He viewed many different movies over the years and many kinds of television programs. In this respect I do not suppose he was so terribly different from most people. The difference, however, was that he did not read or watch movies simply for entertainment. He was always looking for ideas.

Sometimes he would watch things on television that surprised me. When I asked him why in the world he had any interest in a certain program, he would always say: "You never know what idea I might get from this program." There were even some Christian programs that were, well, how do I say it without being uncharitable? The program had not been produced in a professional fashion or perhaps the sermon was a little off-base scripturally.

When I questioned him, however, he would say, "You have to be eclectic. I dismiss the questionable or scripturally incorrect things, but I pull out the good things." There is a large caveat, however: Before any of us can be safely eclectic, it is imperative to be well-grounded in the scriptures as Dad was! We must first be able to rightly divide the word of truth, as discussed in 2 Timothy 2:15.

—I will never forget a particular Regents meeting at ORU when things did not look good from a financial perspective. The University needed money, well, there was not really anything unique about that particular situation. Bringing in sufficient finances was a constant concern, however, what caused that specific occasion to remain in my memory was a statement Dad made which I had never heard. He said: "Faith sees where sight is blind." Despite the financial picture, he was full of faith and confidence that the Lord would pull us out. And He did!

In my Father's house are many mansions. If it were not so, I would have told you...

–John 14:2 (KJV)

"MANSION OVER THE HILLTOP"

Chapter 13

S oon after my husband and I were married, Mother invited us to dinner in their home. This would have been in 1971 when Dad and Mother were still living in "La Casa de la Paz," their house just next to the Oral Roberts University campus in Tulsa. I had been sixteen when we moved into that house, then left when eighteen to live in a dormitory on the ORU campus, then later married. As there were just the four of us for dinner that evening, we ate at the breakfast table, adjacent to the part of the kitchen containing a double-sink and dishwasher. On the other side of the table was a built-in desk on which Mother had placed a small television so she and Dad could watch the news while eating breakfast.

A Rather Big Story

On this particular evening, we had just finished dinner. Ron and Dad were still sitting at the table talking. The television was on but no one was paying particular attention to it, that is until we heard the voice of Dan Rather mention Oral Roberts. Of course the four of us were all ears and instantly became quiet as church mice—so we could hear what the famous reporter was saying. Mr. Rather was telling the world that Oral Roberts had made so much money over his lifetime that he had given a million dollars to each of his four children.

I suppose what made the news report so noteworthy to us was that as Dan Rather was making the comment, I was standing in front of the sink rinsing the dishes—wearing my mother's rubber gloves—and Mother was standing to my left, loading the dishwasher. In the dead silence, which ensued in the kitchen after that stunning remark, I turned to my mother, looked her straight in the eye and demanded: "Where is my million dollars? I never got mine!" Of course at that point, our uproarious laughter could no longer be contained. It was so absurd! Well if any of my dear readers know Dan Rather, I wish you would ask him if he is aware of the location of my million dollars. So far at least, after approximately forty years, it remains in an undisclosed location.

I tell you that story in order to aid your understanding of the reality of Dad's financial status. Now I hasten to point out that we lived well and certainly not as paupers. However, the standard of living in our family in my formative years would never have made the cut for "The Lifestyles of the Rich and Famous." Mother and Dad did send me to a private school up until I was ready for the seventh grade. And, I know the tuition would have been dear at Holland Hall. However, I can tell you that when I spent the night with classmates from that school, as did so many girls in those days, most of the other girls appeared to be in far better financial positions than my family.

They all seemed to have servants everywhere I looked. Several of them had a full-time cook. It was actually pretty neat. When I stayed at the house of one of my school friends, I did not have to help prepare dinner nor with the dishes afterwards. They actually had servants to do such things! What luxury!

Unassuming

In comparison to most of my classmates at that private school, I felt poor. In fact, I eventually prevailed upon my parents to allow me to leave the private school after completing the sixth grade. I so wanted to attend a public school for my junior high and high school years. I simply did not feel comfortable with many of the other children with whom I had attended school, because most of them flaunted the obvious fact that

they were richer than my family. While there were certainly exceptions to this pattern, many of my fellow students spent a great deal of their time bragging about their riches and I found it rather unpleasant. (By the way, I'm the scraggly one in the middle row, second from the right.)

While I truly have no goal to disparage my former classmates as some of them were far different from the others, I suspect that my experience will give you a more concrete idea as to the reality of the standard of living in the home of Oral Roberts. We did live well and I am very grateful for that. Mother did have a maid—although she would have to "clean up after" some of those individuals once they left the house. She was German. What can I say?

Also, my father had access to an airplane that was owned by his ministry. However, even though I was not allowed to go with him on a great many of his trips as I was in school, I knew my father's habits. He was simply not any fun at all! He just traveled to the place where he was scheduled to preach, studied his sermon in his hotel room, went to preach the sermon, came back to the hotel room, ordered room-service, then went to bed.

Now he did often play golf in the mornings, but afterwards, he returned to his hotel room and took a nap. Upon waking, he studied his sermon...well, you know the rest. Apparently when he preached in Africa, he did go to see Victoria Falls, but I only know about that because such jaunt was a gigantic exception to his normal routine. In all of my experience, I never saw my parents live the high life! While Mother and Dad went out to dinner on occasion, especially after church on Sundays, Dad almost always preferred to stay at home.

After all, at most restaurants he could rarely take one bite before being barraged by others wanting to talk to Oral Roberts. While all of these people were not kind, most of them were very well-meaning. It was just that there were so many of them that it was impossible for my poor father to enjoy his meal. And, if Mother felt a compunction to clean up after some of those maids she hired when I was a little girl, I cannot imagine how she could have tolerated a cook. My mother was actually a very good cook, at least until she got older. She took pride in her cooking. I still miss her biscuits and white cream gravy with country ham. I have never had anything so good!

Once in a great while, I remember Dad making hamburgers. However, Mother and I eventually banned him from cooking, for we had to face the resulting layer of grease that covered the entire stove and its environs for several feet in every direction. Oh, what a mess!

But what about when Dad was in town during the crusade days? I told you briefly in an earlier chapter that during those days, we lived outside of Tulsa, on what we for some reason called "the Farm" although it was more analogous to a ranch. Although it is basically considered

PHONE 19-F-53

Robin Hood Farm

REGISTERED
ABERDEEN-ANGUS CATTLE

ORAL ROBERTS
OWNER

ROUTE 2
BIXBY, OKLA.

"in town" these days, in the 1950's when I lived there, it was a long way from anything. Back then, there was no expressway in order to shorten the drive into Tulsa. It was perhaps 20 miles one-way from Tulsa's main airport to the farm, which was on the opposite end of Tulsa, near 121st Street South near Mingo in Bixby.

At that time, Dad's ministry owned an aero commander, an airplane that seated perhaps six, not counting the pilot. Because the farm was so far from the airport and given the amount of Dad's traveling in those days, he arranged for a landing strip on the property so that he could avoid that long drive from the airport to our house. Since Bob DeWeese,

Dad's associate evangelist, was a pilot himself, having a plane was made far more feasible than it would have been otherwise.

You may view being able to fly into a landing strip near to your own home as luxurious, however, you might have seen things far differently if you had had the opportunity, as I did, of riding in that plane all the way to California from Tulsa.

I believe the term was that the plane was not "pressurized." Lacking understanding of things aeronautical, I can only tell you that we were often obliged to use oxygen on that plane. Perhaps doing such can be far more pleasant now than it was then and of course, having to "go on oxygen" was certainly unnecessary on commercial planes even of that day. All I know is that using oxygen meant that I had this creepy, cloying feeling—accompanied by this noxious, sickening odor which I was compelled to use for hours at a time. However, that in itself I could have endured far more easily than the fact that there was no restroom. It took 6 hours—six *hours*!—to fly to California in that plane. I was a very shy, sensitive girl. Need I say more?

Dad often referred to the years when we lived on the Farm as some of his happiest. They were not happy at all, however, for my mother. I told you earlier that my father was the spender and Mother was the saver. Dad apparently found a short-lived form of recreation in attending cattle auctions which resulted in his purchasing cattle, the expense of which was collectively more than my mother felt was reasonable, given our financial circumstances. At any rate, she eventually "got her way," they sold the farm and we moved into town.

While I honestly do not remember if there were any rumors "noised abroad" during those years regarding where we lived, I certainly do recall many rumors and claims made about Dad's lifestyle after my childhood. So perhaps you might be interested to learn my thinking on some of those items.

"The Compound"

The first rumor, which I personally experienced, was perhaps in 1967 or so when it was rumored around my high school, Memorial, that Oral Roberts had a gold bathtub. At the time those stories were circulating, we had long since moved into town and were living in the house I told you about earlier, which was on the ORU campus. (We did live in a house which was on the campus even earlier than the one my mother called "La Casa De La Paz," however, that house was apparently never the cause for any rumors, at least not as far as I can remember.)

La Casa De La Paz was inside what was referred to as "the compound" which encompassed several acres, basically adjacent to the campus. While I have no idea what unimaginative individual named the area, I personally felt it was an apt title, for to my mind at least, it felt like being in jail! It was behind security gates, which meant that you could not have a friend over without first contacting ORU's security department. My children were under those restrictions as well, when we lived in one of the houses after Ron and I were married. (The area contained six houses as I recall.)

Of course while it was strictly a matter of inconvenience and isolation as far as I was concerned, I did understand that Dad certainly needed security. As I mentioned earlier, there seemed to be no end to the "crazies" who could and did show up at any time of the day or night, sometimes just to gawk, sometimes to treat Dad as if he were the new Pharaoh, and occasionally toting a firearm.

So why didn't Oral Roberts have *just* his own home behind a security gate? Why include all those houses within the secured area? I think Dad had concerns that one of those unhappy individuals might take out their anger on one of his children or their families. However, I do not contend here that all of those homes were truly necessary. For what it is worth at this point, I can tell you that near the end of his life Dad regretted ever building those homes. He came to the conclusion—if somewhat belatedly—that while the compound had at least kept all of us safe, on the whole it simply was not worth the maintenance headaches, not to mention the terrible cost nor the hassles. Further, the secrecy created so many negative feelings that, looking back, it simply had not been worth it.

The front patio of the house in the compound, where our dog, Samson, had been exiled one Sunday afternoon.

So what was our house like? Did it have a gold bathtub?

No, but it did contain a sink in the guest bathroom which was painted the color of gold. Does that count? Well the house my mother had named "La Casa De la Paz" certainly was large in area, somewhere over 6,000 square feet. It was a long, rambling one-story house with a nice view of Tulsa from the living room. Sadly, we almost never spent any time in that room at night when the view was visible—at least when I was in residence.

When the house recently sold, the front page of the Tulsa World carried the story. Their reporter was apparently given a tour and wrote: "Visitors expecting opulence will be disappointed. The house is large but relatively ordinary." While the article was true, I cannot say that it was a pleasant sensation to view the picture and article on the front page of the local newspaper. How shall I describe how that makes one feel? Invaded? Sad? Well, despite my unimportant, probably over-emotional reaction, it was in truth a good thing for folks to be given an idea of what was behind that mysterious security gate.

Perhaps it was the secrecy alone that caused the problem? No, I suppose it was that during some of the years when we lived there, Dad appeared on television asking for money regarding one of his many building projects, particularly the City of Faith. I think that is what came across as so offensive to many people—which was of course fueled by the media, as is so often the case.

One of the most memorable occasions for me personally was the night of a tornado, which is now rather famous to native Tulsans such as this author. It was June 8, 1974. I was "great with child" about one month in advance of my due date. My husband and I had left our home (behind that security gate) for dinner. During our drive home following dinner, the skies over Tulsa were pelting rain. Just before our arrival, the electricity went off so that our button to open the security gate was of course useless. My husband was able to open the gate manually just enough for the two of us to squeeze through the opening. Mine was a much more interesting squeeze than Ron's, unfortunately!

The water had congregated on the other side of the gate and reached beyond our knees. We trudged up the hill, drenched both below and above and finally made it to our house. We decided since we were already so wet, we might as well walk the rest of the way to the top of the hill in order to determine whether Mother and Dad were safe as the storm had been accompanied by lightning. When we arrived, Dad had just received a telephone call advising him that both the roof of the newly built Aerobics Center on campus and the roof of his ministry building (OREA) had been totally lifted off in a tornado. (Both were later repaired, in case you are wondering!)

Ron and Dad both raced to the carport and drove to the campus to see what they could do to help, if anything. (By that time, a security guard had been successful in opening the gate sufficiently for a vehicle to pass through.) Of course both my father and my husband were totally unfair to me. I wanted to be of assistance as well, but simply because of my advanced pregnancy, I was shunned and forced to stay in the dreaded compound. Can you believe it?

The truth is that as harrowing as that evening truly was, it was still rather exciting—so I suppose I should not complain. Suffice it to say, though, that living behind a security gate was not always as wonderful as others may have believed. I, for one, have always preferred to live in a regular house in a regular neighborhood with regular neighbors and so forth. However, there is no question that at the time Dad built that compound, right or wrong, there was in fact at least some reason for him to be concerned about his own safety and that of his family.

Shucking Corn

Some will remember as well that during the first years of the University, Mother and Dad opened our home to scores of guided tours of the President's home, particularly during the beginning of a school year. I can remember having many other groups arriving as well, faculty groups, groups from the Tulsa community and so forth. Those were, in fact, the only events in which I ever remember Mother not doing all of the cooking herself. Well, with her faithful Tonto (me!) at her side. On those occasions, the food was provided by the University. Former or even current ORU students will remember Saga Foods although not always with delight! At any rate, Saga sent students to help serve and to clean up after the event. But you guessed it. First of all the food could not compare to my mother's cooking and secondly, she and I had to "straighten up a little" when the Saga folks left the house.

At the risk of revealing my family as the country bumpkins, which perhaps we were, I will relate an incident which occurred when I was maybe 16 or so. Every summer, Mother and I drove to Bixby (near where we had lived on the farm when I was very young) in order to buy as many bushels of sweet corn as would fill the car. When we returned home, Mother's parents would often be there, ready to help with the shucking. Was my dad in attendance? Hardly. If he was in town, his comment at the beginning of such venture was generally: "Hey, I'll help you when you get finished!" Oh well!

Forming an assembly line outside under the carport, by the end of the day we had lots of luscious corn divided into small containers in the freezer, ready to eat the following winter. This was one of the few household tasks that truly received my serious disdain. It was not that I minded the work and I certainly enjoyed the fruits of our labor. No, it was the worms. I ask you, how did those little critters always manage to end up only in the ears for which I was responsible? It was simply unconscionable!

At any rate, on one of those Saturdays, we had been working for an hour or so when we heard the phone ring inside the house. When I rushed into the house to answer, it was my date for that evening wanting to set the time to pick me up for the movie. When he politely asked what I had been doing that day, I answered in a matter of fact fashion:

"Shucking corn." While he said little at the time nor that evening, by the following Monday, everyone at school seemed to be aware that Oral Roberts' daughter had spent her Saturday shucking corn! They all thought it was so hilarious.

Here I am in the dining room of our house in the compound when I was living there as a teenager.

It took me a few minutes to understand the joke, as shucking corn had always been a part of our family's routine. Obviously, the expectation of my fellow students was that a family with such a famous man at the helm would be far too uppity to consider doing what was necessary to prepare sweet corn for the freezer. What my high school friends could not seem to understand was that our family never felt we had "arrived" or that engaging in such tasks was somehow beneath us. I will admit to dreams of foisting off those pesky worms onto someone else, but no matter what I did...

Homes in California

But what about the homes in California which seemed to be a source of never-ending discussion? How could Oral Roberts afford to buy a house in California on the strength of his rather small salary from ORU?

Because the University supplied us with a home on campus.

You may be familiar with the concept of a parsonage and that was, in effect, the working idea here. Now I hasten to point out that parsonages are typically far smaller than the house I described to you earlier in this chapter. On the other hand, the ministry, which Dad continued to carry on, brought in far more money than the typical church which provides a small parsonage for its minister.

When I was a young girl, Dad and Mother owned a house in California. The first house itself was perhaps 4,000 square feet but was certainly nothing to shout about in itself. However, the home was on a cliff overlooking an absolutely gorgeous view of the Pacific Ocean. It was purchased basically to provide a little distance between Dad and the pressures of his ministry in Tulsa. He wanted that view specifically in order to be more creative in both his writing as well as in preparing sermons.

Dad was a prolific author, having produced over 100 books during his lifetime. Looking back, I rather doubt such accomplishments would have been possible had he been "stuck" in Oklahoma all the time with the daily pressures and challenges in both the office of his ministry and on the campus of ORU.

As a young girl, I had absolutely no appreciation for the view—or for California for that matter. I wanted to be home with my friends! Okay, I know what you must be thinking. I was spoiled, correct? Yes, I suppose in that way I was in fact spoiled. It is just that I never realized it. I thought I was being mistreated by being forced to leave home for the summer, never having the appreciation for the ocean, the sand or the waves, which I should have had. Just think, I could have been down there with Gidget and Moondoggie! Oh, the ingratitude of youth!

Years later, Mother and Dad sold that house then later purchased a house in Palm Springs. While it was nicer and bigger than the one on the ocean, it too was an old house and one could not call it opulent by any stretch of the imagination. It was, however, close to a country club Dad joined. As I said before, golf was Dad's only recreational activity and even on the golf course, he made friends who often gave large donations to his ministry and to the University.

You may have heard something about the house purchased I believe by ORU toward the end of the 1980's in the Beverly Hills area. Ron and I visited there on maybe three or four different occasions. It was an old home needing vast repairs, and was therefore gutted and totally redone. It eventually was a lovely home, perhaps 6,000 square feet in an expensive area, not far from the famous Sunset Boulevard. The hope was that over time the value would increase and bring in money for the school while in the meantime, Dad would be able to create as I have described earlier. Alas, no view.

I recall it was in that house where Dad, with my mother's assistance, recorded his commentary on the entire Bible. I remember Mother having this very small, unsophisticated tape recorder with which to record Dad's voice and seeing them both totally surrounded by Bible encyclopedias and the like. Later, he did a new commentary of the New Testament alone, which was much more in-depth, but as I recall, both were recorded while Dad and Mother sat on the couch in that house. The house was eventually traded for a building and we were told that the increase did eventually translate into finances in aid of the University. I will leave it to my dear reader's own discretion to decide whether the University's purchase of the house in Beverly Hills was simply a misuse of God's money or whether it was a reasonable venture.

My own view is that if such was necessary for Dad to do his best work to produce those commentaries, it was well worth the expense and resulting controversy. While the original full Bible commentary Dad prepared was acceptable, the New Testament commentary which followed was—dare I say it?—brilliant. His depth of understanding of the heart of Jesus was an incredible boon to anyone who loves Jesus and enjoys Bible study. To me, it would have been impossible for Oral Roberts to produce something so imminently valuable while in Tulsa. Believe me, once it became known that Dad was "in town," the phone both at home and in his office rang incessantly.

Country Club Memberships

I have already mentioned that Mother and Dad became a member of a country club near their home in Palm Springs. Also, they were members of Southern Hills in Tulsa. These memberships, particularly Southern Hills, served several purposes. First, they provided a place for Dad to play a relaxing round of golf and enjoy himself for at least a few hours. Personally, I do not believe it was that much to ask for a man who worked basically seven days per week. (For those of you who are purists about Sundays, remember, Dad was an evangelist and not a pastor. It was perfectly acceptable to prepare sermons on Sundays!)

However, the golf course was *never* only a place for Dad to relax. For one thing, it was not until Dad reached his 80's that he even understood the meaning of relaxation! Dad's activities at a country club were never simply for fun and enjoyment as with other executives. The golf course was a wonderful way for Dad to get to know people who had the financial resources to make large gifts to the University, and many of them did! We used to say that Dad "ate, drank and slept ORU." If there had been a way to be productive on ORU's behalf in his sleep, he would have done it!

Additionally, belonging to a country club gave him at least some privacy when he ate out—where he would not be deluged by people. Unfortunately, as the years went by, the other members eventually learned to be more comfortable having "that evangelist" around and arrived at Dad's table as well, however, the numbers were much more manageable! Thank God, they were usually kind!

Dad's Expensive Suits

I have already described Dad's poverty-stricken childhood. I related that he was often pulled away from his school as a boy in order to pick cotton and to do other chores. Dad most definitely did *not* enjoy the humor when members of his father's church joked about the poverty of their pastor and his family. Please, I do not mean to castigate those who said such things. They were no doubt repeating what others may have said before them. And, had they realized how their words would mark a sensitive boy who stuttered and stammered so much that he at times was unable to state his own name, well, perhaps those words would never have left their lips. And it was not simply the lack of money so disturbing to that little boy. Rather, it was the reproach that *accompanied* those limited finances Oral Roberts so fiercely wished to escape.

There is no question that the memory of being "too poor to paint and too proud to white wash" as Dad would say, never left him. During one of the earlier years of our marriage, Ron and I purchased pairs of matching overalls we had found on sale. When we wore them to Mother and Dad's house for dinner that evening, we were both stunned at Dad's reaction. "Don't you have anything else to wear?" It was obvious from the look on his face that our attire truly distressed him.

We had purchased the offending items with the thought that it would be fun to wear them when we were together—and simply for casual events such as an informal family dinner. After all, they were on sale and Ron and I lived on a limited budget. We never dreamed our attire would offend my father, but it did. He asked us never to wear them again in his presence, for it reminded him of the days he had nothing to wear BUT overalls. I learned later of a dress-up high school dance he had attended—you guessed it—having nothing to wear but overalls. The stigma of that terrible poverty never left him.

And perhaps the above may give the reader a glimmer of understanding why Oral Roberts later purchased beautiful Italian suits. I would not say that he feared being poor again, however, I would say that the state of Dad's finances as a child seriously colored the remainder of his life.

His abject poverty was only a part of the reasoning, however, for the admittedly expensive purchases. If he were sitting by me as I write this paragraph, he would insist I tell you how much he had to be on television and therefore, he had no choice but to dress well. He would want me to tell you that he had to look nice when he met with all kinds of community leaders, sometimes presidents and other national leaders, sometimes world leaders and so forth. He would also have me tell you that he was extremely serious about being a role model for the people to whom he ministered.

After all, how could he possibly expect to help them rise out of their poverty if he had not obviously risen from that terrible state himself? He might even tell you that things were different then. While these days, the adage that "the clothes make the man" is often out the window, it certainly was still in vogue up until perhaps the last ten years of Dad's life.

And yet while all of these things are perfectly true, I am convinced that there was a deeper reason. I suspect that his poverty had so marked him that he never lost that deep sense of insecurity, even many decades later after...well, perhaps after his mode of dress simply no longer mattered, to anyone but himself. To Dad, you had to be dressed properly to be "somebody." He never allowed Mother to wear jogging outfits or shorts as other women. Oh no. At the very least, she had to wear a nice pair of slacks with a nice blouse tucked in—every day, even after they were in their late 80's and had absolutely no plans to leave the house for the entire day! Of course I ruined it all when I showed up at their house wearing jogging outfits and the like. And, it is a sign of my father's true regard for my husband that he made few comments when Ron showed up, in nothing dressier than shorts.

So Was He Rich?

If you were to investigate the average annual salary of a college president, I believe you would find that Dad's salary as president of Oral Roberts University was nominal in comparison. However, as you are no doubt already aware, he certainly had access to some luxuries, for example, private air travel. On the other hand, as I mentioned earlier, Dad wrote more than one hundred books during his ministry and ORU days. He never took those funds for himself. They originally were split between his children, then later given to his ministry. I have already told you earlier as well that when Dad started Oral Roberts University, he used virtually everything he had in order to plant the first seed toward that project. The truth is that when he left the University in 1993, Dad and Mother had their retirement and little else. Remember, they had been living in a house provided for the President of Oral Roberts University. When they retired from the University and moved to California, they were obliged to obtain a 100% loan on a condominium which they purchased in Newport Beach, California.

Even though he had officially retired, Dad had to somehow earn an income in order to pay off the loan. He was 75 years old, but thankfully, not without friends. Pastors began inviting him to speak in their churches. As the President of the University, if Dad was given an offering after a speaking engagement, the money had gone to the University. But for the first time, Dad was free to actually deposit the money into his own bank account! He also wrote several books during those years, and for the first time, did not donate the proceeds somewhere else.

Also, young ministers began to schedule time with him in his condominium in order to ask him all sorts of ministry questions. Dad never asked to be compensated for his time and advice, however, many of them did make offerings to him out of gratefulness for his help. After all, who could give you better advice about starting or continuing a ministry than Oral Roberts?

It never failed to amaze Dad that he was actually "in demand" despite his age. At the point when he was no longer physically able to travel, or rather, when my mother put her foot down once again(!) many of those pastors transported their television equipment into his condominium to enable Dad to preach sermons without having to leave his living room. The good news is that it did not take all that many years for the loan on his new residence to be paid in full.

As it turned out, Dad made more money in his old age than what he had made in past years at the University and in his evangelistic ministry. Be that as it may, never let it be said that Oral Roberts worked for financial remuneration alone. That would have been totally outside his character. The truth is that he loved what he was doing. He was the kind of person who simply had to have something to do. He in fact continued giving into the lives of other ministers up until a few days before the fall that ended his life.

I have laid out the question, followed by the facts as I know them so that you can formulate your own answer. Just the same, you may find the following instructive in deliberating your own opinion:

Before Mother and Dad moved to California, they had a little study in their house on the ORU campus. On those few evenings when he and Mother were home, if Dad wanted to watch a basketball game and Mother wanted to watch, well, anything else, she would quietly leave the study and go to the den in the front of the house. In the little study, Dad had a picture of two young boys in a large frame hanging on the wall. It was an old, black and white photo and had obviously been enlarged many times. The boys were standing next to an ugly, rusted contraption that must have been a gas meter. The older boy looked right into the camera, a confident expression on his face. The younger boy had his head down. His eyes were looking up just enough to give you a fleeting glimpse of the obviously shy, retiring boy within.

If you had been alive in, say 1929 and been asked to guess which boy would become a famous evangelist and college president, which one would you choose? It simply must have been the boy with all of the swaggering confidence, correct? Actually, no, that was my Uncle Vaden. Oral Roberts was the one with his head down. And believe me, at the time that picture was taken, no one outside of perhaps his mother and God Himself ever dreamed that that little backward boy would ever escape the dismal shell within which he dwelled. Obviously, "little Obadee" in bare feet and overalls would never have been chosen by anyone as the one most likely to succeed—at anything.

In any event, had I been as anxious to escape poverty and a stuttering tongue as my father, that picture—with its memories—might have been the first thing to go! But not so my father. No, he deliberately had the photograph enlarged, framed and hung on the wall in a place where he would be certain to see it often. Why? Because it reminded him where God had brought him. Who better to help poor suffering people than that lonely, hurting little boy? Perhaps there were excesses in his life; he was never one to do things halfway. And yet, despite my love and deep respect for him which must be patently obvious by now, I know I have good reason to be proud of the richness he brought into people's lives as a result of his life and ministry.

God has promised His servants that the house of God has many mansions. Some translations of the Bible employ the word "rooms" rather than "mansions," but whatever they are, they are fine indeed. Dad wanted to help people come out of that "poor mentality," the terrible belief that you must have nothing financially in order to be "good"—and the stigma which trails right behind it. And he did help many people to escape as he had escaped.

Oh, I am certain that if you searched long enough you would find some who were disenchanted after they started following the principles they learned due to the ministry of Oral Roberts. And yet I have heard accounts from people all of my life, events that date back to the late 1940's, testimonies which relate the most astounding miracles of financial provision. I will tell you only one at this juncture.

William Skrinde had invented some kind of equipment (as I recall it was an extremely technical sort of contraption—well, just about any machine would be too difficult for me to understand!) and he had failed after many efforts to sell it to the government. Mr. Skrinde had finally given up and placed the contraption in a forgotten corner of his attic. He later found himself in one of Dad's crusades and heard Dad preach a sermon, one which said something to the effect that "miracles are coming toward you and going past you—constantly—all the time."

William Skrinde heard Oral Roberts say that these miracles could be his if he would just reach out and grab them. He learned that *each* of us have ideas in our minds which can be turned into miracles, *if* we will turn those ideas over to the Lord. When Mr. Skrinde left the tent that night, he was encouraged for the first time in many years. He went home and immediately dragged out his invention. He wiped off a thick layer of dust, made a few adjustments, and offered it to the government again the following day. This time, they bought it—for what was to him a huge sum. I do not remember the amount of money involved, but I do know that Mr. Skrinde made enough money through the sale of the machine that his tithe alone given to Oral Roberts University represented just under $200,000 over the years that followed. He had reached out and grabbed his miracle.

I do not know if you would have called Oral Roberts rich during his lifetime, but I know he is rich now.

> I've got a mansion just over the hilltop;
> In that bright land where we'll never grow old
> And some day yonder, we will never more wander
> But walk on streets that are purest gold.

... [T]here is a friend that sticketh closer than a brother.
–Proverbs 18:24 (KJV)

"I Found A Friend"

Chapter 14

The first time I introduced my new boyfriend, Ron Potts, to my father, Dad was less than impressed. His comment was: "He seems nice, but he won't last!" At the writing of this chapter, we have been married for over 39 years! Interestingly enough, despite the many times Dad truly heard from God "loud and clear," when it came to his family, Oral Roberts admittedly had few prophetic gifts. Actually, though, at the time I was quick to agree with Dad's assessment, as I did not yet see Ron as someone I would wish to marry. Ron is a person who sort of creeps up on you. There is much more to him than meets the eye. It was only after knowing him for a time when either Dad or I realized Ron's true character. He has so many layers!

While I will admit it would be more than tempting to write a chapter about my love for my husband and our relationship together, this is a book about my father. I have therefore committed this chapter to detailing the amazing friendship that developed over time between my father and my husband.

In retrospect, one could have predicted that Oral Roberts and Ron Potts would have almost immediately found common ground, for they had grown up in remarkably similar circumstances, albeit over thirty

years apart. Like my father, Ron was born into a poor family. Like Oral Roberts, Ron's father was a Pentecostal preacher. Both Dad and Ron felt confined within that church although I am not certain Ron felt as strongly as my father had in that regard.

Ron even picked cotton when growing up like my dad had been obliged to do all those years before. Additionally, both Dad and Ron played basketball on their respective high school teams. However, once when I was making these comparisons to my husband, Ron was quick to disabuse me of the notion that their "economic circumstances" had been quite so similar. Ron stated emphatically: "No, I wasn't as poor as your father. I always had shoes. He didn't."

Ron was the middle of five children. Upon graduation from high school, he initially followed his love of basketball to junior college in Burlington, Iowa. While upon graduation from that two-year institution, Ron had absolutely no plans to continue his education, his grandmother felt quite differently. At the last minute, due in large part to the urgings of his grandmother, Ron decided to follow in the footsteps of his two older brothers (David and Leslie) who were already attending what was then considered a fledgling university in Tulsa, Oklahoma. Ron was one year ahead of me at Oral Roberts University but we soon met—on a blind date. While I agreed with Dad's initial appraisal that Ron would not play a large role in my life, it was not long afterwards that my sentiments changed—180 degrees.

In 1970, by the time ORU's Christmas break came and Ron returned to Iowa to spend time with his family, we had already made plans to write each other daily while apart. I had been living in an ORU dorm during the fall semester of 1970 but went home to Dad and Mother's house for the Christmas holidays. When letters from "that boy from Iowa" began to arrive, sometimes two a day, both my parents noticed, particularly my mother. I was at that juncture the last one of their children still unmarried and they apparently were not quite prepared for me to have a serious interest in a young man, even if he was a preacher's kid like me, and a fellow ORU student!

Calling Ron Potts!

Once Ron returned to Oklahoma for the spring semester of 1971, my mother expressed a specific interest in Ron's Christmas gift to me. While it was in fact a ring, Ron carefully explained to my mother that it was not an engagement ring, but merely stood for "friendship." While that was a true statement at Christmas, well, sort of, the "friendship" soon grew into something far different. Never being reticent in these matters, classes had not been in session very long when my mother decided to take action.

Picture how Ron felt when innocently returning from a class to his dormitory room only to be faced with a large entry on the blackboard… *in the lobby where it could be seen by all.* In huge letters, there was a notice that the president's wife was urgently attempting to reach Ron Potts. Can you imagine the tittering that went on in Ron's dormitory that afternoon? Ladies, they say we are the only ones who gossip, but let's get real. The guys in that dormitory simply *never* allowed Ron to forget! He of course was mortified by all the attention and looking back, it is a clear tribute to his character and stamina that he continued to date the daughter of the president at all!

Over the months that followed, my mother had many discussions with Ron, apparently hoping to convince him to postpone our upcoming marriage until we were older. (We were both 20 at the time.) However, the "Solid Rock" which was my mother had met her match in Ron Potts. To their credit, once Mother and Dad learned that we were not to be swayed in our intentions, they accepted our coming marriage with grace and aplomb.

Soon after our marriage in May of 1971, one fateful day Dad decided to take Ron with him to play a round of golf. While Ron had always been an excellent athlete, he had never hit a golf ball in his life.

The budget of a preacher's son in a small town in Iowa simply did not include golf outings! Not having even an inkling of the difficulty of the sport, Ron readily agreed to join Dad's match. Not surprisingly, Ron's first few holes did not exactly show him to be a budding Tiger Woods.

Undaunted however, Ron was more than willing to continue the match. Dad, on the other hand, was not. Once he realized that Ron had absolutely no golfing expertise, Dad pulled him aside and told him to wait in the golf cart—for the remainder of the match! While Ron was horrified, and more than a little frustrated, Dad stood firm. Much to his chagrin, Ron was allowed to do no more than ride in the golf cart and watch the others play…for the rest of the afternoon!

At the conclusion of the match, Dad apparently felt at least a modicum of remorse and made an offer to his new son-in-law. "If you will promise not to attempt playing on a golf course until I say you're ready, I will pay for your golf lessons." Unfortunately for my father, Ron would make him regret his offer—and then some. Dad had no way of knowing that Goliath had encountered little David! Ron did start taking those golf lessons at Dad's expense.

Approximately one year later after who knows how many lessons, accompanied by bills received by my parents totaling around $10,000, Ron received a call from my mother. And it was not for a friendly chat!

You will remember that it was my mother who paid the bills in my parents' household. There would be no more lessons and that was final! But the "revenge of Ron" did not reach its zenith until he began to soundly beat my father in golf. Now you would think Oral Roberts might have been angry and perhaps feel at least somewhat humiliated given the preceding scenario, but he in fact seemed to accept it all with remarkable self-possession. Never one to admit that someone had bested him, Dad took it all in stride and began to brag to his friends of the remarkable golfing abilities of his son-in-law. It was actually my mother who huffed and puffed much more than my father. And, her consternation seemed to have been evenly distributed between her son-in-law *and* her husband!

But what was to fashion the enduring relationship between the two to an even greater degree were the three years or so in which Ron worked for my dad. One might refer to their relationship as schizophrenic in the sense that it had two completely different manifestations. On one side, it was a typical "gopher" job. Ron traveled with Dad and "waited on him hand and foot" as Ron later described it. He served as a sort of valet, keeping Dad's suits in a wearable condition, cleaning up after him (and my Dad was a mess, believe me!), making plane reservations, running errands, and also being a sort of chauffeur. At the same time, however, over time Ron and Dad began discussing the events of the day and of course, what our family always referred to as Dad's baby, Oral Roberts University.

Over the years Dad had found very few friends. When your name is world famous, as Dad's certainly was by the 1970's, it is far easier to attract sycophants to your side than true friends. Certainly, strong individuals often find "yes men" who say solely what the man with the power wants to hear. There is no question that Oral Roberts was plagued with users for most of his adult life. Some would listen to him, then quickly "share" everything, which had been said with each and every one of his friends and acquaintances alike. Ron, on the other hand, had been trained by my father-in-law, Chester Potts (who could have been tortured in a dark dungeon before he would pass on anything to anyone) and I am truly not exaggerating. Remember, Ron grew up in the home of a preacher. To put it mildly, indiscreet preachers are not exactly appreciated by their followers!

Ron rarely offered information to Dad, however, when Dad asked him specific questions, never let it be said that Ron was bashful with his replies. There was a certain "je ne sais quoi" about their relationship, which kept Dad listening during those years when Ron expressed opinions that were at times contrary to those of my father. While Dad did not necessarily adopt Ron's opinions, he listened to Ron's perspective. As one would imagine, there were those within Dad's inner circle who were not all that pleased with the relationship between their boss and my husband. After all, Ron was just a kid married to the boss' daughter!

But more importantly, Dad taught Ron so much. While never classified as a businessman per se, Dad had become truly savvy over the years, in some cases due to negative experiences, coupled with his extensive reading and excellent mind. He also had a grasp of numbers and finances that was quite amazing despite his lack of formal training in matters of business.

Of course he always hired trustworthy accountants and lawyers, however, he was a keen observer and had eventually become anything but a pushover in the business affairs of his ministry and later the University. Thus, by the time Ron began working for Dad, Oral Roberts had amassed a certain amount of wisdom and business acumen. And Ron paid attention. Additionally, while Ron had a God-given ability to "read people" as he would describe it, observing Dad's talents in that area increased his own natural abilities.

A Temporary Parting

I doubt the reader will find it surprising when I relate that eventually, things did not work out between the two. Such pairings in employment rarely do. The truth is that, well, it was inevitable, wasn't it? Ron was hurt. Perhaps Dad was hurt as well, although I suppose I would have been the last to know if such had been the case. Again, nothing I have told you so far in this paragraph may seem all that remarkable. What is noteworthy, however, is that despite the "break-up" or whatever you deign to call it, the severance of Ron's employment seemed to do little to decrease the innate trust and respect which each had for the other. They also developed an understanding for each other's ways that is unprecedented, at least from my experience between fathers and sons-in-law. And perhaps this could best be described as a comfort level in each other's presence that only grew over the years.

Fast forward now, if you would, to Dad's final years, particularly after the passing of my mother in 2005. By this time, Dad was already 87 years old. For 66 years, Mother had taken care of paying the bills, she had deposited the checks, kept the bank accounts, made sure there was food in the refrigerator and clean sheets on the bed. Here was my mother gone to heaven and Dad had no idea if he even had any money in the bank! He had no idea which bank Mother used.

In the meantime, after his employment with Dad's ministry had come to an end, Ron had worked in the business world a few years. There had come a time when he and I decided that Ron should be the one to stay at home with our children and that I should work outside the home. However, even during those years, Ron increased his own knowledge in the area of investments. He became involved in several different financial ventures over the years, most of which were successful. Having learned from my father to read voraciously and maintain a good working knowledge of world affairs, Ron's understanding of financial matters had grown exponentially over the years.

Again, in his younger days, Dad had had quite a knack in understanding financial statements and the like. However, by his late 80's his mental processes could not have been as acute as before. While others seem to live in denial when such things begin to occur in their lives, Dad was the first to recognize his need for help—and he called upon Ron.

In fact, upon my dad's request, Ron left with Dad directly from my mother's memorial service to accompany him to California to help him sort out, well, so many things. That trip was followed by many others over the years between the passing of my mother and Dad's departure to join her. During that time it was almost as if the 30-year interval had never been and the two were again at home with each other. With Ron's help, and with the help of several different caregivers—to whom we are eternally grateful!—Dad was able to organize his household to create an atmosphere which was at least livable without the presence of my mother. Of course he soon learned (finally!) that before her death my little 88-year-old mother had been doing the work of about three people!

But with all of the personal business affairs with which Ron assisted my father, there was something Ron brought to the table that was even more precious. Ron was always someone with whom Dad felt he could "let his hair down." He was able to express his feelings without concern that Ron would betray his trust or expect anything in return.

But it was again very much like their employment relationship had been all those years ago—well, this time with Ron as a volunteer. Ron had no problem doing all those little personal things that elderly men need—things which I would venture to say most sons-in-law and even some sons find repugnant. As is common with the elderly, as Dad had grown older he experienced terrible difficulties with staying warm. Conversely, I have often referred to my husband as "Nanook of the North." I can wear three sweaters in the wintertime and be miserably cold, while Ron wears shorts and still complains that the heat should be turned down!

Given the above, can you imagine Ron's discomfort in the bathroom while helping Dad take a shower? Of course he wanted to make sure Dad stayed warm. During the times when I could come along with Ron to visit Dad, Ron would show up on the other end of Dad's condominium (where I was) after he had helped Dad to get prepared for the day. Ron would be drenched with perspiration from head to toe. Though

Ron did not complain, we did get quite a laugh regarding his appearance on those mornings!

Ron would say, however, that he gained far more than he gave during those times in which he acted as a personal servant. For just as before, his time with Dad did not consist merely of personal care. The two of them spent hours—usually at the dinner table—wherein Dad would recount some of the most awe-inspiring things that had happened over his lifetime. While he had of course reached his 80's, his amazing memory had not totally lost its edge. After many of those evenings, Ron would call me in Tulsa close to tears over things which Dad had told him. In fact, some of the insights I have shared in this book came from what Ron learned about Dad on those occasions.

On the other hand, there were other things Ron learned from Dad which were intended to be private—for in those discussions he also expressed the pain, the rejection, the criticism which he had experienced over the years.

While I suppose Dad could have written a book about such things, a book that would have embarrassed more than a few people, he was content to simply share the information with Ron. In fact, I believe Ron was the only one with whom Dad ever discussed much of that information. And believe me, wild horses could not draw them from my husband's mouth. While many women would have made the lives of their husbands miserable until he told them—especially now that Dad has "gone on to glory"—I respect my husband's integrity and wisdom in keeping my father's trust. He felt that while some of those things would have a positive purpose in sharing, many others were meant only for his ears, and for his ears only. Dad simply needed another human being with whom he could express some of the feelings he had never shared— according to Dad—even with my mother. I am so grateful that Ron was able to be there for my father in those last days.

True Value

While at their first meeting, Dad clearly underestimated what was below the surface of the man I was to marry, once discovered, he was quick to capitalize upon Ron's true value. He truly found an earthly

friend in my husband and I am so grateful. Of course as wonderful as this friendship was, it was something that only served my father during his time on the earth. That friendship is simply not worthy to be compared to Dad's friendship with Jesus, his Savior and Lord.

And, while remembering and writing things about my father's friendships certainly brings a few tears to my eyes, the most important thing I could tell you about friendship is the only friendship which has eternal value. There is Someone who truly sticks closer than a brother, as expressed in the old song: "I Found a Friend." And He can be your friend today as well.

I found a friend when life seemed not worth living;
I found a friend so tender and forgiving.
I can't conceive how such a thing could be
That Jesus cares for even me.
Because He came my soul will live in glory.
I'll praise His name and tell my Savior's story.
What friend so true would give His all for you?
I found a friend and life began anew.
I'm sure you'll find that He is your friend too.

And he shall turn the heart of the fathers to the children,
and the heart of the children to their fathers...
                                        —Malachi 4:6 (KJV)

"LET ME TOUCH HIM"
Chapter 15

D id you foolishly believe a daughter would or even could be capable of writing a book about her father without including a chapter about herself? I saved this story until toward the end of the book, thinking that possibly by the time readers were ready to begin this chapter, they would have had more than enough information about Oral Roberts. After all, perhaps I have already relayed to you the most important information about Dad. Certainly, his relationship with his younger daughter would have little importance within the overall scheme of things. So for those of you who decide to trudge through this chapter...well, I will let my dear readers finish that sentence for themselves.

A Father, Finally

No one knows what a child feels unless he is that child. Most of my life I have lived from within. While this was a protection in some ways, it also became a thorn. Not knowing how to express how I felt without either crying or anger was very difficult. Being so much like my father in some ways made our relationship—well, thorny at times!

I really do not know how to tell you this. How do I say it without making you think less of Oral Roberts? And yet for this to be a credible account, I must. Dad did not really function as a father, at least not toward me—actually until perhaps a year or so before his passing when I was nearing 60 years of age. His focus was on his ministry and Oral Roberts University. His children were secondary, particularly his youngest. The only time he seemed truly interested in one of his children was when he believed that one of them could be helpful in his ministry. He first focused on Ronnie, my older brother, as the one to carry on his ministry, then later switched to Richard, my other brother.

Of course even during the best times Dad and I had during his last days, it would be wishful thinking to imagine that we were as close as so many other fathers and daughters. Even then, I cannot help but be realistic enough to admit that much of the love Dad truly showed to me at the last may have been a result of his terrible disappointment with other things in his life. This may have also been coupled with guilt for having spent so little time with me over the years.

All right, now what I have said in this paragraph so far may sound scintillating, especially to those Oral Roberts-haters out there, however, lest you believe that his remaining daughter has written a "tell all," negative book about her father, you must promise to complete this chapter. I implore you to allow me the opportunity to thoroughly explain myself before you come to a conclusion that is simply unmerited.

Child-like Faith

Oral and Evelyn Roberts gave birth to four children. I had an older sister, Rebecca, born in 1939, who was 11 years older than me. My older brother, Ronnie came along in 1944. After Ronnie, my brother Richard was born in 1948, and lastly, this writer—at the tail end of 1950.

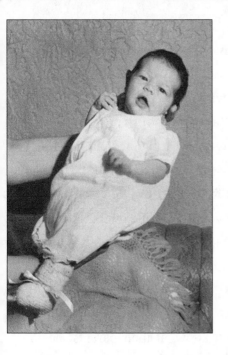

Dad always said that of his children, I was the one who looked most like a Cherokee and I have always been terrifically proud of that fact.

To set the time, when I was born, my father's evangelistic ministry had only been in full swing for about three years. While I now regret some of the things I felt so deeply as a child, it is important to tell you of my terribly mixed and confused emotions about my father. On the one hand, I was so incredibly proud of him. That evangelist who stormed around the platform holding onto the microphone, doing a Jericho March and telling the people about Jesus was my father!

I absolutely loved his ministry, remembering many of Dad's sermons and the principles he espoused quite well even now. And I not only memorized the principles but integrated many of them into my life as well. I suppose what I have been describing in some detail could be referred to as childlike faith. I accepted the principles without question, and they *worked*.

On the other hand, I had no concept of and no understanding of why my father was gone from me so much. He seemed to be out of town more than he was in town. And, when he was in town, he was most often busy and away from our house. If he was at home, I was recurrently asked not to disturb him. He was busy studying for a sermon, or perhaps napping or meeting in the den with one of his associates in the ministry so I was expected to be quiet.

Of course I missed my mother as well, as the two of them often went out of town together, although my mother was certainly far more accessible than my father when she was in town. I remember many times going into my mother's closet while she was gone somewhere with Dad. Her clothing still carried a faint scent of the lady who was my mother, despite the fact that she was not wearing them at the time. I remember the stacks of hat boxes. Of course I peeked! And, her closet was a delightful place in which to hide from the babysitter. Actually we had some truly wonderful people staying with us while our parents were both out of town, but many of them, well, they were not always so great. And of course even the nicest ones simply could not cure the terrible loneliness of being without my parents.

So how did I deal with all of this? How is it that I now hold no resentment against my parents? As you know, at their parents' death, many children of well-known parents cannot wait to tell the world of each and every mistake their parents made while they were living. I can think of several of them and you most likely can as well. More often these days, children tend to blame their faults on their parents. Personally, I would say that is very convenient. How nice to blame all of your failures on someone else! Perhaps their refusal to take personal responsibility for their own actions keeps them from facing who they really are.

I, on the other hand am far too realistic for such an approach. I believe God can help us to overcome whatever hurts we may have experienced as a child. Blaming our faults on our parents is a stupid, useless cop out. After all, if everyone used that excuse, no one would ever achieve any-thing at all because, face it, none of us had perfect parents.

While blaming others for our own faults seems to be particularly in vogue in the 21st century, joining that "club" simply had no interest for me. No, I chose to serve the One who appeared to me as a little girl. All right now, I am not being wacky or weird here. For any of you Oral Roberts detractors who have not yet discarded this book in disgust, I am not saying that a 900-foot Jesus appeared to me, okay? No, I am saying that where other children had imaginary friends, I had Jesus. He was similar to an imaginary friend in that I could *not* see Him. And yet, He was so very real to me. He was my imaginary friend who was not imaginary.

I cannot remember a time before I knew Jesus was my friend. Oh I do not claim to have understood the deep things of God as a child, however, Jesus was always there for me. You see, He never went out of town. He was always there. He was the one my father was talking about in those fiery sermons of his. How did I know? It is hard to say. I just knew. From a very early age, I learned to fill my life with Jesus in the lonely times.

The Prophecy Teacher

While I had what church folks call "memory verses" as a little girl, I began studying the Bible in depth when I was a teenager. I loved Bible prophecy then and now. I remember having this big chart of all the coming events described in Revelation, Daniel and other parts of the Bible. Many times when I had invited a girlfriend to spend the night at my house, I would spread out my chart on the bed and "teach" my friend everything I knew (or at least what I thought I knew!) about Bible prophecy. My mother would inevitably spy the light coming from beneath my bedroom door during the early morning hours and assume that we were giggling or perhaps talking about boys as was the custom of most girls. (Well, we did do that too!)

You might assume that Evelyn Roberts would not have been surprised to walk into her daughter's bedroom only to find the girls poring over the Bible, but she was in fact surprised. While she must have become dreadfully tired of driving me all over town and picking me up later for all sorts of Christian youth meetings, she did not complain, well, not much anyway. (However she did finally draft others like my sweet Aunt Kathleen and a gentleman named Frank Reeder to help her with those transportation duties.)

I am not saying that having Jesus in my life made all my difficulties fly away on the wings of some angel. I am simply telling you that with Jesus as my friend, those difficulties were not—well, they were not as tough to bear. I wish I could tell you that my love for Jesus at an early age caused me to take on all of His attitudes. Despite my sincere love for Jesus, as a child I did feel a great deal of resentment for both of my parents. I remember times when Dad would be home and he and Mother had invited a few people over for dinner. With his friends all in view, he would often ask me to come sit on his lap—but I refused. I was angry that one of the few times he paid attention to me was when we were in the presence of others, in my mind, just so that he could "show me off."

Of course I must admit that I was also tremendously shy and that did influence my reticence to a degree. The plain truth, though, is that at those times and others as well, I felt like a puppy taken out of its cage just long enough to be petted and pampered, then sent directly back to my cage. My, how embarrassing that is for me to admit, for looking back, mine was a stupid, foolish attitude! If I had just had the personality of my brother, Richard, for example, perhaps my father would have enjoyed being around me too! However, I lacked the discernment to see any of those things in those days.

Unrealistic

I was clueless that Dad simply did not know how to approach me, or how to show his love for me. For while he certainly did ignore me, I have a feeling that such was the result not only of his busyness in his work, but also because of my own hyper-sensitivity and intense shyness.

Part of it was because I could not bring myself to put into words the deep love I had for him and my huge desire to be close to Oral Roberts. I had retreated into myself to such a vast degree that I had incredible difficulty expressing my feelings to anyone with the power and presence of a man like my father. I was totally intimidated by him. Besides, one of my greatest faults has always been that I expect people to know when they have hurt me. They should understand—never mind how—why I am upset with them. Then they should come to me of their own accord and profusely apologize. I was yet to learn (and still have difficulty remembering even now) that such omniscience rarely occurs among mortals. My expectations were simply unrealistic as most folks, especially men(!), often have no earthly idea that they have hurt you. I was Eliza Doolittle throwing those slippers at Henry Higgins while the professor was concurrently ducking and wondering why on earth his pupil was so angry.

Despite the foregoing, however, I did manage to have many happy times growing up. One fun thing about having a rather famous father is that sometimes you get to meet neat people. I remember a time when Mother and Dad along with Richard and I were in a restaurant in the Los Angeles area. My absolute favorite television star as a little girl was the man who played Wyatt Earp, Hugh O'Brian. Richard and I spied him in the restaurant and immediately started begging Dad to approach him so we could meet the actor. I ordinarily complained about strangers approaching *us* because of Oral Roberts being at our table at a restaurant, but this was different of course! (What a hypocrite I was.)

Despite the fact that Dad had never met Hugh O'Brian, he very kindly accommodated our wishes. It was so tremendously exciting when "Wyatt Earp" actually walked over to our table! Wow, he was even more handsome in person than he was on our television set! The only problem was that either his pants were too tight or his zipper had somehow gone south of its own accord and he, unfortunately for him, did not notice the problem until he was standing at our table. Of course he quickly zipped his pants while standing before us, but Richard and I had fun laughing about that for simply days! Even so, it was a huge thrill in my life.

Then there were the confusing moments as the daughter of an evangelist. On those Sunday mornings when Mother and Dad were out of town, before getting ready for church I looked forward especially to turning on the radio. Dad had a radio program in those days. It started with a wonderful quartet singing a song or two. While I do not remember it all in perfect order, I do recall that at some point in the program, my mother would start talking.

I would get really excited at that point because I so loved hearing her voice, but I would also be confused. She would always talk about someone in her family who had had some life-threatening disease and tell how the Lord had healed them. I would say to myself: "I didn't know that my sister Rebecca ever had cancer!" or

Here is my mother reading one of those testimonies for Dad's radio program. Aren't the sunglasses and purse the coolest?

"When was Ronnie paralyzed? I don't remember that!" Being much too shy to ask anyone, I was relieved to learn, years later, I might add, that my mother was simply reading letters of testimony which had been sent to Dad. It was people saying that they or a loved one had been healed in Dad's ministry—and Mother was simply reading their letters out loud.

The Mural

Then there was my confusion about the Abundant Life Mural. When I was growing up, the office of Dad's evangelistic association (OREA) was in downtown Tulsa. There was the neatest thing on the ground floor of that building which attracted many tourists. People from all over the country came and took guided tours of the building, which culminated in seeing the Mural. The Mural was what must have surely been considered an avant garde presentation for the 1950's and 60's. It told the story of creation and gave the entire salvation message from the Bible. You walked into a room without windows and took a seat.

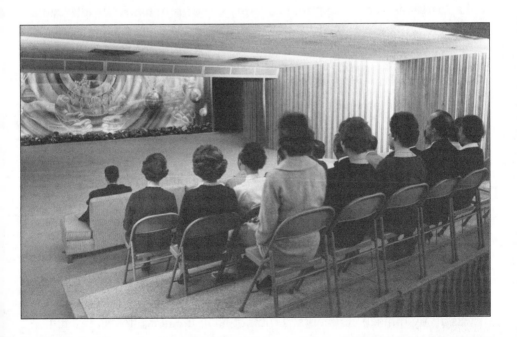

The auditorium could accommodate about sixty people at a time. The entire front wall of the room was covered by a mural that consisted of all kinds of things that looked like plastic to this author, but perhaps were something else.

At the beginning of the presentation, all the lights would go off and it would be dark and eerie while these big blue curtains slowly opened. Then lights would shine on different things at different times during the presentation during which a deep, resonant voice would speak. The voice talked about the earth being without form—and was void—and how God had created the stars and so forth, then the voice would say: "And it was good." Of course I know now that these were basically quotes from Genesis, but at the time, in my child's mind, I thought it was God Himself speaking! I thought the Mural was just about the neatest thing I had ever seen or heard. At the end of the presentation, I would hear my Dad's voice asking if there was anyone who wanted to give their hearts to the Lord. As much as I loved my father, I had to admit that that part was very disappointing to my childish mind. After all, Dad's voice was high-pitched next to the voice of God!

There were very nice ladies who had the ability to turn on the presentation and even when tour groups were not there, I bothered them often to turn it on—just for me. God knows how many times I watched the presentation, but I certainly do not. The affect that presentation had upon my life is inestimable. I absolutely loved it. Then one day, I was upstairs outside Dad's office when all of a sudden, I heard *GOD* speaking! It was so amazing because He was in my Father's office. Wow!

God Himself had come to see my father and to talk to him! I was totally enthralled, but then a man walked out of Dad's office and went downstairs on the elevator. Once he left, everything was quiet. I finally gathered the courage to venture into Dad's office to see God, but my Dad was all by himself! Of course I did not have the nerve to ask my father where God went. It was actually not until years later when I learned that "God" was in fact Bob Daniels, the current crusade soloist. I learned that it was Bob Daniels who had narrated and spoken for God in that presentation of the Mural. What a shock! Oh, the crazy misunderstandings of childhood!

I mentioned earlier that Mother and Dad sent me to a private school through the sixth grade, however, I finally convinced them to allow me to go to public schools for my secondary education. I must say that both Nimitz Junior High School and later Memorial High School in Tulsa were much more pleasant to me as, for the first time in my life, I was allowed to feel "normal." Certainly, the lifestyle of our family seemed to fit in far better with my fellow students at public school than it ever had at my private school.

On the other hand, it was not until I arrived in public school that I heard comments about "Oral Roberts" or was asked about my father while at school. For the duration of the years prior to high school graduation I did experience many comments—mainly negative—from my classmates. After all, this was the 1960's during which "Oral Roberts" was truly a household word in this country. The other students appeared to be particularly caught up with the fact of my father's notoriety. I suppose the most commonly used expression was for one of them to walk up to me and say emphatically "Heal!" Of course this was basically shouted to me in a school hallway—causing the other students to stop and stare. Obviously, they were mimicking what Dad often said while he was praying for someone in one of his crusades.

In my high school, if there were any big "he-man" athletes in my classroom, they always seemed to sit in the back. I would walk into the room, the only entrance being toward the front, and the athletes would say in unison: "There's Oral!" It seemed I no longer had a name of my own.

Then there were those fellow students (and so many others outside of school!) who were syrupy sweet, hoping to gain something from Oral Roberts' daughter. Shy as I was, however, those things did not trouble me nearly to the extent of feeling unimportant at home. I suppose it was the contrast of the expectations of people outside our home—assumptions that of course I was close to my father!—which hurt the most. I did not mind the assumptions in themselves. I just minded that they were untrue.

But please, I am not telling you such things to elicit sympathy.

Far from it.

How I was treated in school helped to make me strong, and they did not have a major affect upon my life. The good news also is that my teachers seemed to like me, perhaps because I was a good student and made every effort to follow the rules. I wish I could say I was compliant because of my strong desire to learn. No, that was not at all my reasoning. I just knew I could not have handled the embarrassment of ever—even once—being called down before the other students by one of my teachers. The major concern was that my conduct might obliquely bring disdain upon that famous personage: "Oral Roberts." I therefore made every effort to keep such ignominy from occurring and was largely successful. Whew!

Dad could not make my high school graduation as he was preaching somewhere (I never even tried to keep up with his incredible schedule) but my mother came and for that I was grateful. I have told you earlier how much I truly loved both my undergraduate and graduate years as an ORU student. However, I do need to fill in to some degree the years between my undergraduate and graduate years. During those eleven years, Ron and I had our two children then eventually moved to Colorado in 1977. Ron both taught and coached in high school and I was a legal secretary. We had been living in the Denver area for almost seven years when I received a telephone call from my father, asking me to come back to Tulsa, to work for him.

Tending a Marriage

Even now, this story is so very painful that I have to force myself to tell you. I just ask again that you temper my remarks by understanding that the facts as I understand them are from my own perspective. None of us really have any more than that. There is no such thing as an unbiased reporter. No matter how hard we try to be objective, every single person on earth views things through the haze of his own imperfections. We cannot help but be self-serving, even when we try so terribly hard to be truthful.

So what I tell you must be measured by that yardstick.

I can only guess at my Dad's perspective and I have no doubt that from *his* perspective, he was not trying to harm me. It is just that it seemed that way to me. So here it is.

At least my father could never say he had no advance warning of what the tenor of my actions at ORU would be. I remember standing in our kitchen in Colorado on the telephone with my Dad and Richard. It had been several years since Ron had worked for my father, as I discussed in an earlier chapter. Ron and I had grown tired of living in Tulsa where being related to Oral Roberts forced us to live inside a goldfish bowl.

It was not that we necessarily wanted to do things which were considered wrong by church folks or my family, it was just that we wanted to go where we were just as unnoticed as everyone else. A place where no one would whisper when I walked into the room: "Oh, there's Oral Roberts' daughter!" After awhile, that sort of thing wears on your consciousness. But more importantly, we found it impossible to become one as husband and wife—as long as my parents were around. We wanted to be in charge of our own lives.

Richard and I were very much alike in that we did not want our parents controlling the way we lived or thought. However, that is where the similarity between my brother and I ends, for we each chose totally different paths as a result. There are two ways most adult children react to control from a strong parent. Some give lip service in the parent's presence, then secretly do what they wish outside the parent's presence. Others live the way they feel is best and are up front with their parents about their choices.

Richard chose the former. He, as well as his first wife and later his second wife, became very adept in that regard. Ron and I, on the other hand, chose the latter. We were far too rebellious to pretend! We did not always agree with things Dad was doing at that point and when asked, we told the truth of our feelings. Of course that never bodes well with a dominant man such as my father.

So there came a time when Ron and I sensed that if we were ever to have the kind of oneness which marriage is all about, we would have to remove ourselves from the influence of my parents and the world surrounding them—to live totally on our own. Please do not mistake my meaning. My parents did nice things for us and meant well. It was just that that goldfish bowl which was Tulsa had become far too confining for us.

So by the time of the phone call I referred to earlier, we had been living in Colorado for several years and loving it. Over time, my husband and I had finally come into our own as husband and wife. We had learned to depend upon the Lord and each other, oh not perfectly, but in a far greater fashion than had ever been possible in Tulsa under the gun of the public eye. So when Dad asked me to return to work for him in Tulsa, I cannot say that I was unaware of what things would be like.

However, by that time it is true that Ron and I had truly become a family along with our children, and we felt far more competent to endure the slings and arrows of Tulsa living. Besides, no one was more adept at putting a guilt trip on an individual than Oral Roberts! I was hearing things like: "The family needs to be together," "We miss having you here" and other such platitudes.

I remember telling Dad that if I returned to Tulsa, I wouldn't be a "yes" person. I made it very clear that I would not be controlled—and yet I suppose I knew, in my heart of hearts, that Dad would expect such as he always had. So why did I fall for it? Was it the excellence of Dad's persuasive powers? Well, he did make it all sound so great. He actually made noises that I would have an important role at the University. Looking back, I realize he was anything but specific. My, Dad would have made a great lawyer or politician. If anyone had a "silver tongue," it was my father. He could make things sound a certain way without having made any clear, definite pronouncements!

Worse for my husband and I, however, was that soon after we arrived in Tulsa, with little money in the bank and therefore, now totally dependent upon my father, Oral Roberts paid a visit to Bob Foresman at the now defunct Tulsa Tribune. As a result, there was a front page article seen of course by all. The drift of the headline was that Dad's son, Richard, would be "Mr. Outside" at ORU and his daughter, Roberta, would be "Miss Inside." It intimated that Richard and I would eventually share control of the University. However, I was to learn very quickly that instead of having a true position waiting for me at ORU, Dad in fact had no idea what to do with me.

While he seemed honestly glad I was around, Dad apparently had not taken the time to come up with any real work for me. However, this actually worked to my benefit for Dad did finally arrive at an idea that definitely appealed to me. He asked me to go through each department, first at his evangelistic association—OREA, then at the University, sit down with the department heads one by one and learn the "business" of each. While I suspect some of the department heads were suspicious that the "boss" had sent his daughter to spy upon them, most seemed frankly happy to let Dad know, through me, just exactly what it was they were doing.

I typed long descriptions of each department and passed them on to my father. In actuality, I did learn a great deal and certainly do not feel that time was wasted. However, after that assignment came to a conclusion, one of the few tasks remaining was in attending certain events such as chapel services, laymen's seminars, Regents meetings and the like. While I had a lovely office—far better than that to which my true role entitled me—I have never been the sort of person who was willing to accept a salary in exchange for, well, very little work. My husband has always referred to me as a "worker bee" and I suppose he is essentially correct.

Again, however, Dad's seeming reluctance to give me the sort of all-consuming assignment, something I could "sink my teeth into" which I craved, worked to my advantage. While I had been accepted to the law school at Tulsa University when Ron and I were first married, I had basically relinquished my dream of being a lawyer since Ron and I had moved away and had two children. However, by the 1980's, ORU had a law school of its own. One afternoon I found myself grouching a little about having so little to do to "earn my keep" to Carl Hamilton, ORU's academic dean in those days. Dr. Hamilton's response was: "The best thing I know to do in an 'I don't know period' is to go to school." He had remembered my dream of a law school education from past years.

Of course while that sounded great, I assumed that going to law school would not be possible for me as long as our children were young. However, when I talked with my husband, he quickly volunteered to take care of the children so that I could attend law school—and he meant it! Dad got on the bandwagon for me to attend ORU's law school as well, perhaps because he was tired of me coming to him so often asking for something to do! But again, while law school was the most arduous and tedious task of my life up until that point, it was a tremendous opportunity for me.

While I did have some assignments from Dad and certainly had expectations upon me regarding attendance at many different university and evangelistic association events, there remained sufficient time to begin law school at least on a part-time basis.

Despite the fact of my disappointment in Dad's role for me in the University, I remain deeply appreciative of the opportunity to obtain a graduate degree. Thinking back, perhaps Dad had even been "a little bird" in Carl Hamilton's ear—anything to keep me busy, however, there is no question that God used it for my good. After all, a law school education unquestionably opens a brand-new world for an individual and while it was exceedingly grueling, it worked to make me a better person as well. It helped to toughen me up and forced me out of at least a measure of my shyness, things I would certainly need for the coming days.

A New Position

I should tell you as well that Dad and I for some reason always seemed to clash—at almost every point. When the two of us sat down to converse, it seemed inevitable that some sort of upset would result. I suspect this was partially because we were so alike. We both wanted our own way and we both wanted to be right—all the time! At that point I had not learned the art of persuasion that I believe I have learned after practicing law for twenty years. I did not understand then that a frontal assault is often unsuccessful! When I argued with my father, I backed him up to the wall and he had nowhere to go but back at me! My methods, or lack thereof, soon became a recipe for disaster between the two of us.

Once I graduated from law school and, thank God, passed the Oklahoma Bar examination (although I am embarrassed to tell you that I did not pass until my second effort), Dad at least did finally agree to give me a real job at the University. I became the transfer counselor and international student advisor in the Admissions Department of ORU. No, it was certainly not a role one might consider *important*, however, there is no question that my experience in that department did prepare me in many ways for my future.

That position also gave me a true opportunity to become more closely acquainted with many of the ORU students. What a wonderful experience that was. My, ORU has been so blessed of God over the years to draw some absolutely wonderful people to its campus. Oh there have been those who simply did not belong at ORU, but all in all, the students have been an incredibly gifted and bright group of young people. And, at this point in my account of those years, I can thankfully exonerate Dad somewhat because after awhile, he did call upon me to serve the University as its Dean of Student Services.

How I loved that! All of a sudden I was responsible for the recruiting, registrar and financial aid programs of the University. I dug in immediately. I think perhaps my most favorite task was changing the financial aid area into a more user-friendly department. That seemed to be the most criticized department in the entire University community.

In order to determine the specifics of the criticism, I requested that the maintenance department construct a large suggestion box for students to use while waiting in line during registration and oh my, what an education I received! I learned the real story from the students. It was not at all that the employees were bad people. It was just that they had put their own convenience first, before that of the students. Of course there was nothing unusual about that mentality—such seems to be in vogue amidst corporate America these days as well—but I was determined to change things in any department over which I had responsibility!

With the help of some incredibly dedicated and hardworking fellow employees like David Owens, Dr. Bill McFarland, Dr. Jeff Ogle, Dr. Sheree King, and many others, it was amazing what we were able to do. Over time, things began to change and I absolutely loved working with the students. After all, as I told my staff perhaps like a broken record, the students were what ORU was all about. It was the students for whom God had raised up the University. It was the students whose tuition paid our salaries. It was the students who would go where God's light was dim. It was all about them and not just making things easy for ourselves!

And yet, while I was ensconced in the challenges of my own areas of responsibility in the University, compromises were being made in other areas in order to pave the way for new leadership at the top. The honest truth is that once my employment at ORU ended, I became determined not to dwell on the specifics that had caused me to tender my resignation. Therefore, while I certainly remember some details, there are many events I have not considered for a very long time.

Suffice it to say, then, that there were compromises, financial irregularities and so forth with which I felt I must no longer be associated. You may be thinking, "Well, you probably remember only those things which speak well of you, while forgetting your own mistakes and shortcomings!" And there may be some truth in that assumption. I will just say that I erred on the side of the vision of the University and on the students, while there was another who seemed to be trying to go somewhere as an individual.

While I was largely left alone by the top administration, there were notable occasions when I was expected to allow what I saw as impermissible shortcuts, for example allowing certain students exceptions to official school policies which were not available to other students. At first I went along—albeit reluctantly—with some of the things I was asked to do. However, by 1990, I came to a decision that I could no longer be a part.

Now I hasten to point out that the things of which I speak were not necessarily illegal. I just felt that they were categorically wrong. I also should point out that I have always been a stickler—one who typically saw black and white and no gray areas. Later in my life, particularly after having practiced law, I have learned that there are in fact gray areas but I did not see that at the time.

Having said that, however, the major cause of my demise was inextricably linked with the new way of doing things which were in keeping with the new leadership which was to come. Of course I can criticize my father and brother all I want, but the fact remains that I was not so perfect either. My attitude was certainly not always what it should have been on many occasions. In retrospect, I wish I had been more persuasive, and made what might have been seen as more gentle efforts to cause things to go in a different direction—rather than going in like a bull in a china closet.

Carl Hamilton told me once that ORU did not really need an efficiency expert. There unfortunately may have been some legitimacy in his comments, however painful to admit to you, dear reader. On the other hand, there is simply no way to whitewash the fact that Dad was preparing the way for his successor as the next president of the University. As Richard and I had always seemed to be at loggerheads, Dad was correct in assuming that such would leave absolutely no place for the likes of me, daughter or no.

A Terrible Misstep

While both my husband and I warned Dad both orally and in writing of the danger of his plan, he absolutely could not accept our urgings. As I told you in an earlier chapter, I certainly did not have any desire to be the president of the university. I was really pretty happy with where I was at the time although admittedly, I did have a desire at some point to have a higher standing as to the academic side of the University. But at that time, I only knew that placing my brother in charge of the University would be a terrible misstep. Is that an indictment of my brother? Not really.

The truth is that he simply did not have the capability of running a University and was not all that interested in education or academia. It simply was not his bag and I suspect that in his heart of hearts, Richard has always known that. Place yourself in his shoes for a moment, however. Would you have said no if your father had offered you a University? Few would have done so! Although warned by many others as well, Dad simply could not see things as they were.

And I hasten to remind you that each of us has blind spots. Despite his true greatness, my father was not immune to this all too human frailty. We *all* share the frightening propensity to press on in a plan or program despite the prognostications of doom which are everywhere around us. In fact, often our most perverse stubbornness comes to the fore *because* of those predicted negative outcomes. Then later when the full reality of the situation is before our eyes and can no longer be denied, we look back and wonder how we could have been so blind! The problem with being so hard on others though—is that we later have few excuses when faced with our *own* frailties. I love the way the NIV translates Matthew 7:1: "Do not judge, or **you too** will be judged." Oops! No one wants that and no one can stand up to honest judgment because we all have warts. If practicing law has taught me anything, I have seen that—and how!

How can I describe leaving the University of my dreams? It was clearly one of the saddest, most devastating days of my life. Although Dad and I disagreed as to how to carry out the vision of the University as to his successor, I never once doubted the vision: to raise up students to hear God's voice. That vision which had captured my heart as a young girl was no less dear to me, even upon leaving what I saw then and still see today as the hallowed ground of Oral Roberts University.

The rejection I felt was so intense that I began to wonder how I was going to go on. It seemed the end of everything for me. And yet, as angry and hurt as I was, I was somehow able to separate the wrongs I felt Dad had done to me from the Jesus I had learned to love—you guessed it—because of my father. One thing I did understand was that when we face problems, the most infantile reaction is to run away from God.

My not so imaginary friend was still there for me, just as He had always been. It was such an amazing day when I discovered a verse in Jeremiah which I had no memory of ever reading before. It was Jeremiah 29:11 (NIV): "For I know the plans I have for you," declares the Lord, "plans to prosper you and not to harm you, plans to give you hope and a future." The day I discovered that verse within the dark caverns of the writings of the weeping prophet was a time for celebration! I wrote out the verse in huge letters and put it on the mirror near where I dressed every morning and dressed for bed every night. I said it to myself—over and over again—for months.

I did the same thing with Philippians 4:8 which tells us the kinds of things to wrap our minds around. I was having difficulty with the admonition to dwell on a good report (as the only report I knew about my own life) was sad indeed. I had a law degree but was too devastated to have come across well in a job interview. Perhaps the Lord was protecting me when I was not granted even one interview after sending my resume to an unknown number of prospective employers. Thus the only "good report" I could find was our older son, Randy's report card. It contained only A's. So I took his report card and taped it to the cabinet in the kitchen. Every time I cooked a meal, I saw it and rejoiced.

But what is more important is an event for which I shall forever be grateful to God. The evening of the day I left ORU, I received a call from a friend with whom I had attended Memorial High School, Joanie Elmore. She and her husband, Jason, had somehow learned of what was for me a catastrophe at ORU and insisted upon coming over that very evening. I did everything short of downright rudeness to discourage them from coming. I was simply in no mood to hear what she and Jason would say. After all, Jason was a pastor and I knew the drill. I was supposed to forgive, right? Well I was not ready to forgive! I was angry and wanted to continue being angry. I had no interest in those worn-out platitudes typically offered at such times. However, Joanie absolutely insisted that she and Jason come to our home and bring dinner. If it had been anyone but her—if not for our longstanding friendship—well, I would have declined and not necessarily in a tender way! However, I finally relented.

A Life-Changing Conversation

I do not know how I sat through dinner that evening, but I was honestly hoping to "shoo" them off within five minutes of desert. However, they insisted upon sitting down with us in the living room after dinner, just as I had feared. (Have you figured out yet that my attitude was less than Godly at that point?) With almost no preamble, however, Jason looked at me right in the eye and said: "Roberta, you get to forgive!" I responded "Oh, you mean I *have* to forgive, right?" "No," stated Jason.

"You don't have to forgive. It is your choice. But the only way to be free is if you *choose* to forgive."

The conversation we had with Joanie and Jason that evening changed my life. I had already put away the framed picture of my parents that had been sitting in the living room. At least I had not given in to my desire to stomp on it! And I cannot say that forgiveness came overnight. It did not. However, once I made a conscious decision to forgive—over and over—when the bad thoughts came, a forgiving attitude began to get stronger and stronger. I began to feel better and better.

I kept notebooks on all kinds of scriptural things. I had nothing else to do anyway when the boys were in school. It was also during this horrendous storm that I began praying that the verse above from Malachi would come true in my life, that my father would turn his heart toward me and that I could somehow turn my own heart back to my father, to forgive him for the throbbing anguish underway in my life. Oh, how I longed to touch him.

A few months later, Ron encouraged me to begin a law practice with a friend of ours, Fred Stoops. While I learned a great deal during that first year, it was not long before the Lord gave me the courage to strike out on my own. With Ron's incredible assistance, we started our own law office. It is still so amazing when I look back at how much God has blessed us, and our law practice over the years. We have not become rich, but the Lord has always been faithful—for over 20 years now—to send clients to us.

And yet that time of hiatus, between leaving ORU and practicing law, is precious to me as well because God was all we had and we clung to Him. God had something great on the other side, but He gave us that time of preparation. We learned in minute detail that God is always faithful.

It was also during that time that a young man whom I had met while he was an ORU student asked me to become a volunteer co-host on the Roadshow, a program on the Oasis Network. The folks at the Oasis Network provided exactly that for me and I am so grateful. God knew how much I needed that acceptance during that time.

It was during the initial years of law practice when our children grew old enough to attend college. ORU was simply out of the question for either of them—from two vantage points. First of all, both of them had themselves lived through the trauma of our exit from ORU. ORU had been our very lives. Our boys had tender memories of ORU from the time they were small. They were also very defensive of their mother. When I left ORU there was some "to do" in the Tulsa community, felt particularly by the fellow students of our boys. While their fellow students and even their teachers were incredibly supportive of their mother, who was seen as a sort of victim in the situation, at the same time I am sorry to say that there was a very negative feeling about my brother and my father. I believe these negative feelings reinforced in the minds of our children that ORU should be the last place they would attend college.

Secondly, while Ron and I could not force from our hearts the love we had for our alma mater, we knew that attendance there for our children, so recently after the termination of my employment there could be nothing but awkward for both of our children, and for my brother who was by then the president. It is with indescribable sadness that I inform those of you not already aware that both of our children went far away from the teachings of God they had learned in our home.

Now we ask ourselves, should we have sent them to ORU? Would things have been different if we had sent them to ORU? I honestly do not know the answer to those questions. However, Ron and I have not given up on their return to the true Godliness we saw in our children while they were living in our home. We press on, believing that both of our boys will choose to return to the God of the Bible, so loved by their parents.

But fast forward, if you will to one of my birthdays—perhaps four or five years after we left ORU—when my husband received a telephone call from my mother. She and Dad wanted to take us out to lunch. Although there had been a few cordial but rather stilted occasions in which we had seen my parents after the end of my employment at ORU, such had been rare. Ron immediately accepted the invitation and I went, but only reluctantly. While I truly had worked on forgiveness as I told you above, it was as if I expected my birthday to be a "day off" in that direction.

But my husband would have none of that! And, I realized later that he was correct, as usual, in accepting the invitation. However, I realized that I had not come quite as far as I had imagined in the process of forgiveness! Just when you think you have conquered something negative in your life, it seems that the adversary always raises his ugly head.

And yet, the good news is that that lunch was the beginning of a better relationship between the four of us. We were even invited to visit Mother and Dad in the condominium in California to which they had moved after my brother became president of ORU. While at first Ron and I became adept at staying with "safe subjects" like the weather and my parents' health, things gradually became much better.

With all of my faults, I can tell you truthfully as well that I had prayed faithfully for my parents, particularly my father, that the Lord would turn his heart to mine, as stated in Malachi. While Ron did not seem to struggle even occasionally with a bad attitude toward my parents as did I, he had admittedly lost all hope that Oral Roberts would ever turn his heart to his little girl. But I could be just as stubborn as my father and would not give up! I prayed and I prayed and, well, I prayed some more.

A Wonderful Day

Then came October 28, 2002, a day which shall live in…happiness! I was visiting Mother and Dad in California and for a reason I have now forgotten, Ron had not come with me on that visit. One evening, Mother had already sought her bed, but Dad and I remained awake, sitting in the den. By that time, Dad's hearing was not what it had been, so to communicate with him, one had to sit within a close proximity.

Seemingly out of nowhere, Dad actually apologized to me for the way he had treated me when I was at ORU. It was the first time he had ever apologized to me for anything in my entire life. He was so abjectly sorry that he almost broke down and cried. I was, well, I do not have the appropriate words to describe my excitement. It was not one of those apologies which states: "If I hurt you, I'm sorry" or "I didn't mean to." On the contrary, it was heartfelt and so very sincere. My heart went out to him as his struggle to force the words from his mouth was patently clear. The only time I had ever seen such transparency and warmheartedness from my father had been when he was praying for the sick—and then usually just with strangers who needed healing. Caring for hurting people came easily to him. That had been God's greatest gift to him. But it was far different to show that side of himself to someone he knew, particularly, well...to me. No, he had never shown that side of himself to me, but he did that night.

You would think that I would have gloried in his pronouncements of sorrow for past conduct and would have wanted him to go on and on and on. After all, I had waited an excruciatingly long time for any kind of softness to come toward me from my father, of all people! But no, I ached for him far too much to allow him to continue. I interrupted him and said, "Oh Dad. I forgave you a long time ago!"

What was so amazing to me about that night we had together was his response. He said "I know. That's what has bothered me all these years. I knew you had not only forgiven me but were praying for me, and have been for a very long time." I almost lost it then. It is one thing to pray for someone, but when that person KNOWS and really feels your prayers, well, I would need a ghostwriter to better express to you the emotions I experienced that evening. Phenomenal, incredible, awesome…none of those words are sufficient to express my gratitude to God for that night!

The following morning, when my mother and I were fixing breakfast, I told her what had happened the night before. She said, "I've been telling him to apologize to you for a long time now but he just couldn't do it. I'm so thrilled he's finally gotten the words out!" He whose very name meant "spoken word" had a tough time expressing himself? He who could wow audiences with his uncommon oratory had difficulty saying what he meant? Yes, even him!

But it actually was not until after my mother's passing when Dad and I finally began to have a more normal father-daughter relationship. A good deal of the credit for that is legitimately due to my husband. Ron understood as no one else, least of all Dad and me, that while Dad and I still seemed to clash, much of it was because we were so alike. He it was who suggested that I start writing letters to Dad.

By that time of course, Dad was terribly lonely after losing "his daring wife, Evelyn." While we had urged him to move back to Tulsa upon my mother's death, I suspect that part of his reluctance was a desire to allow my brother, Richard to have free reign at the University but also because my father was a little too proud to let the good folks of Tulsa and the ORU community see how old and feeble he had become. Oh the male ego! It cannot be tamed any more than the tongue! At any rate, Ron believed that letters from me to Dad would not only help with Dad's loneliness but might somehow assist in pushing the two of us beyond the initial threshold which had always stopped the bulk of communication between us.

So I began writing letters to Dad and Ron's observations proved to be correct. I believe for the first time, Dad began to see the heart of his younger daughter. He was overwhelmed at the principles of his ministry I had remembered and applied to my life over the years. He never knew. It is interesting that, years before, when encouraging his partners to write letters to him, Dad would say: "There's something about a letter." And he had been correct all those years before.

Perhaps only two or three months before Dad's passing, he started saying that I simply did not write him enough letters. He even talked of collaborating on a book together, a book in which our letters to each other would be published. Even though my father's life ended before this was possible, there are no words to express the change that had occurred in Dad's perception of his only living daughter. Some of the people who stopped by my Dad's condominium during his last days told me later that Dad had actually read my letters to them out loud! He was proud of me!

Now granted, by this time, Dad had realized many things about my brother. By this time he had lost ORU and was continuing to suffer due to the events of that time. Ron did not tell me until after Dad's passing that during this time, Dad told Ron that all those years ago, he had never known how much I loved his ministry and the University—until it was too late. I have no regrets, however. I realize more than anyone that I had contributed to the years of our lack of understanding for each other by my own stubborn pride. Even more importantly, however, is the fact that God used all of these things in my life for my good. The hurt had only strengthened me. The hurt had only driven me to the things of God.

And in the end, my little girl dream of "Let me touch him" finally came true and he was finally proud of me.

And while he was gone so often when I was a little girl, and while he could be so remote even when home, he touched a lot of other people, in such dramatic ways. Who knows how many people are now in Heaven or on their way to Heaven because of my father? Only God knows. I am so proud of what he did for the world! He did bring God's healing power to his generation. And overall, I have still managed to have a great life, despite the hardships I have related in this chapter. I married a wonderful man. His family—his brothers and sister and especially his parents, bent over backwards to show me the love I missed in my own family.

What was significantly more important, however, was that I met Jesus at an early age. I met the One who has never made a mistake, who was always in town, and as Dad used to say: the One "who was closer to me than the very breath in my nostrils." How could I possibly complain?

You will see above that I named this chapter after a Vep Ellis song called "Let Me Touch Him." I played that song on the organ many times in my Dad's crusades. I remember Vep singing that song before the great audience under the crusade tent. Although I experienced that feeling about my father ("Let me touch him!") up until a year or so before his passing, at the same time God Himself was longing to touch the people He had created, and He chose my father.

He chose Oral Roberts to reach out and touch those people, many of whom were themselves longing to touch their Creator. When Dad heard the voice of God for the very first time—calling him to bring God's healing power to his generation, he had two options. He could ignore the call and thereby be at home for this little girl—as so many fathers are for their daughters. Of course had he made that choice, it would have been as if fire were shut up in his bones, as described in the Book of Jeremiah. Or, he could carry out the call of God as best he could, thereby causing his little girl to believe that he was simply ignoring her. And he could trust His faithful Creator to show Himself to his daughter, even when she was almost too young to understand who He was.

So am I sorry he made the choice that he did? Absolutely not! He did the right thing, for Jesus did in fact show Himself to me. Here I am 60 years old with few regrets. Because Jesus showed Himself to me as a child, I escaped many of the painful memories which have now come back to haunt many of my contemporaries. Yes, when I was a teenager many of them saw me as "little miss goody two shoes," but I did not care. God meant it all to me for good!

And the icing on the cake is that finally—after all the years and all the excruciatingly painful misunderstandings between us—I got to touch my father. We developed a closeness we had never, ever experienced.

But more importantly to my own individual existence, I got to touch Jesus, because of my father. How can I possibly argue with the decision of Oral Roberts to touch the world, for when my earthly father was gone to reach those hurting people, my heavenly father was with me. He never goes out of town!

I can still see Vep Ellis standing on the platform of Dad's crusades singing this song:

> Let me touch Him, let me touch Jesus.
> Let me touch Him as He passes by.
> Then when I shall reach out to others,
> They shall know Him, they shall live and not die.
> Oh, to be His hand extended,
> Reaching out to the oppressed;
> Let me touch Him, let me touch Jesus,
> So that others may know and be blessed.

For my yoke is easy, and my burden is light.

—Matthew 11:30 (KJV)

"KNOWN ONLY TO HIM"

Chapter 16

Having already appropriated an entire chapter in order to discuss Dad's relationship with this author, I would of course omit an important part of my father's story if I did not add to the material I have already related to you about Dad's other three children.

My sister, Rebecca, was the oldest of the four children of Oral and Evelyn Roberts. She was almost a second mother to me, especially during my teenage years as Mother and Dad were out of town so often. This may also have been the case because she was 11 years older than her little sister, Roberta. Rebecca was born when Mother and Dad were pastoring before he began the evangelistic ministry for which he became famous.

In some ways, she and I had different backgrounds for by the time I came along, Dad was already a famous evangelist. I did not have the pressures Rebecca felt, as her girlhood was spent with a daddy who was a pastor. For those of you who were not raised in the church, at least in the early and mid-1940's, when your daddy is the pastor, certain things are expected of you. It did not take Rebecca long to understand that if she did not meet those expectations: hair always perfect, dress ironed perfectly, etc., etc., etc., she would face certain ostracism not only from her parents but from all of those who attended her daddy's church.

While there were certainly expectations placed upon me, the intensity was on a lower level as I did not face the scrutiny of those lovely ladies in the church as had Rebecca. It was certainly not easy for her as the older child of Pastor Roberts.

When she was 19, Rebecca married Marshall Nash. In 1977, my husband and I were living in Colorado. Rebecca and Marshall had been on a vacation in another part of Colorado when they stopped in Denver to see us. They were considering whether or not to purchase an airplane and asked Ron to travel with them on a "test run." At the last minute, Ron decided not to go. It was on that flight when the plane carrying Rebecca and Marshall crashed over Kansas, killing Rebecca and Marshall as well as the pilot and his wife.

The affect on Dad and our family was immense. I suppose I should tell you about the television special Dad made, requiring the presence of each of his remaining children and their spouses to participate. Perhaps I was wrong to have had a bad attitude regarding being pressured to appear on that program. Some said that the television program about Rebecca and Marshall's death was very moving and was something that helped them to face their own struggles. I certainly hope it did, however, I have to admit that being expected to take part in a television program—to be aired all over the country—so terribly soon after losing my only sister was beyond onerous for me.

The only reason I mention that long ago event, however, is because I believe it will give the reader additional insight into the individual who was my father. We are all different of course. My reaction to the pain of losing my sister was to retreat even further into myself. My last response would have been to discuss any of my feelings on nationwide television. However, once he passed his shy childhood years, expressing his feelings publicly became a part of what Oral Roberts was all about.

While even my father had certain things in his life he preferred to keep to himself, I suspect opening our hurts for the world to see and hear may have been cathartic for him. As difficult as it was for me, the program seemed to aid my father with continuing on, despite the terrible loss.

Ronnie was the next of Dad's children to be born after Rebecca. He and I were very close, although not as close as Rebecca and I had been. Ronnie had been brought up to be Dad's successor but never seemed comfortable with that plan, or with his life for that matter. Although some have blamed Ronnie's eventual suicide in 1982 on my parents, I have never subscribed to that viewpoint. Yes, my Dad did exert a tremendous amount of pressure on Ronnie. However, those pressures alone were insufficient, at least in my view, to have caused such an extreme response.

No, Ronnie was fighting other demons in his life, some of which I discussed in an earlier chapter. And, as much as I loved him, I would be less than honest if I did not tell you that he was simply not a strong person. Having said that, he was one of the most caring individuals I have ever known. He had a tender heart that was, well, an indescribable loss.

While both Rebecca and Ronnie deeply loved their father, it is difficult for me to put into words the occasional acrimony felt and shown by each of them toward their father. All three of us came to a time in our lives when we realized that if Dad had any strong interest in his children, it was much more for our brother, Richard, than for any of us.

Richard, who is two years older than this author was always so full of life—from the time he was a small child. He had such obvious talents, such abilities, such potential. He was personality plus, an attribute which, well, none of the rest of us had. While each of the children of Oral Roberts had their own God-given talents and abilities, it was those given to Richard which were so tangible. To be sure, the capabilities of the rest of us were there, but they were not nearly as apparent.

Have I told you too often in this book that Dad's ministry and the University was his life? Almost every thought was geared toward his ministry and actually, in Dad's mind the University was simply an extension of his ministry. If he saw an entertaining program on television, he only watched it to see if there were any ideas he could use in his ministry. If he liked a movie, it was because he learned a concept in the movie which he could either use in the University or use as an illustration in a sermon. Even when he played a round of golf, it was never to simply relax as most men do. Oh no, not my father. He was either dreaming some new dream or striking up a relationship with a person who could potentially help ORU. Or maybe he was thinking about a sermon he was getting ready to preach.

Even the hours he spent talking about athletics to my husband and to so many others over the years was never solely for the sake of athletics or for his own enjoyment. No, it was so that ORU would have good teams, which would put ORU on the front page of the newspapers, which would bring in donations and help recruit students. I honestly cannot tell you of one thing in Dad's life which did not somehow relate to his ministry. Yes, he relaxed his body on occasion, but the wheels in that brain of his were almost constantly turning. He was always learning, always searching, always looking for one more idea, one more dream, one more way to get God's Word to more hurting people. Of course that is why he had such difficulty sleeping—because he could not seem to stop those wheels in his brain from their continual whirring.

He ate, drank and slept ORU as I have said, bringing in students, keeping the physical plant sharp, maintaining the academic excellence, raising the funds which were necessary in order to subsidize the tuition paid by the students, and so forth.

His ministry—which encompassed Oral Roberts University—was the focal point of his life, the very meaning of his existence. If Dad met a person he had never met before, his first thought was: "Could this person help the ministry?"

Since he looked at his children in the same way, what do you suppose he found? It was Richard who had the musical talents, at least to a far greater degree than the rest of us. It was Richard who had the incredible gifts so easily recognized by the naked eye. It was Richard who was perfectly comfortable on a platform even as a small child. Looking back, it is far easier for me to understand why Dad was so drawn to Richard. What father in Dad's position would not have seen Richard as the one who could carry on the dreams and visions he had received from God?

So were the rest of us jealous of Richard? Yes, I suppose we were in varying degrees. I suppose what is so ironic is that with all the attention which Dad lavished upon his younger son, Richard was willing to accept the benefits, but without ever having a strong commitment to meet the expectations which came with those benefits. On the other hand I have to say on Richard's behalf that he felt smothered. He felt incredibly pressured and at one time told Dad: "Get off my back!" I am not sure that in his innermost being Richard was ever truly interested in "receiving" a ministry and University from his father, however, he could not bring himself to say no.

At any rate, it was not until several months after lawsuits were filed against ORU (mentioned in an earlier chapter) when Dad began to realize who Richard really was. He so wanted Richard to be a "little Oral Roberts" and of course, no one could have been what Dad wanted even if they tried much harder than Richard ever had.

I cannot totally exculpate my brother, though, as he seemed all too willing to bask in his father's love while never, at least in my mind, understanding the dream and the vision of the University. The purpose of course was to help people—to meet people at the point of their needs just as in Dad's ministry. I am not sure that Richard ever truly appropriated that notion to himself, nor was the University ever Richard's passion as Dad had so hoped.

In the end, once the true reality dawned upon Dad, it was the greatest disappointment of his life. With all of his triumphs, and despite whatever other mistakes he had made, Oral Roberts died with an almost incurable pain and disappointment that his son was far more interested in himself and his family than with the concerns of the University which

God had asked his father to build. And why was this the case? Because it was a bad fit for Richard in the first place.

Interestingly, when Richard was married to his first wife, Patti, in the early 1970's, I remember her begging him repeatedly to leave his father's ministry and go with her—anywhere—in order to remove themselves from the pressure his father was putting upon him. Had Richard been willing, would things have been different for him? We will never know, but I will say that we judge Richard far too harshly when we totally castigate him for the things I have described to you above.

He had expectations put upon him he simply could not handle and for which he was ill-equipped from the beginning, for, it was not his dream. It was his father's dream and never something that became a part of his own psyche as it had his father. You cannot put your vision onto another person. You cannot cause a vision you received from the Lord to be transferred into the mind of another person. We must each have a vision from God ourselves. Vision cannot be passed on from father to son. It must come directly from God! Yes, an individual can be called to another person's vision, but only if that person chooses such, not because of the pressure from another.

Okay, I realize that all the pastors and evangelists who are reading this book may now feel like throwing this book into the nearest trash can, where there is weeping and gnashing of teeth. Yes, it is common for ministers to pass on their ministries to their sons or to other family members. I would just say to those who have decided to plod through this chapter despite their outrage, that it is incumbent upon a minister to hear from God as to his successor.

A ministry is not like a house or car or bank account which can be given to a person in your will. It is not yours to give. It belongs to God and never, ever to a person. Only God knows the future of a ministry. Only God knows the end from the beginning. And only God can raise up a successor. That person may well be the son or perhaps another relative of the founder. Conversely, the successor chosen by God may have no biological relationship to the founder!

When these decisions are made by man, it puts a yoke on the person chosen but not called of God for a specific task. Man's yoke is heavy and ill-fitting. God has a yoke alright, but it fits! Whatever mistakes Dad may have made, the yoke upon his shoulders was what God had raised him up to do—whether it was praying for the sick or educating young people to change the world. God's calling upon Dad fit, and it fit beautifully.

There was a song which was often sung by Bob Daniels in Dad's crusades which I remember well. It carries a message we Christians sometimes forget:

> Known only to Him are the great hidden secrets
> I'll fear not the darkness when my flame shall dim.
> I know not what the future holds
> But I know who holds the future
> It's a secret known only to Him.

And what shall I more say? For the time would fail me to tell of...

—*Hebrews 11:32 (KJV)*

"THE WONDER"

Chapter 17

"Paraclete" is a Greek word Dad used, particularly when he taught a course on the Holy Spirit at ORU. He often spoke of paraclete as meaning "one called alongside to help." Of course he was speaking of the Holy Spirit and my purpose is not in any way to equate human beings with the Holy Spirit. Having said that, however, I find that the term paraclete could also be employed to describe those individuals called of God to make it possible for Dad to do what the Lord had asked *him* to do. A book about Dad would be far from accurate if I failed to mention the scores of people who were there for my Dad, in so many different ways.

Now I will ask you, dear reader, to forgive me for any lapses in my memory. Or, perhaps I did not mention a certain individual because I am unaware of the contributions that were made. And of course, I have already mentioned some of the individuals who were so instrumental in Dad's ministry. So I implore you to have some understanding and realize that the following chapter is simply an effort, albeit incomplete, to say thank you publicly to at least a few of those special people who answered the call of God to help my father.

And by the way, if you have not already discerned it from previous chapters, Oral Roberts was not exactly a person who was easy to please, nor was he always so nice to be around. Sorry, folks, I cannot tell a lie. He was susceptible to mood swings. More importantly, he was driven. The Bible tells us that tribulation brings patience, therefore, let me just say that these folks must have acquired vast quantities of patience. They sometimes endured *great* tribulation when working for or with, or sometimes even just being around my father for long periods of time. Need I tell you that those folks received very little financial remuneration for their incredible contributions? All I can say is, great will be their reward in Heaven.

While it is a wonder that these folks were willing to deal with the downside, they must have realized that lurking beneath the short bursts of temper was something incredibly valuable for the world. As I type these words, I am imagining my Dad reading this over my shoulder. I know what he would be doing. He would be chuckling and saying, "Well she's got that right!" For despite his sometimes difficult side, he also had a sense of humor, and thank God, well recognized at least most of his faults.

The Wonder

Telling my readers that it was a wonder for so many people to have been willing to help Dad in what he was attempting to do for God over the years reminds me of a man named David Ingles. While David Ingles is now the CEO of a radio network (The Oasis Network based here in Oklahoma), in the early 1960's, he was a fledgling songwriter. You will remember me mentioning Bob Daniels earlier in the book, one of my Dad's crusade soloists who I formerly (and mistakenly of course!) believed was God Himself. David Ingles had just written a song called "The Wonder" and wanted Bob Daniels to sing it in Dad's crusades. So he brought the song one day to the office of Dad's evangelistic association (OREA), in downtown Tulsa at the time.

David Ingles' visit that day must have been ordained of God because he not only was successful in "pitching" his song to Bob Daniels, but he also met the woman of his dreams, Sharon Tucker, who was at that time working there. At any rate, while the song is certainly about Jesus, I believe it is not inappropriate to quote its chorus in order to express my gratefulness to those wonderful people who, despite the difficulties, did come alongside my father to help:

> *The Wonder*
> Dear Jesus, dear Jesus what a wonder you are,
> You are brighter than the morning star;
> You're fairer, much dearer than the lily that grows by the way,
> You're more precious, more precious than gold.

I begin with a precious woman of God named Ruth (Hanson) Rooks.

She was Dad's very first employee and began working for him when she was a young girl in 1947. Over the years, she considered herself "on call" virtually night and day for anything Dad might need. By the time of Dad's death, even though Ruth no longer received a salary, she continued to volunteer on his behalf and is continuing to do so at the time of this writing. That is in the neighborhood of around 63 years, by the way! While I could easily pen an entire chapter on this lady, Ruth has always abhorred attention, therefore for her sake, and only for her sake, I will limit my remarks.

I want the world to know—despite her reticence—that she was without question one of the most loyal people God ever created. She it was who would listen kindly when this author complained about her boss (are you shocked?). After my complaints, she would quietly and patiently remind me of one of the good points of the man who was my father. And of course all of this was despite his incredibly demanding nature which she experienced on a daily basis. Well, all I can say is thank you, God, that you called Ruth to help Dad. What a lady!

I have already mentioned Bob DeWeese, Dad's associate evangelist. I will never forget his booming voice and his incredible sense of

Here are pictures of Ruth, both when she first started working for Dad as a stenographer in 1947, then later at the University in 1976, along with Jan Dudley, Vivian Smith, Ferne Howell, and this author who was about two months away from delivering her second child!

humor. As I noted earlier, Bob preached in the afternoons at Dad's crusades. I suspect as well that Bob may have been one of the best friends Dad ever had. If there was time, the two of them would venture onto a golf course in the mornings before they were both scheduled to preach later in the day—Bob in the afternoon and Dad in the evening. Here's a picture of Dad enjoying a round of golf as well as one with his "partner in crime," Bob DeWeese!

Say, "Amen!"

When I was in high school and playing the organ for Dad's meetings, I simply could not wait until the afternoon service had concluded so that I could rush back to the hotel, change into my swimsuit and bake in the sun. Of course I would only have an hour or so before it was time to shower and prepare for the evening service, however, to the teenager that I was, an hour was better than nothing.

So one day just before the afternoon service was to begin, I asked Brother DeWeese to keep his sermon short so that I would have more time to sit in the sun. All right, I admit to being immature! He responded, "Well, when you think I have preached long enough, just say "Amen" in a very loud voice and I will take that as a signal to finish my sermon. So after he had preached for perhaps thirty minutes, I said "Amen" at full volume. However, the sermon continued for at least another hour!

After the service, I asked Bob what in the world he was thinking and why he had the audacity of destroying my hopes for time in the sun. He responded with an ornery little gleam in his eye that when he heard my "Amen," he became so inspired that he just had to preach a little longer. And that was the last time I ever said "Amen" during a sermon.

But Bob DeWeese's story would remain untold if I did not tell you about the rousing duet he and his wife, Charlotte sang in Dad's crusades. They sang a song that pre-dated "Oh Blessed Holy Spirit" by Vep Ellis which I have discussed in an earlier chapter. "Pentecostal Fire is Falling," though, was just as powerful in its day. I cannot forget the two of them standing on the platform singing that song. The best part of the song for me was toward the end. The chorus went like this:

> Pentecostal Fire is Falling, Falling,
> Praise the Lord it fell on me.
> Pentecostal Fire is Falling;
> Brother, let it fall on thee!

Never let it be said that Robert F. DeWeese was shy about what he believed! Speaking in tongues was controversial then as it is now. On the last line of the song instead of merely singing: "*Brother*, let it fall on thee," he and Charlotte would point at members of the audience at random, at my father, and at the sponsoring pastors while singing boisterously:

Brother, Sister, Baptists, Methodists, Presbyterians, Lutherans, Brother Roberts, and Sponsoring Pastors, "Let it fall on THEE!"

For those of you who are unaware, many of the folks in the above denominations do not believe in the Baptism of the Holy Spirit! Therefore, the song took great courage—and yet, Bob and Charlotte had such loving smiles on their faces that it was difficult for any offense to be taken. The song contained both power *and* charm!

Talk about an unsung hero, Collins Steele was the man who was responsible for hiring the temporary workers to put up the tent and to later take it down. He and his sweet wife, Lois, acted as an advance team to put everything into readiness for Dad's crusades. Because of people like Collins Steele and others, Dad was able to simply walk onto the platform and begin preaching. But it was no small undertaking for Collins to make all of the arrangements for a large crusade to actually happen. The truth is, I have no idea of the things that had to be done both before and after—for I was sheltered from all of that. But oh, what a blessing Collins and Lois were to my father—and to me.

There was E.J. Fulton who was responsible to recruit and train volunteers to follow-up and add a personal touch for the people who met Jesus, as a result of Dad's sermons. Music even played a part in his training of the volunteers. Each volunteer was given a packet of information, including materials such as helps in studying the Bible to hand to those who came to the altar. The packet also included a badge that would identify the volunteer as a "personal worker."

As the crusades lasted anywhere from five days to several weeks, Brother Fulton did not want the personal workers to forget their badges on each successive evening. So he came up with a cute little ditty, sung to the song: "Give Me That Old-Time Religion:"

> Put your badge in the packet,
> Put your badge in the packet,
> Put your badge in the packet
> And put it in the box!

He was one of those rare individuals who could give instructions and make it fun for all. Inside the packet was a card for each person who had been converted to Jesus in the meeting, to fill in the name and address. When the crusade was over, those cards would be divided up (evenly!) between each of the sponsoring pastors. Many of those pastors went door to door after the meetings, visiting with those folks—and doubled the size of their churches!

It was E.J. Fulton's son, Bob, who played the organ at many of Dad's crusades (after Roberta and Geneva Millard). Oh what a wonderful organist he was.

I have talked about the great songwriter and singer, Vep Ellis, many times already but I simply must tell you how particularly kind he was to me. When you are the very shy daughter of someone who everyone (well, at least the people I was around anyway) thinks is so special, you tend to feel a little lost. Vep Ellis was so incredibly kind to me. Without ever saying it, Vep showed that he understood my plight—my loneliness, and was so kind to a little girl who so often just felt in the way.

One particular morning while waiting for my mother to bring something to Dad at his office at OREA, I found myself in front of Vep's desk. We talked for a bit and then, inevitably, I needed to use the restroom but could not remember where it was. An artist as well as a talented musician, Vep drew a quick sketch for me, mapping the exact directions to the restroom. What was so notable was that he used quick drawings of his co-workers as guideposts. In the drawing, George Fisher was drawn as a big fish, Bill Armstrong was depicted as a strong arm, and so forth. While I unfortunately lost that little map long ago, I do still have some of Vep's drawings.

He was pretty good, wasn't he?

There were people like my Dad's brother Vaden, George Stovall (who just retired after 55 loyal years!), Al Bush, Ron Smith, Hart Armstrong, Hilliard Griffin, Myron Sackett, George Fisher, Bill Sterne, Dub Jeffers (who later developed "Discoveryland!" just outside of Tulsa with a beautiful rendition of the Broadway play "Oklahoma!), Pearl Curtis,

J.O. Work, Bob Fraley, Pat Griffin, Leon Hartz, Joe Jewell, May Long, Charles Ramsay, Howard Dessinger, Bill Armstrong, Elaine Drain (Taylor), Manford Engel, Willard Mason, Diane Peterson, Barbara Favors, and so many, many others who helped Dad in the evangelistic association.

There was Jim Nash who took pictures of the crusades. (His brother, Marshall Nash, later married my sister, Rebecca.)

Over the years, Dad was very wise to obtain excellent legal counsel. It should not surprise you that I cannot cannot resist the opportunity of touting my own profession! Men like Saul Yager, Don Moyers, Jack Santee and others. Without Don Moyers' influence, there would have been no building called "Mabee Center" at Oral Roberts University— for it was Don who originally had a relationship with individuals at the Mabee Foundation in order to make that gift possible. I am so grateful to God that Dad was able to find lawyers such as the above.

Then there was Rex Humbard of the fame of Cathedral of Tomorrow in Ohio who went to one of Dad's crusades and was the first to tell him: "You must put this on television!" Only God knows the difference which was made in people's lives because of this great man of God.

While I complained earlier about being with babysitters so often, it is true that these folks made it possible for Dad to do his work. As I mentioned, some of them were not so great, however, others were absolutely jewels, for example Opal Kay (Bullock), Elizabeth Burnett and Bob and Anita Pratt. What a blessing they were in our lives!

Then when the University came along, there were the founding Regents and others who came later to serve on the Board, people like Ernest Simpson, Michael Cardone, Sr., then later, his son, Michael Cardone, Jr. What a fine family of folks in love with Jesus!

I remember a fun trip when our family visited the Cardones in Philadelphia when I was a teenager. I recently ran across this picture, taken of Mother and Dad in the Cardone's living room.

Even the famous Pat Boone put down his "Love Letters in the Sand" long enough to become an Oral Roberts University Regent. There was Darrell Hon and later, his son, Barry. What a wonderful contribution they made, in so many ways. There was Velmer Gardner, Frank Holder and Jerry Melilli, Lowell Merrill, John Wellons, John and Nona Askew, Frank Foglio, Irby then Jack Shaw, Jere Melilli, Charles Trebilcock, John Whitsitt, Nick Timko, Bill Swad, Bob Zoppelt, Charlie Watson, Bill Howard and later his son, Scott, Jimmy Pattison, Martin Wirkkala, Eldon Thorman, Dr. John Barton, and Bill Reiff. The first Chairman of the Board was S. Lee Braxton, a man with innumerable contacts who loved my father as a brother. Bob DeWeese, who had been that loyal associate evangelist in Dad's crusades, was Chairman of the Board after Lee Braxton's retirement.

There were many folks who were able to help with large financial donations like Eleanor Reese Hamill, Marajen Chinigo, Sam and Isabelle Graham, Anna Vaughn Benz, Mike Hammer, Barbara Newington and Bailie Vinson. Of course I have already mentioned the wonderful people of the Mabee Foundation.

And one of the stories I remember, funny, yet oh-so-serious. Toward the beginning of his effort to begin Oral Roberts University, Dad had attempted to obtain a rather large loan from several Tulsa banks, but to no avail. There was one particular bank with which Dad wished to do business, but simply could not get past the front door. It was Walt Helmerich who came to the rescue, however not in a way you might think. Now this was about 50 years ago, so my facts will not be perfect.

What I remember, though, is that Walt Helmerich had a relationship with a competitor of the bank with which Dad desired to do business. I do not remember the exact relationship, but whatever it was, it was strong indeed. But more than that, the Helmerichs were and still are movers and shakers in the City of Tulsa. Their word was gold, if you will—and they liked and I believe, respected my parents.

When Walt Helmerich learned that Dad was having difficulty obtaining the loan, he simply invited Dad to lunch. How would that help, you ask? Well, he took Dad to lunch at a restaurant where he "just happened to know" the president of the other bank would be eating that day. Dad and Mr. Helmerich had a nice lunch, and ostensibly, that was all. It was later that afternoon, though, when the president of the bank from whom Dad wanted a loan called Oral Roberts and said: "You can have your loan!" One of the first buildings constructed on the ORU campus was begun with those funds. So what difference did the lunch make? Apparently, when the bank president saw Oral Roberts having lunch with Walt Helmerich, he began to see Dad in a completely different light, and I suppose he assumed that he would lose a lot of future business, perhaps in more ways than one, if he did not make the loan. And the rest, as they say, is history.

Although I do not remember ever hearing how Dad and Mother had become so close to Walt and Cadijah Helmerich, I do know how they valued that friendship, not only because of the influence of the Helmerich family which I have described, but also because of their many kindnesses to my parents over the years.

Of course, there were others in the Tulsa community who helped smooth Dad's path in so many ways. People like John Williams, Doug Mobley, Otis Winters, Charlie Kothe and Whitley Cox.

I have mentioned a number of individuals who gave large gifts to the ministry and also to the University. Dad was so incredibly appreciative of those gifts. I have already told you about the partners in a previous chapter, however, if people in Heaven can get angry at people on earth, Dad would be very frustrated with me if I did not mention these folks again and again and again in any book about him. These were the ones whom he knew he could rely upon month after month after month, if for small amounts.

The partners were the lifeblood of his ministry and he well realized it. Therefore, Dad spent a great deal of time writing what he called the monthly letters. These were letters to his partners and no, there was no time for Dad to personally write an individual letter to each of his partners. Such would have been a physical impossibility. There were so many of them, thank God! However, he did spend many hours every month writing a letter he knew that with the help of his co-workers in his evangelistic association, would reach his partners and would minister to them. He wanted to give something back. I simply cannot overestimate how Dad valued every single person who ever gave gifts to his ministry, whether large or small.

There was Demos Shakarian who founded the Full Gospel Businessmen's Association. Oh what a friend he was. In difficult times, Dad would often call on Demos. I can hear Dad changing the pronunciation so that what was supposed to be a short "o" became a long "o" so that his friend's name sounded like: "De Most." It was clearly a term of endearment, just for Demos.

There was Steve Strang of Charisma Magazine, Jenk Jones of the Tulsa Tribune, and other members of the media, who were Dad's true friends.

Then there were the administration at ORU. It was Dr. John Messick who most emphasized to Dad the idea of academic excellence. There were men like Bill Jernigan, Charles Ramsay and his son, Chuck, Carl Hamilton, Bob Eskridge and Bob Brooks—and oh, so many others.

There were Kenneth and Millie Cooper who inspired the Aerobics Center at Oral Roberts University (a place which claims responsibility for much blood, sweat and tears over the years—well, mainly just sweat but...)

And how can I appropriately thank the faculty? People like Harold Paul, R.O. and W.R. Corvin, Howard Ervin, Gene Eland, Bernis Duke, Harold Greenlee, Joyce Bridgman, Steve Durasoff, Seong Ja Park, Verbal Snook, Barbara Trisler (now Silvers), Nate Meleen, George Gillen, Bill Epperson, Roy Hayden, Grady Walker, Henry Migliore, Sherrod Braxton, Warren Straton who also designed the Abundant Life Mural which I described earlier, and later his wife, Eileen joined the faculty. There was my wonderful history professor, Franklin Sexton and later his wife, Ruth. There was Duane Thurman who I can still hear saying that it took just as much faith to believe in evolution as it does to believe in the Bible! There was John Tuel, Ray and Carole Lewandowski, Grant Moore, Betty Knott, Tomine Tjelta, Evelyn Davis, Irvine Harrison and I have already mentioned Lavoy Hatchett and Alice Rasmussen.

There was Roger Tuttle who encouraged his law students to "go out and fight the Philistines!" And how could I forget John Eidesmoe who taught us to integrate the Bible into the law. There were other wonderful professors in ORU's law school such as Tom Goldman and Gary Lane. And no matter how you feel about Anita Hill (who later spoke before Congress in opposition to the appointment of Supreme Court Justice, Clarence Thomas), I remember her as a wonderful person when she taught—ironically—a course on employment discrimination!

And these people are representative of many others who have taught at ORU over the years—at great personal sacrifice to their own incomes. What an influence they had upon us when we were at such impressionable ages.

There were people such as Jo Frailer in the ORU dorms. Jo was pretty hard on me, I recall, and guess what? She was exactly what I needed. Then there was my sweet aunt, Kathleen Green (my mother's sister) and her co-worker Sarah Robertson who held down the fort at the ORU switchboard for more years than they would appreciate me conveying to you. There were people like Tommy Tyson, Julie Tierney, Sheree King, Jeff Ogle, Bill McFarland, David Owen, Bill McQueen, Dr. Don Loveless, Vernon Hale, Dorothea Heit, Vivian Smith, Dave Weeden, Phil Cooke, Ed Blotevogel, Gwen and Jerry Culver, Roger Rydin, Adam Sewards, Bill Montgomery and so many others.

I will never forget the intervention of Larry Johnson, a man who provided security for Dad. Picture this. We're at Mabee Center watching a basketball game. Larry was on the aisle seat, with Dad and Mother next to him, then Ron and I next to them. I'm just watching the play by play action, totally oblivious to anything else. Right before my unobservant eyes, Larry had jumped out of his chair, run down the steps, cuffed a man who was attempting to harm Dad, and was ushering him out of the building before I even realized what was going on! It all happened and was over within seconds. While unfortunately, that was just one of the times when Larry and others protected my father from "crazies," it was the only time I actually witnessed such an occurrence.

I thank God for Larry Johnson, Gary Gibson and other such observant individuals!

There was Rocky Roberts (my Dad's nephew) who handled things from a maintenance perspective. And Rocky's brother, Bill Roberts, was the one to whom Dad gave the credit for having saved the University at least a million dollars in building costs for the Mabee Center. I suspect that out of all of Dad's family, it may have been Bill Roberts who believed in Dad's ministry the most. There was Elsie Fisher who was for years the campus hostess after her husband, George who I mentioned earlier, suffered an untimely death.

There was of course O.W. Coburn, who gave the seed money for the law school. Every day when I went to class, I walked under a quotation engraved in large letters on the wall. It was former Chief Justice Burger saying, "Lawyers can be healers." I have never forgotten that in my twenty years of law practice and have endeavored to carry out that admonition.

Many of its graduates appreciated the wonderful influence which Oral Roberts University had in their lives. Ken Copeland is a notable example of these folks. From the time of his graduation, Ken began giving of his substance to ORU and stood by Dad through so much. "Thank you" is so inadequate to express my father's appreciation and deep love for Kenneth Copeland.

Of course there were other famous preachers who were wonderful friends to Oral Roberts and to his ministry. What is most interesting to me is the diversity of Dad's friends. How was it that he was friends with people as different as Billy Graham, Kenneth Hagin and Benny Hinn? Actually, a full list of Dad's friends would most likely shock the reader. Just as one example, consider this: Dad's list of friends included people like Creflo Dollar, Fred Price, E.V. Hill, Benson Idahosa and many other African American preachers and evangelists. And yet, when George Wallace, the famous pro-segregationist, was seriously injured by an assassin, can you guess who was willing to pray for him? (I understand Governor Wallace eventually apologized for his earlier position.)

And by the way, the concern of Oral Roberts for George Wallace was not demonstrated merely with a quiet prayer in a secret telephone call. Not my father! Oh no, he told the former Alabama governor that an ORU chapel service was about to begin and to wait for prayer until Dad could arrange for a line to be connected with the public address system during Chapel. He wanted the students to be backing him in prayer as well, plus I believe he was setting an example before us. And believe me, we got the message!

And what a remarkable chapel service that was. It took place before Christ's Chapel was built when chapel services were being held in Mabee Center. By the time the chapel service had almost come to its conclusion, some of these folks I have been telling you about—who were truly "wonders"—had managed to connect the phone call in time. This was in 1972, long before the Internet and other technological advances with which we are currently so blessed. I will never forget when Dad stood at the podium and asked us, students, faculty and administration, to reach out our hands in prayer to George Wallace.

Of course there were many African American students in the audience that day, but I do not remember hearing any complaints. We had been taught by our president that when someone asked for prayer, you were always there for them. I am not certain that the relationship between Dad and George Wallace would qualify as friendship. Perhaps one would see the two as merely having been acquaintances. However the relationship is framed, though, Dad showed us how to express the love of Jesus that day, in spite of the widely divergent viewpoint of the recipient.

There were wonderful pastors such as Ralph Wilkerson and Jeff Walker who were Dad's true friends. And there were so many others who came to Dad for mentoring during his final days on earth. Yes, Dad certainly gave into their lives, however, they gave into his as they helped to give Dad a sense of usefulness, particularly after my mother passed away.

Thank God for Dad's caregivers during his last days. Lovely ladies like Sunny Howard and others made life easier for him—and for his children!

Of course the newest "wonder" are the Green family, who heard the voice of God during one of Oral Roberts University's most trying hours. The Lord sent new wonders, people like Dr. Mark Rutland, ORU's new president, who were willing to, well, take us from where we were to where we needed to be.

And "What shall I more say? For the time would fail me to tell of..." well, so many more who truly were and are "wonders" in our eyes and more particularly, in the eyes of the Lord. I thank God that He called them to be paracletes to my father and that they answered the call. I thank God for their tremendous faithfulness and for the great sacrifices they made for His Kingdom. I pray He will reward them—as only He can!

Jesus answered, "I am the way and the truth..."
–John 14:6 (NIV)

"TELL IT LIKE IT IS"

Chapter 18

I n an earlier chapter I discussed Ralph Carmichael's role in Dad's television specials. His song entitled "Something Good is Going to Happen to You" would no doubt be the song now most associated with Oral Roberts. However, much of the other Ralph Carmichael music was featured on those specials as well. One of those songs was "Tell It Like It Is." The song, in part, proclaimed to those long-ago audiences:

> Let's tell the truth about the world we live in.
> Let's look at life and all that we hold dear.
> Let's check it now before it quickly passes.
> Truth is like a sphere-shaped object, more than just one simple side.
> Wait till all the facts are assembled; calmly think and then decide.

Thus, I simply must not conclude this book without giving you a few more personal insights into my father's character—some humorous and some—well, not so humorous. He was a man who could light up an audience by simply walking on stage and announcing to all: "Something GOOD is going to happen to you!" So who was that masked man?

"I Don't Have Time!"

—He loved basketball! Once the ORU basketball games were played in Mabee Center, he made certain that the seats reserved to him and my mother were away from the aisle. The trouble was that when people caught a glimpse of Oral Roberts at a basketball game, they wanted to talk to him. Apart from one instance I remember, these folks were almost always simply well-wishers. But he would have none of it, for he was unwilling to miss even one play of the game.

He was engrossed from the tip-off until the final second. I can still see him jumping up in his chair when a referee called a foul on the other team, and yelling to whoever would listen: "I saw him do it, I saw him do it!" And then if the ORU fans interpreted a foul as a "bad call" and filled the arena with "boos," Dad would stand up and wave his arms, attempting to stop the booing. I do not remember a time when Dad's efforts seemed to make an appreciable difference with the raucous crowd, but he was totally undaunted and never gave up trying!

—Sometimes people, particularly wealthy businessmen contacted Dad during a crusade, demanding an individual prayer because "I simply don't have time to sit through a long meeting!" And apparently, some of these folks had incredibly serious diseases. Dad's response could at times be sharp: "Well, you have time to die, don't you?"

—Dad had an incredible love and deep appreciation for the Jewish people. I was taught as a small child that you simply never criticize a Jew—not for any reason. Any judgment of the Jews that was appropriate was to be left only to God Himself. I was taught (and still believe strongly) that they are God's chosen people and that God's love for them will never be diminished, come what may. I would say that Dad took a middle ground as to what some are saying these days. He certainly did not agree with those who feel Jews are on a "different track" and therefore do not need to know Jesus.

On the other hand, they were still so very dear to him, despite the veil over their eyes described in the New Testament regarding Jesus being the Son of God. After all, they gave us the Bible, the entire Bible! Jesus Himself told us to live on every word that comes from the mouth of God. (Matthew 4:4) How can we call ourselves Christians—"little Christs" as they were named in Antioch—and legitimately sit in judgment of God's chosen people?

A King-Sized Question

Over the years, Larry King interviewed Dad several times on his popular "Larry King Live" program. While Larry King was always kind to Dad, he never failed to ask the difficult questions. Of course you may be aware that Mr. King is Jewish. I remember a particular interview Ron and I were watching on television at home. I always watched Dad's live interviews with a degree of anxiety, as it is oh so easy to say something that can easily be misunderstood. At any rate, it was toward the end of the program and I was beginning to relax when Larry King asked: "Oral, do you think Jews will go to Heaven if they don't accept Jesus as their Messiah?"

My first reaction was sheer panic, thinking, "Oh Lord, how is he going to answer that without offending Larry King, but at the same time not compromising what he knew to be true about Jesus?" Obviously, I should have known that Dad would be prepared for such a question, and he was. He reminded Larry King of a very long, now unfortunately obscure conversation between God and Abraham found in Genesis 18:23-33. Abraham was asking God whether or not He would still destroy the evil cities of Sodom and Gomorrah, even if they contained righteous people. In the course of the discussion, Abraham asked God a telling question: "Shall not the Judge of all the earth do right?" After describing those verses, Dad said: "God is the judge, not me. Whatever God's decision, He will do what is right!" Larry King was totally non-plussed. Unable to come up with a clever rejoinder, he simply let the subject drop.

You might be interested in knowing as well that Dad assigned a very kind gentleman, Dr. Myron Sackett, with the task of placing New Testaments written in Hebrew in many caves, both in Israel and Jordan. This was of course an evangelistic effort on behalf of the Jewish people, hoping particularly that those scriptures would be discovered during those coming days in which the Bible predicts a time of "Jacob's trouble." (Jeremiah 30:7)

Meeting Ben Gurion

I remember when Dad had an opportunity to meet with the first prime minister of Israel, David Ben Gurion. He met with Mr. Ben-Gurion in the kibbutz to which he had retired after the years of his incredible service to the young State of Israel. Dad and Mother visited Israel many times over the years, even before the Temple Mount in Jerusalem had become a part of the new State of Israel (in 1967). I am so incredibly proud of him for his stand for and love for the Jewish people.

—Unless it was truly necessary to keep something secret, my father often had difficulty—or perhaps he never even tried—keeping secrets. Funny how he seemed to be especially unable to keep the secrets of other people! He would tell his secretary, Ruth Rooks, not to let anyone know something, then later, he just could not seem to keep from spilling the beans. As Ruth used to say, many of those things were not really so secret. Dad just wanted to be the one to tell the secret!

For example, when I was pregnant with our first son, Dad persuaded Ron and I not to announce the upcoming birth for a while. The reason now escapes me. I just remember that at the time, his thinking sounded rational. That very evening, Dad was scheduled to preach in a Layman's Seminar on the ORU campus and I was scheduled to play the organ. This was 1974—in those long ago days when organs were still used in church services. Before he began his sermon, Dad could stand it no longer and announced to the audience that his younger daughter was expecting. Well, there went that secret!

Ron and I did not really mind, it was just that...well, you know. My revenge came by referring to my father for several months afterward as "Big Mouth," well, behind his back, anyway!

Living It

—While scoffers argued that the concept of Seed Faith (discussed in a previous chapter) was merely a disingenuous scheme used to increase his offerings, no one who knew him personally could have believed that of Oral Roberts. Dad did not just preach Seed Faith. He and my mother as well *lived* it. After Dad's passing, I had the opportunity to meet a Jewish gentleman who had attempted to teach Hebrew to my parents. I am embarrassed to tell you that I have since forgotten his name. Sir, if you are reading this book, I hope you believe in forgiveness!

According to this kind gentleman, it was apparently my mother who was much more serious about her studies, while my father was always having to reschedule or cancel his lessons due to other things taking place in his life. (Well, he was the president of a major university at the time!) At any rate, the man told me that in all the times he came over to their house, Dad would never let him leave without giving him something.

Sometimes it would be a book, sometimes it would be food or something of that sort. One time, Dad looked everywhere for something to give the man but simply could not find anything. So he reached into the freezer and pulled out something (I do not recall what it was) and handed it to his teacher! I just hope it was not a ham!

—By the time Mother and Dad left ORU to "retire" in California, they did not even have enough money in the bank in order to make a down payment on a house. Granted, California was a far more expensive place to live than Oklahoma, however, the point is that it seemed that every time my mother had managed to put a meaningful "nest egg" into the bank, Dad would start a new project. It might have been a new building at the University, or later when he began the City of Faith or perhaps he needed new equipment for broadcasting on television.

Dad would have a big fund-raising meeting somewhere, then come home to Mother full of excitement and yell: "Evelyn, how much do we have in our savings account?" He wanted to give to the new project! Mother generally began her protestations with: "Now Oral..." but within a few minutes, well, he would talk her out of a large chunk of whatever amount they had in savings! Now those amounts would have been small in comparison to what a wealthy person could have donated from *their* bank accounts, but in relationship to my parents' income, their gifts were always a very large amount. In fact, I do not remember any project Dad started without first giving what was for him (and my mother!) a large amount of money himself, as seed for the project.

A specific example of that was Mabee Center, ORU's large arena, which seats over 11,000. One afternoon Dad was sitting around a table with several other men. At that time, ORU's basketball team was playing ball in a small domed building on campus called the "Health Resources Center." Actually, I have wonderful memories of what students called "The Old Gym," but it could only hold maybe 3,000 people and was

by 1972, woefully inadequate. Now dear reader, it should be no surprise to you by now that Oral Roberts, the one who always said: "Make no little plans here" dreamed of a larger place for the team to play. Sitting around that table, he told the men about his dream and before long, each of them—including my father—emptied their wallets and laid their money at the center of the table.

The stack of money on that table, which must have seemed so small, eventually snowballed into an amount somewhere around $34 million and built a fabulous arena. And, in case you are wondering, after Dad's days of poverty as a child, he never carried less than $1,000 in cash in his wallet. I know because I peeked, more than once! (At least I did not abscond with any of it!)

Elvis Has Left the Building

Since that time, Mabee Center has hosted stars such as Elvis Presley, Frank Sinatra, Luciano Pavarotti, Garth Brooks, Kenny G, Tom Jones, Johnny Cash, Michael Bolton, Jay Leno, Kenny Rogers, the Beach Boys, Barry Manilow, Chicago, Reba McEntire, and many, many others. I wonder if any of the individuals who attended those concerts ever realized that they were sitting in a miracle?

—And speaking of miracles, for a man who grew up in overalls and bare feet, Oral Roberts managed to meet and talk with an astounding number of individuals most of us consider "important." Heads of state, government officials, people in the entertainment world, businessmen and leaders from many other walks of life as well. And he lived the Gospel before these folks. Romans 2:4 tells us that it is not judgment—but the goodness of God which leads people to change their lives and repent of their sins.

This was where Dad's love for people stood out like a beacon. He had a way of showing love to those who were far away from the Lord, without compromising the truth of the Gospel. Lots of famous "sinners" absolutely loved him for that. Occasionally they changed their lives for the Lord. More often than not, there was no visible change. However, they will never be able to go before the Lord and say "I didn't know!" if they met Oral Roberts. Even his fellow golfers saw the love of Jesus in Dad. Dad's sharpest criticism of this author, in fact, was that I was far too judgmental. While it  was slow in coming, I have made real strides in that area. He was certainly a wonderful example in my life.

—He was a terrible driver! He always had the strangest things happen to him as a result of driving. It was in the early 1970's when cars were first mass-produced with a "talking" mechanism inside. Dad had just purchased a new car but he was never one to spend hours poring over the instruction manual as some men. After he proudly drove home to show Mother his new car, he told her he planned to take the five-minute drive to the Aerobics Center at ORU in order to walk around the indoor exercise track.

The Aerobics Center contained a garage—for the sole use of the ORU President—and could be accessed with a "clicker," similar to the garage many of us have adjacent to our homes. The garage had no windows. On that occasion, over an hour after he left the house, Mother received a call from Dad. He was beside himself!

He had driven into the garage and closed the door behind him, intending to open the car door before the garage door was fully closed. You guessed it. Instead of grabbing the car door's handle, he mistakenly hit the automatic door locks and was quickly surrounded by total darkness. There he was—locked in the vehicle in a room which was pitch black, frantically attempting to break free! He was finally able to escape his temporary prison after about thirty minutes of incredible frustration. The best part of the story, though, was his phone call to Mother afterwards.

He kept repeating to Mother: "Evelyn, there's a woman in that garage! She kept talking to me but I could never find her!" No matter how many times Mother explained that what he had heard was simply a computer on his new car, Dad remained unconvinced. He was certain that there was a woman in that garage!

Banned

Speaking of the Aerobics Center, the road that leads to that building from the main part of the campus originally contained a rather sharp curve with a creek running many feet below. One afternoon, Dad was driving home on that road. As usual, he was concentrating on the next sermon he planned to preach—certainly not his driving. In short, he did not quite make the turn and it was only the guard rail which prevented his car from landing in the creek below. At least he did not attempt to hide such events from his wife.

Once he confessed his inattention at the wheel, my mother felt strangely "inspired" to forever ban him from driving. After that adventure, his darling wife Evelyn arranged for an ORU employee to drive him wherever necessary from that point forward. I can state unequivocally that such was a mercy—to us all! Amazing, when I subsequently began representing the innocent victims of negligent drivers, I did not feel led to make any connection whatsoever to that fateful incident.

— The memory of the impoverishment in which Dad found himself as a child never totally left him. Jesus was correct when he predicted in Mark 14:7 that there would always be people who were poor, and driving through poverty-stricken areas, particularly in Oklahoma, bothered Oral Roberts greatly. I recall an occasion when my husband had planned to drive him to speak in a different part of Oklahoma.

Dad decided at the last minute to fly rather than drive, despite the fact that driving would have taken no more than two hours or so. While he would never have admitted it to us, we understood that his reluctance was based upon what he knew he would see during that drive—coupled with those horrendous memories. He so desired to help people rise from their poverty.

Beloved

—He was loved by the ORU students, and then some. As a group, they referred to him as "The Big O" and he—naturally!—basked in their affection. Not satisfied with merely shouting "The Big O" when Oral Roberts appeared at a basketball game or perhaps at a chapel service, the students almost in unison raised their arms over their heads to form an "O." For his proud daughter, their loving gesture always brought tears, particularly after he reached his 90's.

—He never forgot where he had come from and was so grateful to God. He never forgot that God had raised him up from a sick bed of tuberculosis. There was a movie which Dad and Mother watched in a rare moment of relaxation, about an individual suffering with that dread disease. Mother related to me later that they had to leave the movie before it came to its conclusion because Dad started sobbing uncontrollably. And perhaps that is why he had such compassion for hurting people. He never forgot.

—At times he could have a pretty good sense of humor. One evening he was backstage, ready to go on the air as part of Jerry Lewis' famous Labor Day telethon. Many Hollywood stars and other celebrities were milling around, also waiting to be guests on that program when a lady walked up to him. She was apparently there only to obtain autographs of famous people. One wonders how she was allowed backstage! At any rate, she looked at Dad carefully, then asked: "Are you anybody?" His swift response was: "I guess not!" She pondered that a moment, then said: "Well... go ahead and sign anyway, in case you *become* somebody!"

There was also a time he was walking in the downtown area of New York City when two "ladies of the evening" propositioned him, in broad daylight, no less. He looked at them and said: "Don't you know who I am? I'm Oral Roberts—a preacher!" One of the ladies listened with a blank stare, but the other responded: "Oh, I've heard of you! You must be the one my grandmother's always talking about! Can I have your autograph?" He of course signed his name for her and, in case you are wondering, decided not to avail himself of...well, you know!

—Dad was extremely proud of his heritage as a Cherokee Indian. He often had crusades for Indians from many different tribes and was named Indian of the Year in 1963. Bob Daniels, that wonderful singer I described earlier, provided me with a picture of Dad praying for a little girl at an outdoor meeting in Window Rock, Arizona.

Even three months before his death, Ron and I drove him to preach at a small Indian church a few miles outside of Tulsa, pastored by a very kind man named Negiel Bigpond.

There was Oral Roberts at 91 years of age, still preaching! And by the way, he stayed until he had laid hands on every person in the auditorium who asked for prayer. Now granted, there were only about sixty folks in attendance, however, such was still quite a drain on a man his age.

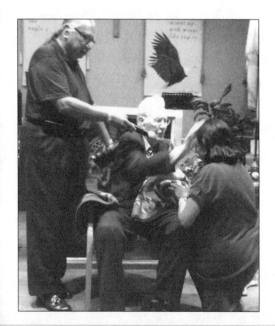

The funny part, however, was that he had been away from Oklahoma so long that he had no idea how the Tulsa area traffic has grown, nor about our new expressways. His stubbornness came to the forefront and he insisted upon going to the church on the road he would have traveled about 20 years before. I kept explaining that in the 21st century, that road (Memorial) was full of stoplights and heavy traffic and that it would be far better to take Highway 75 instead. Well I won the argument, but only because I was driving! He was so worried about being late for the entire drive.

Dad was always punctual to any speaking engagement. I never once remember him being late, to anything. So our drive to Hectorville, Oklahoma from Tulsa was, well, not all that pleasant, if you can read between the lines.

We arrived at the church with one minute to spare, resulting in a deep sigh of relief from his driver. However, we waited quite awhile for the service to actually begin for, as the Pastor put it, his congregants were "on Indian time." Of course Dad never admitted that his driver had in fact steered him in the right direction; perish the thought! Let the reader understand, though, that when the last amen had been said, lunch completed, the last hand shaken, and it was time to return to Tulsa, my tired father insisted upon returning by the exact route by which we had come. Men!

—Along that line, one of my favorite "Oralisms" came directly from Dad's heritage as what is now referred to as a Native American. When on one occasion I was grousing about the fact that there are so few lawyers who were true Christians, his response was "May your tribe increase!"

—I describe myself to others as a fuzzy, not a techie. That was also true of my father except that it is an incredible understatement regarding the dearth of his technical abilities. At least I can operate the remote control on a television! Mother had to put tape on certain buttons on the remote, lest Dad would push the wrong button and the TV would no longer have a picture at all!

—In comparison to most public figures, I would say that Oral Roberts talked to the press far less than many others in the limelight. He rarely responded when slammed by the media. It seemed that when he did agree in advance to talk to members of the press, the final version of the interview had been edited in such a way as to make whatever he said appear, well, twisted. It was his experience that although the person assigned to interview him may have intended the article or program to be positive, once the editor finalized it, the results seemed to vary dramatically from Dad's original expectations.

While it certainly bothered him, my father typically suffered the blow, then continued on with his ministry saying very little in response. After all, we learn from 1 Corinthians 2:14 that the things of God must be spiritually discerned and often appear as foolishness to the "natural man."

A Cowboy at Heart

—In his few leisure moments, I would say that he was a cowboy at heart, at least in his younger days. When he was young he enjoyed hearing western groups sing, groups such as the Sons of the Pioneers. He also enjoyed riding horses.

When I was a little girl living in the house on the farm (discussed in a previous chapter), Dad absolutely loved watching westerns. Unfortunately, it was the 1950's—long before one could play a DVD or access a movie by TiVo or DVR. Movies were not available anywhere but at a theatre, well, that is unless you were extremely enterprising! If you were willing to drive about 20 miles one-way, you could rent movies on 16 millimeter reels. Oh, did I mention that you had to have a concomitant projector in your home and that you also had to be knowledgeable in properly threading the film through the intricate parts of that projector?

As you can see, it was no small undertaking, however, I remember times when my dear mother did just that. I often traveled in the car with her all the way to the other side of town (long before all of the current expressways were in place, I might add!) and rented these wide, heavy reels that contained an old movie western. Films with John Wayne, Roy Rogers and Dale Evans, Gene Autry, Audie Murphy and the like.

Dad would have invited several other western movie buffs for a rousing evening. Mother prepared all sorts of snacks for the group, but it seemed to me that the most difficult part was for her to thread the machine. She of course knew better than to let my father touch any part of the film or projector! My memory is that we had those movie evenings perhaps once every few months. I can still remember how exciting it was to actually be able to watch a movie on your own couch! Wow! Even though I never cared for westerns all that much, it was still quite a thrill. I must confess however, that the best part of the evening did not necessarily emanate from the movie, but from the reactions of my dad and his buddies.

You should have seen *and heard* them when the cowboys won a battle against the outlaws. They would be whooping and hollering to beat the band. It seemed like they yelled through a good part of the movie, and oh, did I love it! I even liked those few mushy parts when the cowboy would get the girl and kiss her, toward the end of the movie. You should have heard them then: "He's gonna kiss her! I just know he is!"

Of course the next morning, Mother and I would trudge all the way across town again in order to return the film. While I am not sure that my mother enjoyed the total event as much as I did, even she enjoyed seeing her husband unwind, if only for a few hours!

Dad also enjoyed going to cattle auctions and bidding on cattle and horses. Unfortunately, he often spent what my mother saw as too much money on cattle so it was not long before she finally "put her foot down" and we moved back to Tulsa.

—His political views would most likely surprise you. He probably would not want me to give you a lot of information on that subject. However, I can tell you that for him, the Christian's job was to spread the Gospel, to help keep people out of Hell, to prosper and be in health while they were on the earth, not to change the world from a political standpoint. He did not necessarily feel that it was wrong for Christians to engage in political activity. He just believed that his calling, and the calling of the University he built for the Lord, was to do the former and not the latter.

When I was his employee at Oral Roberts University, I was bitterly opposed to his thinking on this issue, believing that part of ORU's role in the world should be political involvement. I remember long conversations wherein Dad painstakingly reminded me of the conduct of Jesus Himself during His life on Earth. He revisited the history of Rome— how during the time of Jesus and Paul, slavery and other vast injustices were everywhere, yet early Christians never directly opposed those injustices. He concluded that while injustice was never to be condoned, the primary reason for being a Christian was to further the Gospel, not to bring about political change.

Having said that, however, Dad certainly did his part regarding one specific injustice which was rampant in our part of the country in the 1960's. From the start of the University, many of the African American athletes were married and therefore required housing which was of course not available in dormitories that had been built to accommodate single students. While there were vacant apartments near the campus, the landlords in those days would not consider renting to "Blacks," as they were called then. So these young men and their wives had no choice but to rent apartments on the north side of town, in substandard conditions I might add.

When Dad learned of this, he was incensed! How could you expect these students to drive perhaps fifteen miles one way, just to go back and forth to campus? So Dad built an apartment complex just south of the campus. Apartments were rented to others as well, but the original purpose of the construction was so that the African American married students would have a nice place to live near the campus.

— He loved cornbread and beans. You would think that having lived through the Great Depression in Oklahoma, in that now famous "dust bowl," that when he could finally afford to eat steak, he would never again be willing to eat cornbread and beans. But not my father. Cornbread and beans was his absolute favorite meal. Of course one had to add onions and ketchup in order to make the meal complete. Then if there was any cornbread left over at bedtime, he would often get a small glass of milk and add pieces of the leftover cornbread to it. Okay, you have to be from Oklahoma!

A High Honor

—One of the thrills of Dad's latter years was when he was honored by the Oklahoma State Legislature that turned out to be only a few months prior to his death. Dan Newberry, one of our State Senators, conceived the idea and oh, what a great day it was. I think the best part for me was that while we were waiting to go into the Senate Chamber, the room seemed so chaotic. People were talking at the front with relatively few giving their attention to the task at hand. People were walking around, whispering and not always so quietly. I thought, "Oh no,

it's going to be totally embarrassing for Dad to have flown all the way from California to Oklahoma, only to be ignored!" And admittedly, for the first minute or so after Dad began to speak, few appeared to notice.

However, despite his advanced age, it did not take long for Dad's presence to take an ascendance I had witnessed so many times. To see and hear that Chamber grow quiet was astonishing. As I stood there watching proudly I was wondering, how many times does a man whose parents could not always afford to buy him shoes have an opportunity to address his state's governing body? While I hasten to point out that Dad had addressed Congress at one point in his life, I suspect even that may not have been as meaningful as speaking before his own state's legislature. Being honored by his own—particularly his home state over which he had dreamed of being the governor—well, that was unquestioningly a banner day.

The picture below is with Pam Peterson, who was there that day with us, a current member of the Oklahoma legislature, my friend and a fellow ORU graduate.

The following morning, while I knew he would be fatigued from the excitement of the day before, I asked Dad if he had saved any energy for a radio interview. You may remember from an earlier chapter my discussion of David Ingles and the Oasis Network. Wouldn't you know it. David Ingles married Sharon Tucker and they eventually had a son, David Warren Ingles, who attended ORU and who I met while working at ORU. For many years now, I have had the opportunity to serve as a volunteer on the radio network on "The Roadshow" with David Warren. While I did not ask David Warren in advance, I had a feeling that if I could somehow pull it off, he would be more than happy to interview my father.

At any rate, Dad surprisingly agreed to the interview and such was, to my knowledge, one of the last interviews he granted before his departure to Heaven.

Even the next day, during that interview, Dad was still quite overcome with the honor that had been bestowed upon him by his native state. Only in America!

— A final word to the detractors of my father's accomplishments. Personally, I have made a decision that:

- when I have preached to millions about God's concern for each of us as individuals;

- when I have broken down both of my shoulders in order to lay *my* hands on over one million people in a prayer of faith for their healing, and

- when I have built a major University which has graduated over 30,000 souls trained to bring the Gospel into every person's world, then perhaps I will have earned the right to denounce Oral Roberts.

Consider this: Paul states that each of us will one day stand before the Judgment Seat of Christ (2 Corinthians 5:10). I can picture it: Roberta Potts standing there—perhaps leaning on one foot, then another with a certain degree of fear and trembling, wondering how she will be seen by the One sitting on that throne. I have a feeling that at some point during the process, Jesus Himself will tell that anxious soul how many people are already in Heaven or on their way because of *her* efforts. So the question is, what number did He tell Dad on *his* arrival to that throne? I can already tell you without the need of a fancy calculator that my Dad's number will exceed mine—exponentially!

And I do not even have the excuses my Dad could have used for being an influence on so few. Let's get real. I never stuttered! I was not even poor when I grew up. I always had plenty of nice clothes to wear. I never suffered with a disease that threatened to literally squeeze the breath out of my body. Unquestionably, Dad's excuses would have played much better than my paltry ones.

And yet I know there are a vast number of individuals who have already arrived or are on a direct path to Heaven *because* my father lived. So in my view, only those who can boast a higher number than my father would have a justifiable reason to impugn his life, faults and all! Unless and until I can win that contest, I will be incredibly proud of my father for the good things he did. The rest, I will leave to God's judgment.

For our light affliction, which is but for a moment,
worketh for us a far more exceeding and eternal weight
of glory.

–*2 Corinthians 4:17 (KJV)*

DON'T TURN HIM AWAY

Chapter 19

O ne of the most enduring things which happened as a result of the ministry of Oral Roberts was this: My father's ministry, particularly through his sermons and later through Oral Roberts University took religion beyond salvation. He brought it beyond simply going down to an altar to make a decision for Christ and taught people how to integrate that decision into their daily lives. Dad's ministry was designed to give people a better life, the abundant life promised by Jesus. As expressed in Dad's ministry, the things of God could be brought into every area of our lives—our physical bodies, our minds and our spirits. Dad personalized God to each individual. When speaking of Jesus he would often say: "He sat where you sit. He felt what you feel." Dad's emphasis on the Holy Spirit taught people how to pray. I am not referring to what sometimes is reduced to a meaningless exercise with someone reading something from a sheet of paper. I mean prayers that touch the heart of God and get results of Biblical proportions!

One of the reasons Dad had been so dissatisfied with his life as a pastor was that at church, people just came down to the altar. Yes, when they prayed to receive Jesus as their Savior, and if they meant it, that decision would keep them out of Hell. And while I would never in a million years wish to diminish the monumental importance of a sincere salvation experience, let's face it. There can be twenty years, maybe thirty years or forty or fifty years before Hell becomes an issue in many peoples' lives. So what is a person to do about their decision to receive Jesus *in the meantime*?

So often in Dad's experience as a boy, he saw people come to the altar. They had an emotional experience, but when they went home, that experience changed *nothing* with respect to their daily lives. If you cannot incorporate the things of God into your daily life and if your relationship with God is for Heaven only, what good is it while you are here on earth? As Dad often said, you won't need to be healed when you get to Heaven. You will never be sick then! It is here on the earth that you have needs. It is while you are here on earth that you need to be healed. Dad brought religion beyond "pie in the sky in the bye and bye" to the here and now of our existence.

In Dad's day, as a young boy that is, people were caught up in going to church. Being there every service was seen as so very important. It was as if those church services were important *in themselves*. But so often it had become just a church experience, not a *life* experience. Dad did not want to be an evangelist who would simply breeze into town and have a big meeting—then leave and go on with his life. He wanted there to be real change in the people as a result of his coming. And that is the reason why Dad took the names and addresses of each crusade attendee and split them up between the sponsoring pastors. Dad wanted a continuity between what the people had experienced during his crusades and with the rest of their lives!

While certainly the change in people's daily lives Oral Roberts was endeavoring to bring did not happen to all who attended his meetings nor to all of those who have attended Oral Roberts University, that change actually happened in the lives of countless people. While I suppose many of the people who were healed in Dad's crusades have now passed away just like Dad, there is virtually nowhere you can go in this country without running across an ORU graduate.

And of course there are many of them in other countries as well. My point is that Dad's ministry truly changed people's lives and is still changing lives today, even though his physical body has been placed under the earth.

Oral Roberts taught all who would listen that we do not have to wait until Heaven to experience the goodness of God. God's healing power is here right now, today. Dad announced to the world as no preacher had before him, that Jesus is close to us, as close as the very breath in our nostrils. Dad told his world that God is a good God. He said to his world: "Something GOOD is going to happen to you!" He told the world to expect a miracle. He told the world that they could hear the voice of God. And now students of the University which God told Dad to build are going into every person's world—to places where Dad could never have dreamed of going.

I told you earlier of sitting on the edge of my chair in Dad's crusades as a little girl. The tent would be teeming with people, some sitting in folding chairs and others standing just outside the tent, straining to hear what was going on inside, their shoes covered with sawdust. He would come to the end of his sermon, then he would say: "Let every head be bowed and let every eye be closed." Then he would pray the most captivating prayer to the Lord I have ever heard. In an urgent, pleading voice, he would say: "Oh dear God: Don't let a man who heard me preach tonight go to hell. Don't let a woman who heard me preach tonight go to hell. Don't let a boy or a girl who heard the sound of my voice tonight die and go to hell." Even with all of those people inside and outside the tent, you would hear nothing but the sound of Oral Roberts' voice. There was no moving around, or even whispers in the audience. It was as if everyone inside or even near to that tent were caught up in Dad's desperate call to the heart of every person within the sound of his voice.

Then sometimes he would sing a song all by himself. No, his voice was not comparable to that of a professional singer, but oh how captivating it was in that moment. Here are the words of a song he often sang:

Don't turn Him away;
Don't turn Him away;
He has come back to your heart again,
Although you've gone astray.
Oh, how you'll need Him to plead your
cause on that eternal day!
Don't turn the Savior away from your heart.
Oh, don't turn Him away!

And now I come to you, dear reader. If I can be so bold as to speak for my Dad, he would say those same words to you. Please do not read this book and yet turn down the call of Jesus Christ which He is making to you right now! If you were interested enough to read a book about Oral Roberts and stay with me right to the very end, then God is already dealing with your heart. I urge you, as my father would, not to live your life another day without accepting the Lord Jesus Christ into your heart, for there is no other name under Heaven given among men by which you must be saved.

While Jesus never promised that living for Him would be easy, it is in fact quite simple to accept Him into your life. And oh the joy and the peace that He can bring if you choose Him and only Him as your Lord and as your Savior. In order to ask Jesus into your heart, you only need to talk to Him—saying something like the following:

> Dear Jesus, I've made a lot of mistakes in my life. I've been living for myself. I'm sorry. Please forgive me for what I have done wrong. I take you into my heart and into my life. I put you in charge. I want *you* to be the Lord of my life. I give you control. I ask that you save me from my sins. I believe that you are the Son of God and that you love me. Thank you, Lord Jesus.

If you said that prayer and if you really meant it, then you are "saved" as the Bible describes it. This means that you will not go to Hell when you die, but it also means that you have an opportunity for abundant living, full of the goodness of God. I suggest that you find a Bible if you do not have one, or try perhaps www.biblos.com or another website on the internet which displays the scriptures in the Bible—so that you can begin to read what the Bible tells you to do now. Find some good friends who truly know Jesus. Find a good church that preaches the same good news you read about in the Bible.

Keep talking to Jesus. You do not have to pray prayers which sound perfectly holy or with lots of "thees" and "thous." Just speak to Jesus from your heart as if He were sitting in the same room with you, and He WILL BE sitting in the same room with you. No, you will not see an earthly body, but you will sense Jesus' spirit in you and around you. You can have that friend who replaced imaginary friends for me as a little girl, as described in an earlier chapter.

Reviewing my life, I am almost grateful for that loneliness which I have described in this book—for it led me to Jesus. Oh what a heritage I have, both in my father and in my Lord Jesus. I thank God that He chose me, not some other little girl, to be the daughter of Oral Roberts. Yes, it was terribly difficult in many ways, but oh how glorious it is to know that Jesus has become so real in the lives of so many—because my father listened to God. It is so wonderful to know that because of my father's ministry, there are so very many people who made Jesus a part of their daily lives, expecting miracles as my father's ministry had taught them to do.

The fruits which have already burst forth as well as the good things being made possible because of Oral Roberts University students and graduates make the loneliness and any hardships I had to bear just a light affliction, which was but for a moment. And of course it will work *for me* a "far more exceeding and eternal weight of glory."

Perhaps there were others to whom God was speaking in the mid-1930's in Oklahoma, others who might have carried out God's visions and dreams for the world more perfectly, but the fact is that they apparently were not listening to God. Or perhaps they heard but were unwilling to make the sacrifices necessary to obey God. Dad listened and He obeyed to the best of his ability. He was just a poor stuttering boy from Oklahoma who was far from perfect, but who did everything he knew to do to listen to the voice of God, and to obey.